Other books by Alan McKenzie:
The Harrison Ford Story, Zomba Books (1st Ed, 1984; 2nd Ed, 1985)
Hollywood Tricks of the Trade (with Derek Ware), Gallery Books (1985)
How to Draw and Sell Comic Strips, North Light Books (1st Ed, 1987; 2nd Ed, 1996; 3rd Ed 2005)

Other books published by Air Pirate Press
The Art of Brett Ewins (2011)

The Harrison Ford Story
Published by
Air Pirate Press, 62 Cowper Road, London W7 1EJ

First published in Great Britain in 1984 and 1985 by
Zomba Books, Zomba House, 165-167 Willesden High Road, London NW10 2SG
(Zomba Books are no longer trading.)

Cover Design by Steve Cook for Ex-Men Graphics
Interior design by Sydney Falco

Third Edition, 2011

Copyright © Alan McKenzie, 2011

ISBN 978-0956914910

Alan McKenzie asserts his moral right to be
identified as the author of this work.

THE
HARRISON FORD
STORY
by Alan McKenzie

*This is the Hollywood star for the earlier Harrison Ford,
located outside 6665 Hollywood Boulevard.
The current Ford's star is at 6801.*

INTRODUCTION

Back in 1984, when the first edition of this book came out, the first chapter started this way:

SOMEWHERE along Hollywood Boulevard's sidewalk of showbiz fame, where the names of the stars are imbedded in the very concrete beneath the tourists' feet, there is an entry for Harrison Ford. Well, of course there is! Ford is one of the biggest box-office draws of the Eighties. You'll find him in major roles in four of the five most successful movies of all time. It would have been five out of five had his cameo role as Elliot's headmaster in ET: The Extra-Terrestrial *– written as it happens by the second Mrs Ford, Melissa Mathison – not been cut from the movie at the last minute. So if any of Film City's army of 'Stars', Superstars' and 'Megastars' deserves the honour of having his name immortalised in concrete, Harrison Ford's the one, right?*

'Except,' chuckles Ford, 'that's not my star! It was put there years ago for an old time (silent) matinee idol also called Harrison Ford. No, I'd never heard of him, either. Or not until the Screen Actors' Guild told me I'd have to change my name. That's why I'm Harrison J. Ford in two of my earliest films. When I heard the old man had passed on, I called up the SAG about it. They couldn't confirm his death, but I dropped the J. anyway.'

The original Harrison Ford is not one of the better-remembered silent stars. He made his film debut in 1915, in a picture called Up the Road With Sally. *His career blossomed and within a few years he was co-starring with such performers as Lon Chaney, notably* Shadows *(1922). As the Twenties wore on he gravitated towards comedies like* Up in Mabel's Room *and* The Nervous Wreck. *Little was written in the fan magazines at the time. The earlier Ford was just as hard to pin down in interviews as his namesake. 'He has a neat habit,' said one contemporary journalist, 'of placing the blame for good work onto the innocent shoulders of others. "Mary Provost is a great little actress to work with in comedy" or "Phyllis Haver is splendid in it also" are the sort of facts he will remind you of if you compliment him on his own acting.' The first Ford died at the age of 73 on 2nd December 1957, ten years after retiring from acting.*

'If they ever decide to put an entry there for me,' says Ford, 'they needn't bother. It's there already. And I kind of like the idea of using his.' Sentimental perhaps, but the old man would probably have approved.

It's a good story and though a lot has changed since 1984 – most notably the addition of a star for *our* Harrison Ford on Hollywood Boulevard in May 2003 – it would have been a real shame to have left it out completely. But it also contains some inaccuracies and omits some interesting details that have come to light since 1984, so I've made a point of adding them in the relevant places in this revised third edition. The original first eight chapters have been re-written and expanded and further seven chapters have been added to cover the Harrison Ford movies since 1984. And the final chapter, summing up Ford's career has also been augmented with further research. Hopefully, this will give a more complete overview of the actor's career to date.

Alan McKenzie, October 2011
www.thestoryworks.com

CHAPTER 1

HARRISON FORD: THE EARLY DAYS

From College to Contract Player to Carpentry

'My job is pretending to be Indiana Jones, or whoever, and I consider personal information about *me* can only water down the illusion.' Harrison Ford

Harrison Ford has a reputation for being a very private man, and he has spoken little in public of his early life, often responding sharply when asked a question by a journalist he deems too personal. 'I was raised in Chicago,' said Ford once in a rare moment of self-revelation. 'Nothing too remarkable there. Just the usual. Baseball, fooling around with cars. I was a loner type. Not very active in sports. I didn't know what I wanted to do when I was a kid.'

Harrison Ford was born on July 13th 1942 of an Irish Catholic father, Christopher Ford (born John William Ford) and a Russian Jewish mother, Dorothy Nidelman (born Dora Nidelman). His father had started his working life in Vaudeville, the same as *his* father. But by the 1930s the American music hall was in terminal decline as radio and movies rose to become the staple entertainment of the mass market. Ford Sr cannily moved into radio, joining the Federation of Radio Actors in 1938. But within three years he'd changed careers, and became writer at WENR Chicago, though his resonant, baritone voice meant that he still did a fair bit of voice-over work.

Harrison Ford's unusual given name came from his maternal grandfather, Harry Nidelman – 'I think it's Yiddish for "son of Harry",' Ford joked in 1994. His childhood was middle-class and uneventful, though he deliberately avoided trouble by calling himself 'Harry' rather than 'Harrison'. By his own admission he was not an outstanding scholar. Loner he may have been, but he showed no special interest in the traditional pursuits of loners. No long hours with his nose buried in books. No solitary Saturday afternoons immersed in the adventures of John Wayne at the neighbourhood cinema.

'I didn't spend much time at the movies,' he told an interviewer, 'I'm not a scholar of Bogart's mannerisms, so I miss a lot of the film references that people like Spielberg and Lucas toss around.'

Given that Ford's father had strong ties to acting and the entertainment industry, it might seem strange there were few games of 'dress up and make believe' in Ford's childhood. In fact his earliest ambition was to be a coalman. 'My dad would get all dressed up, go to work, come home, sit at the dinner table and bitch like crazy about those bastards at work,' said Ford. By comparison, Ford Jr thought the life of a coalman seemed far more attractive. '*He* didn't go home at night and tell his wife how uncooperative the coal was.' The idea of acting didn't occur to him until much later on.

In 1948, Christopher Ford changed jobs again. He joined a growing ad agency, Needham, Louis and Brorby. With the War firmly behind them, Americans were demanding more and more in the way of luxury goods. And it looked like the new-fangled television was just the way for manufacturers to sell their products to a hungry public. By the mid-1950s, Ford was a manager at NL&B and was earning enough to move his family from the inner city to the suburb of Morton Grove.

The 12 year old Harry Ford attended MS Meltzer Junior High on Ballard Street and almost immediately ran into trouble with some of the tougher kids at the school. Every day he was taken to the top of a hill by these kids and pushed down it.

'They weren't so much beatings as exercises in ritual humiliation,' Ford recalls. 'It wasn't important that I suffer physically, just that I not think that I was the equal of my mates. I knew the ritual had a form and a shape to it, and that it was far more efficient just to tumble down the hill in a satisfying way and then make my way up, rather than have to fight those guys to get back into the parking lot.'

The point of these indignities was never explained, but Ford had an idea of why he was being punished. 'They might have sensed an underlying arrogance that they didn't want to allow to blossom,' he said. 'That probably came from the distance at which I held myself from people. And still do.'

In 1956, Ford moved on the Maine East High School, one of the highest achieving high schools in America at the time. As he'd done at Meltzer, young Harry contrived to keep a low profile. He wasn't athletic and confined his activities to the more nerdy pursuits, like the model railway club and the audiovisual club and, through that, became involved in the school's amateur radio station, WMTH, though as a technician rather than as 'talent'. In the meantime Christopher Ford's star was still in the ascendant at the Needham agency and the family moved to a larger house in a better neighbourhood, North Ridge, in 1957.

Some of Ford Sr's work ethic must have rubbed off on Harry, as he had a string of part-time jobs during his teenage years. 'My parents came through the Depression and we were taught to believe that we were not entitled to comfort,' Ford explained.

One of his first jobs was as a cook on a luxury yacht. He found his recipes in a copy of

The Joy of Cooking that his mother had given to him and tells a story about how cooking a meal for his employers on a very choppy lake while feeling hopelessly seasick, 'was probably the most heroic thing I've ever done.'

His longest running job was at the Evening Pipe Store, which specialized in pipes and special blends of tobacco. It was here that Harry took up smoking, a habit he's not been able to kick.

From Maine East High, Harrison Ford went on to Ripen College in North Wisconsin, a liberal arts college that didn't have too stringent entry requirements, following in the footsteps of another alumnus Spencer Tracy. He spent the best part of three years studying English and Philosophy, but with ever-diminishing results. Casting around for some way to boost his grades – failure was unthinkable with his father shelling out the best part of $2000 a year in tuition fees – Harry Ford approached the drama professor Philip Bergstrom and was accepted onto the course. Ford was beginning to lose his babyface looks and his voice was deepening as he matured. He was cast as the lead in *The Threepenny Opera* at the college theatre, The Red Barn. For Ford, it was a turning point.

An unexpected bonus of becoming involved in the campus drama scene was that suddenly, Ford had access to girls. He began seeing a girl called Mary Lee Franke who'd been in *The Threepenny Opera* with him, but as Mary Lee was 'pinned' to another boy (college-speak for 'going steady'), the pair had to meet in secret.

As Harry entered his final year at college, he wasn't able to muster the energy to be interested in getting a degree in Philosophy. 'I would sleep for four or five days at a time,' he recounted in 1994. 'There was one class I never went to. I remember once when I slept for seven days and finally roused myself got myself out of bed, managed to get dressed – this seemed to be taking an intense effort – and actually made it to class. All of this seemed to be happening in slow motion. I even put my hand on the door of the classroom, but I seemed unable to turn the doorknob. So I let it go and went back to sleep.' To me this sounds less like bone idleness and more like a bout of depression, though no mention of any such condition has ever surfaced in any other accounts of Ford's youth.

Despite all this, Harry Ford started seeing a new girlfriend in November 1963, Mary Louise Marquardt. Friends and teachers all seemed surprised as Ford was, by this time, something of a star on campus, and Mary was a quite sober and studious girl. But for some reason, the two very quickly became inseparable and the romance began to get serious.

By mid-1964, Ford's combined Philosophy/English degree was in serious doubt. 'Suddenly I discovered that I had no idea how I was going to make a living in those two areas, so I just stopped going to classes – they kicked me out a few days before graduation.' Three days before graduation to be precise. 'Bounced in academic disgrace, much to the embarrassment of my parents, who had made a reservation at a motel in town for the ceremony.'

Christopher Ford was far from happy to find out that after spending $8000 on his son's education, there would be no graduation for young Harrison. 'My parents had paid for four years of education and at the end of it there was no degree, ' said Ford. 'It was not taken lightly.'

Ejected from the protected existence of college life, Ford found himself face to face with the real world. So he took two momentous decisions. He would marry Mary that summer and pursue a career on the stage.

'It was important to be able to announce to people what I was going to do with my life, even if it was only to say the thing that appalled them most,' said Ford later. 'It proceeded naturally enough from the fact that I wasn't going to graduate from college. Now I was off on an adventure, with no sense really of what the odds were because I never knew anybody who was in that work. I don't think my family thought it was going to work out, but they never discouraged me. Discouragement was something I was always happy to have. Some resistance, you know?'

Where others might have struggled, Harry had little difficulty finding work as an actor, even in Wisconsin. 'I decided to stick to acting, with drawing room comedy in mind. So I did one season of summer stock (the American equivalent of repertory) immediately after college, in Williams Bay. That's a resort community on the shores of Lake Geneva. Not the Swiss one, the one in Wisconsin.'

It was the old Ford luck that led to his engagement with the Williams Bay Repertory Company. The Company had taken on three 'resident actors', talented youngsters who were to serve a kind of apprenticeship through the summer season. One of these young actors had let the company down and the Company director William Fucik needed a replacement. He asked around if anyone knew of a local young actor who might make an adequate replacement and Harry Ford's name came up.

Harry and Mary met with Fucik and the older man was impressed with Ford's quiet confidence and serious mindset. Fucik had worked for one of California's best-regarded theatres, The Pasadena Playhouse and had coached Paul Newman 15 years earlier at Williams Bay and by then was a well-known acting coach in Hollywood. With the opening of the season just weeks away, Fucik took a gamble and offered Ford the job, figuring that he had the raw material to work with and could bring Harry up to standard in time.

Ford made his professional stage debut on 26 June 1964 in the production of *Take Her, She's Mine*. The next morning, he and Mary were married and the couple spent their honeymoon getting used to being part of a theatre company. Ford went on to roles in *Night of the Iguana* (in which he forgot his lines on stage*), Dark of the Moon, Sunday in New York* and even a musical, *Little Mary Sunshine*. Both audiences and critics enjoyed his performances.

As the season drew to a close, Ford and Fucik discussed Harry's options in the acting business. Through his movie connections, Fucik was acquainted with *Gunsmoke* star James Arness and suggested that Ford try Hollywood, though Ford habitually offers a more light-hearted tale to any reporter who asks how he'd ended up on the West Coast.

'I went to Los Angeles,' he'd recall. 'I didn't know any of the names of the motion picture studios. I didn't know any actors. I didn't know anything! And of course I'm not an Angeleno by birth or by heart – it's just the place where I find myself today. But Los Angeles is where you have to be if you want to be actor. You have no choice. You go there or New York. I flipped a coin about it. It came up New York, so I flipped again. When you're starting out to be an actor, who wants to go where it's cold and miserable and be poor there? Better to be poor in the sunshine than in the snow. That was my idea, anyway. So we loaded all our stuff into the Volkswagen, drove off and didn't stop until we saw the Pacific. As far as I was concerned, that Ocean must mean California – fine! Let's stop here, Laguna Beach. About 60 miles south of LA. I did a play, *John Brown's Body*, at the playhouse there, but the thought of doing it over and over again just stopped me. Luckily, Columbia Pictures' New Talent programme scout saw me and sent me to see the head of casting there.'

That's not an accurate telling of story, but the reason Ford tells it that way is because Fucik was an intensely private man who shunned publicity. Once, when Paul Newman had given Fucik credit for being the best acting coach the actor had ever had Fucik called his protégé and asked him never to mention his name publicly again. In truth, it was Fucik who suggested Hollywood and offered Harry and Mary a place to stay in California, and that's why the Fords loaded up their decrepit VW van and headed west. Ford had simply followed Fucik's wishes and edited him out of the story.

The Fords took regular jobs – Harry working in a boatyard, then in a department store, Mary worked as a doctor's receptionist – while Harry continued to study with Fucik and then with Fucik's friend Bob Wentz. Through Wentz, Ford landed an audition at the Laguna Beach Playhouse and, in February 1965, auditioned for a part in Doug Rowe's production of *John Brown's Body*. His performance gathered good reviews from the local press, including one from the *Laguna News/Post* which said, 'Harry Ford may be the best young actor in the area – and this is his area debut.'

It was during this period that Ford picked up his trademark scar in a 'fast car crash. I was driving through Laguna Canyon. I had come from my job as an assistant buyer in the knick-knacks and oil paintings department of Bullocks department store and as I turned round to put my seat belt on, I ran into a telegraph pole ... later on I ran into a bad stitcher!'

As the run of *John Brown's Body* came to a close, it was Laguna Playhouse musical director Ian Bernard who suggested Ford might want to try his luck at Columbia Studios. Bernard was a former actor turned writer and musician who had sold a screenplay to Columbia, *Synanon*. Bernard arranged an interview for Ford at Columbia with his contact Billy Gordon, head of casting at the time, whom Ford referred to as the 'little bald-headed guy' in his subsequent retellings of the tale. Harry dutifully showed up with his customary quietly serious mindset, hoping the old Ford luck would land him a contract.

Even in the 1960s the major Hollywood studios were keeping scores of young good-looking hopefuls on the payroll and using them in bit parts in movies. Ford told movie journalist Tony Crawley the story of how he was hired and made it sound like something out of a 1930s musical.

'I walked into this small, heated, walnut-panelled office. There was a little, bald-headed guy with a stub of a cigar, white on white shirt, white on white tie, sitting behind a desk. Two telephones. Behind him a man who looked like a racetrack tout on two more phones. I sat in the only chair available, right in front of the desk, and listened to them discussing big names and big money. Then the bald guy looked at me as if he'd discovered a snake in his soup. "Who sent you here?" I told him. He turned to the other guy and said, "Who's that?" "I dunno," the other guy said.

'The bald guy turned back to me. "That's all right ... doesn't matter. What's your name? How tall? How much do you weigh? Any special hobbies, talents, capacities? Speak any foreign languages? Okay, fine. If we find anything for you, we'll let you know."

'I walked out of the office, down the hall and pressed the button for the elevator. When it didn't come immediately, I realised that I had to pee. I went round the corner to the bathroom, went in, took a pee, came out and the assistant guy was running down the hall yelling, "Come back, come back." Obviously, if I'd gone down in the elevator, it wouldn't have been worth his while chasing me.

'So I went back to the office. The little bald guy says, "You're not the type we're usually interested in, but how'd'ya like to be under contract?" Sure, absolutely. And about six months later, I was. For $150 a week. And all the respect that implies.' Ford was told to report to the Head of Columbia's New Talent Program, Walter Beakel, a fellow Chicago-an who had overseen the early career of *Working Girl* director Mike Nichols.

It might seem to some that Harrison Ford's acting career was well and truly on its way. Perhaps Ford himself thought that at first, too. But it wasn't going to be that easy.

Head of the studio Mike Frankovitch was spending a lot of time at the London office of Columbia, supervising pictures like *A Man for All Seasons*, *Georgy Girl* and *Oliver!* So the running of the LA offices fell to a tough-talking ex-producer called Jerry Tokofsky. The two did not get along. In those early days Ford was subject to what seemed like an endless string of ignominies. First, the Screen Actors Guild told him that as there was another actor called Harrison Ford, he'd have to change his name. Ford bit his tongue and added an initial of 'J', even though he has no middle name. The fact that the original Harrison Ford had been dead for eight years by this time seemed either not to matter or be unknown to the SAG. The next outrage to be visited on Harry was to be told by management that his regular, college-guy haircut wasn't right and they sent him to the studio hair stylist. Ford came out with an Elvis quiff and a short fuse. Finally, that same management decided that 'Harrison' was too pretentious and that he would have to change his name. 'I suggested "Kurt Affair",' said Ford. 'After that, there was no more talk of changing names.'

'It was 1965,' he continued, 'and Columbia was still playing 1925. You had to come to the studio every day, in a jacket and a tie, go to acting class, eat in the executive dining room, submit yourself to photo layouts. Six starlets and six fellas playing football on Malibu Beach in front of a Chevrolet Nova for a glossy magazine ... you know the kind of thing, "Photos courtesy of Columbia Pictures." Horrible, really. Worse than any factory. Nobody ever knew your name at the Studio, or cared a damn about you. I went nuts.'

Nevertheless, Ford stuck it out. 'It was less sophisticated than modelling, but it was a way of being acknowledged as an actor while I learned to act.' At least, that was the plan. But if the truth be known, Ford's career was on hold.

'I wasn't learning anything. But around that time I bought a house near the Hollywood Bowl and decided to take out everything I didn't like about it. I'd never done any carpentry before, but I got the books from the library, got the tools and did it.'

THE MAIDEN VOYAGE

Whatever their other faults in the handling of their contract players, Columbia did sooner or later use the better ones in bit parts in their movies. Eventually, Ford's number came up, mostly due to the ongoing support of Walter Beakel. He had a part. 'I played a bell boy in *Dead Heat on a Merry-Go-Round* (1966). One day's work. Nothing uplifting. I had to say, "Paging Mr Jones, paging Mr Jones," or something like that and then James Coburn would wave me over and I'd give him a telegram. That was it!'

For the record, the line was actually, 'Paging Mr Ellis.' But regardless, Ford's first movie appearance didn't set the film community alight. In fact, Jerry Tokofsky was less than pleased with his 'performance'.

'The guy who was the vice-president of Columbia at the time – maybe I'm spilling the beans here, but that guy is no longer in the business and I am – he called me into his office after that film. Now, remember. All I had to do was deliver a telegram, right?

'"Kid," he says – they always called me "Kid", probably because they didn't know who the hell I was – "Kid, siddown. Lemme tell you a story. First time Tony Curtis ever appeared in a movie, he delivered a bag of groceries. A bag of groceries! You took one look at that person and you knew he was a star. You ain't got it, kid! Get back to class, because you ain't going to work again in this studio for six months, maybe a year. Get yourself together.'

Ford was amazed. 'I thought I had to act like a bellboy ... it didn't occur to me till years later that what they wanted me to do was act like a movie star.'

It was as if Ford's hopes for an acting career had been dashed. He was trapped in a seven-year contract with a studio which wouldn't let him act. But eventually he did act again.

In the autumn of 1966, Columbia Pictures took over production of a Roger Corman movie called *The Long Ride Home* (1967, aka *A Time For Killing*) and installed b-movie director Phil Karlson. The movie pitted Glenn Ford's Union soldier Major Walcott against imprisoned Confederate officer Captain Bentley (George Hamilton) in a fairly unremarkable American Civil War drama. 'Harrison J. Ford' turned up playing a young officer, Lieutenant Shaffer. Not one contemporary review noticed the presence of the young Ford.

Columbia then cast Harry in the movie version of a hit Broadway play. 'I got a small part in *Luv* (1967),' commented Ford. Small is right. Having trouble remembering what Ford had to do in that one, I checked the cast and credits of the movie meticulously. Ford was so far down the list that he must have dropped off the bottom. No mention is made of him in the studio's list of actors for that movie. But he played the role of a 'Hippy' who punches Jack Lemmon's character on the nose after a fender bender. He didn't make very much impression in this one either.

But Beakel – and probably only Beakel – continued to believe that Harry had that indefinable something that would take him far in the industry. Beakel's protégé Mike Nichols had been signed to direct the hottest new property in Hollywood, *The Graduate*. Every agent in town with a twenty-something actor on their books was pushing their guy for the choice role of Benjamin Braddock opposite Anne Bancroft's Mrs Robinson. Several well-known names auditioned for the part and were rejected, including Warren Beatty, Robert Redford and even Burt Ward, later to be cast as tv's Robin alongside Adam West's Batman. Beakel persuaded Mike Nichols to see Ford, and despite his inexperience, Harry was called back for a second interview, which must have meant Nichols was taking him seriously, but ultimately, the role went to the more experienced Dustin Hoffman.

'Was I demoralised?' asks Ford. 'You bet I was. I was going nowhere fast. This was the atmosphere when they let me go.'

Tokofsky called Ford into the headmaster's office and to give him another dressing down. 'The head of the studio, Mike Frankovitch, was still in Europe, so this other guy had to make the determination whether or not they should take up the option on my contract after eighteen months.

'"Kid," he said – what else? – "as soon as Frankovitch is back I'm going to tell him we ought to get rid of you. I don't think you're worth a thing to us. But I know your wife is pregnant, you need the money, so I'll give you another couple of weeks. Just sign the piece of paper my secretary has. Okay, boy? Now, get out of here!"'

Ford had had enough. He was tired of being pushed around by men behind desks. He told Tokofsky where he could stick his money and was fired on the spot.

'I had that kind of spirit, but nothing behind it. Three days later, I was under contract to Universal.'

OUT OF THE FRYING PAN?

It was Walter Beakel who once again came to Ford's rescue. He knew an agent, Dick Clayton, who would take Harry on as a client. Clayton in turn knew Monique James who ran the New Talent program at Universal and secured an interview for Harry. Beakel personally coached Ford for the meeting, with the result that James accepted Ford into her 'family' and the young actor was once again under contract to a major Hollywood studio.

It might seem strange that Harrison Ford would give up one studio situation, which he hated, for another which probably wouldn't be a lot better. He still had to suffer through acting classes and the trainee actors were given small roles in tv episodes and 'movies of the week'. But at least Harry was getting roles. 'The situation at Universal was somewhat better. But they never really had the guts to use me outside of television.'

Ford embarked on another round of appearances in such Universal tv shows as *The Virginian* (in the season five episode 'The Modoc Kid', and season six's 'A Bad Place to Die', both 1967), *Ironside* (in the season 1 episode 'The Past is Prologue',1967) and the tv movie *The Intruders* (filmed in 1967, but not broadcast until 1970). Ford was also assigned to a role in another Civil War drama, the 1968 Universal movie, *Journey to Shiloh* (1968), written by *Star Trek*'s Gene Coon. Ford played Willie Bill Bearden, one of seven young Texans who leave home under the leadership of Buck Burnett (James Caan) in search of adventure in the Confederate Army. They plan to join up with General Hood's Richmond Raiders but after several adventures en route – one of their number is killed in a card game, they witness the lynching of a runaway slave, Buck falls in love with a saloon girl, Gabrielle (Brenda Scott) – they are inducted into a Pensacola unit because of their outstanding horsemanship. Suddenly, they are face to face with the true horror of war at Shiloh. The Confederates are routed and four of the youngsters, including Willie Bill, are killed. The survivors of the battle are put to flight and Buck is wounded escaping from the Confederate military police, who are hunting down deserters from Shiloh. Buck regains consciousness in a military hospital, but is horrified to find his arm has been amputated. He learns that the last member of his band, Miller Nalls (Michael Sarrazin), was to be shot as a deserter, but has escaped and is hiding out in a barn severely wounded. Buck defies orders to go to Miller, but finds him close to death. Touched by the story of the seven young men, General Bragg (John Doucette) calls off the military police and allows Buck, the sole survivor, to make his way home.

Ford's role in the film was so minor that it has proved impossible to track down a review that singles out his performance, though *The Monthly Film Bulletin* said of the film in general, 'the acting is often strident and the script too naively emotional not to fall into mawkishness at times ... (but) well worth a look.'

Still, someone at Universal must have been pleased with the work Harry Ford did because he, along with fellow cast members Michael Sarrazin and Don Stroud were flown to New York to audition for director John Schlesinger who was preparing to film *Midnight Cowboy*. Though, in the end, the ingénue role went to Jon Voigt.

Despite not getting the *Midnight Cowboy* role, it seemed that Harrison Ford's luck was taking a turn for the better. Beakel introduced Ford to a producer/casting director called Fred Roos. Roos had been one of the first to see the talent and charisma of a young actor called Jack Nicholson and had cast him in two low-budget movies for Lippert, *Back Door to Hell* and *Flight to Fury* (both 1964). He saw a similar intangible something in the young Harrison Ford, and suggested him for the lead in a new movie by Italian maverick director Michelangelo Antonioni, *Zabriskie Point* (1969). Antonioni had made something of a name for himself as a director whose films reached the lucrative 'now' generation. His earlier film *Blowup* had opened to the bafflement of the establishment critics and the delight of the target audiences.

Roos managed to get Ford in to see Antonioni, but the director couldn't see what Roos saw. 'He was not a leading man in the way they thought of leading men at that time – not pretty enough,' said Roos. 'The strongest quality I saw was his great sense of masculinity. There was a kind of dangerous intensity he had, and combined with all that was this droll sense of humour. And then he had extreme confidence but nothing braggadocio.' Nevertheless, Roos managed to get Ford three days work in the movie as an airport worker.

Zabriskie Point tells the story of a rebellious American student, Mark (Mark Frechette) who finds himself involved in a campus riot. When a policeman is shot Mark is a suspect and is forced to lie low. He steals a small private plane and sets off across the Arizona desert, heading nowhere in particular. He crosses paths with Daria (Daria Halprin) who is heading towards Phoenix in a borrowed car for a meeting with her new employer, Lee Allen (Rod Taylor). Mark lands his plane and is given a lift by Daria. They stop in Death Valley and make love amidst the sand dunes. When Daria is stopped by a police patrol, Mark decides that the only way out of his dilemma is to return to the plane and give himself up to the police. He paints the plane with slogans and outlandish colours and sets off for Los Angeles. But when he arrives, a police reception committee is waiting and Mark is shot dead before he can explain. Daria hears the news on the car radio before she arrives at her meeting and for a while seems to deliberate whether or not to continue. Reaching a decision, Daria presses on to Allen's luxurious mountainside villa and, after wandering aimlessly around the house for awhile, climbs back into her car and drives some distance from the house. She looks back to the villa and imagines it and all it represents being blasted to smithereens by a huge explosion. Smiling, she continues on her journey to nowhere.

As it turned out, Antonioni seemed to experience inordinate difficulties in achieving the results he wanted with *Zabriskie Point*. The script sported the names of five writers and the movie was recut by the director several times. In the cutting and re-cutting Harrison Ford's part ('In fact, the whole sub-plot,' says Ford) was snipped out and consigned to the oblivion of the cutting room floor. Which is probably just as well. *Zabriskie Point* was not a success and did nothing to enhance the careers of any involved with it.

Ford went back to another round of supporting roles in Universal tv shows like, *My Friend Tony* ('The Hazing', 1969), *Love, American Style* (the segment, 'Love and the Former Marriage', 1969) and a couple of episodes of *The F.B.I.* (the fourth season 'Caesar's Wife' and the fifth season 'Scapegoat', both 1969)

Then Universal had one last try to launch Ford in some kind – any kind – of youth-orientated film. They loaned Ford back to Columbia Pictures for the film, *Getting Straight* (1970). The film followed the misadventures of Harry Bailey (Elliott Gould) and his girlfriend Jan (Candice Bergen) as they fight to keep their heads above water on an American University campus beset with student unrest. Eagle-eyed film fans might have spotted Ford in the role of Jake, but the movie was locked in time as a product of the late Sixties and did nothing to open up Ford's career. Though he was growing older and gaining more experience, the parts he was getting were becoming 'smaller and more one-dimensional.

'I was given tiny spaces to fill,' says Ford. 'Nothing where you could take space. Maybe they were right, I probably wasn't ready. But I was getting older. Except, when I was twenty-one every one thought I was seventeen. All soft and putty-like but aging fast on the inside, going crazy. I had to get away from it. Yet I had invested maybe four years and I didn't want give up. I still wanted to be an actor when I grew up. When I started acting, I thought of it as being an awesome task, exciting and frightening and a wonderful way for someone with no degree to live. I suppose being the son of a former radio actor and advertising executive in charge of Chicago's tv commercials, I should have known better. I was not prepared for the disillusionment I found as an actor in the studio system.'

At the same time Ford still couldn't bring himself to play the studio game. He hadn't endeared himself to Monique James with the required sucking up, so it probably came as no surprise when Universal let him go, towards the end of 1969. Ford was unemployed and reluctant to continue hiring out his face for small parts in tv shows.

'I was worried that I'd become over-exposed.' says Ford. 'Used up in three seasons and never have a long-term career. So I decided to stop taking small tv parts and become a carpenter. I'd had no training in carpentry, any more than I'd had in acting. But I set my mind to it. My first assignment was a $100,000 recording studio for Sergio Mendes. Fortunately, the Encino Public Library was three blocks away. I'd be standing on Mendes' roof with a text book in my hand.'

For all Ford's inexperience in carpentry, the business paid well. He made more from that Mendes job than he had for his first walk-on part as the bell-boy in the Coburn picture. Soon, the carpentry game was paying Ford well enough that he could take on his own architects and builders. 'That's when I realised the correlation between money and respect.

'Take a lot of money off people and they'll treat you with respect. They'd ask, "How much is all this going to cost?" And I'd say, "Well, I don't know. All can tell you is that when it's done, it'll be done right."'

At last, Ford was not at the beck and call of the studio heavies. And he was loving every minute of it.

'When I started carpentry,' he recalls. 'I liked it so much partly because it was such a relief from what I'd been doing before. For about eight years in the late Sixties and early Seventies, I did cabinets, furniture, remodelling. It was great! I could see my accomplishments. So I decided not to do any more acting unless the job had a clear career advantage. Altogether, I'd have to say I spent fifteen years in the acting business, but I made my living as a carpenter. I am not a Hollywood success story. Still, I didn't worry about money. I had an understanding wife. I was playing pretty fast and loose with life.'

BACK TO ACTING

During 1970, Fred Roos introduced Ford to a former colleague, manager Patricia

McQueeney. She had worked for Roos and Gary Marshall when they ran Compass Management and was already managing the careers of Martin Sheen, Teri Garr, Frederick Forrest and Cindy Williams. She agreed to meet with Ford to assess his potential. 'He sat on the couch in my office, his head down, his hands between his knees,' McQueeney later recalled, 'and kind of frowned at me, looking up at me underneath his brows, extremely uncomfortable and slightly embarrassed. At the time he was working as a carpenter and had done some parts around town and I can remember looking at him and thinking, "What in the world am I going to do with him?"'

McQueeney, like others before her, soon found that Harrison Ford was his own man and had a very clear idea about the kind of roles he would consider and the kind he wouldn't. 'He was always careful about the roles he chose, even when he was stone broke,' said McQueeney. 'I can never change his mind to do or not do something. I can jump up and down and beg and do a little dance, but it never does any good.'

But whatever happened to the guy who had given him such a hard time at Columbia, Jerry Tokofsky? Incredibly, Ford would run into him – almost – a few years later. He told the story on the *Oprah Winfrey Show* in 1997. When Oprah asked, whatever happened to that guy, Ford replied, 'He's an executive in 20th in the television department . I know that because one day maybe 15 years ago [in 1982] I was sitting in a commissary in 20th having lunch, and a waiter came up to me with a little silver tray with a card on it, which I'd only seen in movies. And I picked up the card, and I looked at it, and on it was the name of the man who I'd had that conversation with. And I turned the card over and it said "I missed my bet". And I looked around the room, and much to my pleasure – I didn't know which one he was.'

CHAPTER 2

HARRISON FORD: BREAKING IN

From Touch 'n' Go to Turning Point

'Acting is basically like carpentry – if you know your craft, you can figure out the logic of a particular job and submit yourself to it. It all comes down to detail.' Harrison Ford

Even though, at the beginning of 1970, Harrison Ford was no longer under contract to Universal and his acting career seemed to be in freefall, his carpentry business was going from strength to strength. Among his clients were the good and great of Hollywood: Sally Kellerman, Joan Didion, and James Coburn. 'I worked mostly for people that were well-off and who could afford to indulge me,' he said.

'What I learned from carpentry, above all,' he continued, 'was a work ethic. I used to be very lazy, but now I find I can't enjoy myself when I'm not working. It saved my life to have another way of making a living. Carpentry gave me the possibility of choice. I didn't want to do episodic tv any more, because I was afraid I'd burn myself out before I got a chance to do any decent feature films. Besides, I was too young. I was 24 and I looked 19.'

So Ford had become a lot choosier about the kind of roles he auditioned for. He continued to make occasional tv appearances, but only if the role had something to offer him. He'd often attend auditions in his workman's overalls and took the position that he didn't need to act to feed his family. 'If they know you're dependent on them, they value you less,' he rationalised.

During 1970, the top film and tv producer Norman Lear, who had such successes as *The Andy Williams Show* (1962), *Divorce American Style* (1967) and *The Night They Raided Minsky's* (1968) to his credit, was putting together a new comedy show for CBS. Based on BBC television's *Till Death Us Do Part*, the new show was called *All in the Family* and was to star Carroll O'Connor in the Warren Mitchell role. Ford was up for the part of the Anthony Booth son-in-law character Mike Stivic. The role would have been a great showcase for Harrison, but he was unable to get past his distaste for the racist character of Archie Bunker and turned the part down.

Around the same time, Ford was offered some lucrative tv commercial work by a fellow Ripon alumnus, Bill Haljum, by then an executive with a Chicago ad agency, which he also turned down, saying that no one in the film industry would take him seriously if he did mouthwash commercials.

Throughout 1970 and 1971, Ford switched between carpentry and acting, appearing in various tv shows like *Dan August* (season 1, 'The Manufactured Man', 1971) and, probably through the influence of William Fucik, a couple of episodes of the James Arness vehicle *Gunsmoke* (the Season 18 episodes 'The Sodbusters', 1972, and 'Wheelan's Men', 1973), sometimes as guest star but more often in a supporting role.

However some imminent changes in Ford's life would mean he suddenly needed to make some substantial money. The old Ford luck kicked in, in the shape of Fred Roos.

'When my wife, Mary, became pregnant with our second child, Willard, I realised my health insurance, that I'd had when Ben was born, allowing us to have a baby for about 25 cents a pound, was no longer in force. Because I hadn't made $1,200 in the previous year. So I had to make $1,200 to keep my health insurance. I said, "Well, I've got to do something." And a friend of mine, Fred Roos, was casting a George Lucas picture and said I ought to be in it because it was going to be a big hit. It *was* in every way.'

This was to be the change in fortune that would set Harrison Ford on his way.

THE WRITING'S ON THE WALL

In early 1972, a young filmmaker called George Lucas was struggling with the Hollywood system to get a pet project off the ground. The movie he wanted to make was a kind of musical autobiography, a story of 1960s teenagers wasting away their lives, cruising the streets of small-town California, to the accompaniment of the local radio station blaring out the rock 'n' roll hits of the day.

Lucas had had a qualified success with his first feature film, *THX 1138*, made for Warner Brothers. That is, critics had spoken highly of the film, but the public stayed away in droves. Needless to say, Warners were not interested in financing what they viewed as an indulgent, un-commercial project, despite the very commercial title of *American Graffiti*.

Lucas had no choice but to hawk the project around the other movie factories in town. He hired former film school classmates Willard Huyck and Gloria Katz to help him develop a 'treatment', an outline of the story, in an effort to give the movie moguls something they could understand. All went well. United Artists gave the go-ahead, and a sum of money, for Lucas to produce a full script. Lucas asked Huyck and Katz to write the screenplay. However, they had just landed a deal to write and direct their own horror picture in Britain, and couldn't find time to help Lucas with the script. (For the record, the horror movie became the undistinguished *Messiah of Evil*, 1972.)

Lucas was in a bind. He told his *Graffiti* line producer, Gary Kurtz, to find a substitute writer. Kurtz suggested another film school peer, Richard Walters. Lucas, sure that his project was in safe hands, set off for the Cannes Film Festival where *THX 1138* was entered in the competition.

When Lucas returned from France, he read the Walters script and wasn't pleased with what he found. Walters had done a good job, all right, but it wasn't the story Lucas had in mind. To make matters worse, Kurtz had spent all the United Artists advance on this one screenplay.

Luckily for Lucas, Huyck and Katz returned from their horror movie expedition to Britain, and agreed to pitch in and help out.

Despite United Artists dropping out of the project, all went well. Lucas managed to interest Universal. A young executive there was very keen to give young filmmakers the opportunity (and a very low budget) to make the kind of films they wanted too. This executive, Ned Tannen, gave Lucas $750,000 to make the picture, provided Lucas's old friend and mentor, Francis Coppola, flush from his *Godfather* success, agreed to become producer.

With the go-ahead from Universal, Lucas engaged Coppola's casting director, one Fred Roos, to cast the film. Roos and Lucas conducted an old-time Hollywood talent search in an effort to find just the right performers for the roles, each of which portrayed (perhaps a little indulgently) a different facet of Lucas's own personality. Finally, Lucas selected four or five actors for each of the principal roles and conducted screen tests using video equipment, an unheard of procedure in Hollywood at the time. The idea was to assemble a cast that worked well as a group rather than relying on a band of actors who were individually outstanding. Strangely enough, the final selection each turned out to have star careers ahead of them: Ron Howard (who later went from the phenomenal success of tv's *Happy Days* to directing feature films like *Cocoon* (1985), *A Beautiful Mind* (2001) and *The Da Vinci Code* (2005)), Richard Dreyfuss (star roles in *Jaws*, *Close Encounters of the Third Kind* and an Oscar for *The Goodbye Girl)*, Candy Clark, Cindy Williams and Kathleen Quinlan. And helping out in the secondary parts were Susanne Somers. Bo Hopkins, Paul Le Mat and ... Harrison Ford.

'I was Bob Falfa – the boy in the cowboy hat,' Ford later remarked. It must have been Ford's new forthright confident air that made Lucas pick him for the Falfa role.

'When I went for the interview, I wasn't there as a person who needed a job to put bread on the table,' said Ford. 'I had, for once, a real life behind me. When you're an out-of-work actor and you walk into an audition, you're an empty vessel. So this was a significant change in my personality. I had got my pride back.'

The film was on a very tight budget and Ford's salary was set at the SAG scale rate of just $485 a week, about half what he made at carpentry. Ford's first instinct was to turn the part down, after all, he had a family to support. However Roos managed to persuade him to take the role by upping his fee to $500 a week. For Ford, it wasn't the money, it was the principle.

In the film, Falfa is a cocky out-of-towner who roars into town in a black hot-rod to take on the resident champion in a drag race. Each time he is seen in the film he is with a different girl, eventually carrying Ron Howard's girlfriend Laurie (Cindy Williams) with him during the final drag race of the picture.

The shooting schedule for *American Graffiti* was gruelling. The night-time location filming began at nine in the evening and broke, just before dawn at around five-thirty.

'It was fun,' smiles Harrison Ford, 'It was like a party, but not a Hollywood party. It was a real low budget movie, even for those days. I only got a couple of hundred dollars a week. There were no dressing rooms. The actors sat in the same trailer as the costumes. '

Ford was the oldest of the principal players on me film, though rather than setting an example of professional sobriety, he was more often than not the mastermind behind many of the pranks played on unfortunate victims during the filming.

At first, bored with all the sitting around waiting till he was needed, Ford took to gunning his hot rod, a powerful, custom-built Chevrolet racer that had been used in the previous year's *Two Lane Blacktop*, up and down the main strip of the location town Petaluma. But the local police stepped in and threatened to arrest Ford and impound the car. Then, joined by his newfound partner-in-crime, Paul Le Mat, Ford embarked on a series of pranks which made the rest of the cast very nervous. They drank beer then climbed up the Holiday Inn sign to leave the bottles at the top, they peed in the hotel ice dispenser and tried to set fire to the director's room. 'Harrison and Paul were pretty wild,' recalled Candy Clarke. 'They were drinking a lot of beer in those days. I found them very intimidating, like Hell's Angels types.'

Another time, Ford and Le Mat were hurling beer bottles from their balcony into the hotel parking lot. One of the bottles smashed the windshield of a Cadillac so Richard Dreyfuss tried to get them to stop. An argument ensued and ended with Harrison and Paul flinging Dreyfuss off the balcony into the shallow end of the swimming pool, two floors below.

Dreyfuss was due to shoot close-ups that night, but emerged from the swimming pool with a cut on his forehead which no amount of makeup could cover. Lucas took the news quite well, better than the staff of the Holiday Inn who asked Ford to leave. He was moved into the nearby Howard Johnson's, separated from the rest of the cast.

'I was a bit of a carouser in those days and was in the company of other hell-raisers,' confessed Ford. 'If I'd been in the company of priests I would have behaved differently.'

However, working with director Lucas was an entirely new kind of experience for Ford. Completely different from the old-school, 'just do it, okay?' directors that Ford had been used to working with in Hollywood, Lucas seemed to be open to suggestions and listened to the people around him. At the beginning of filming, Lucas asked Ford to get his hair cut even shorter than Ronny Howard, Paul Le Mat and Charles Martin-Smith to make him seem different from the local kids. Reluctant to loose the remainder of his longish hair, Ford countered with, 'What if I wear a cowboy hat?' Lucas thought for a moment, then said, 'Yeah, that's a good idea. Let's try it.'

At the 'wrap' party, at the end of filming, Lucas screened a twenty-minute extract for the cast and crew. Most were sure that they were on to something good. When the lights went up. Ford turned to his neighbour, Cindy Williams, and said, 'This is great!'

The film had been shot, on schedule, inside 28 working days (or rather, nights), but George Lucas's problems were far from over. Universal didn't like the movie and wanted to re-cut it. It was here that Coppola really earned his money as producer. He flatly refused to allow Universal to tamper with the film, and offered to write Ned Tannen a cheque for the whole of the budget, in effect, buying *American Graffiti,* lock, stock and soundtrack from Universal. After much arguing back and forth, Tanner sort of got his way and was molified with a couple of cuts, then previewed the film. *American Graffiti* was a hit with everyone except Harrison Ford and Richard Dreyfuss, who sneaked out of the preview before the film ended, because they were so embarrassed at their big-screen appearance.

The scenes that disappeared were Terry the Toad's encounter with a fast-talking car salesman, John Milner and Carol's walk through the automobile scrapyard and Bob Falfa singing *Some Enchanted Evening* to Laurie. Ford's scene, which he had ad-libbed and Lucas has kept, was cut not because his singing was inferior (though, admittedly, it's not Caruso either) but because Rodgers' and Hammerstein's estates, who owned copyright on the song, wanted too much money for its inclusion in the movie (though, for the 1978 re-release, these scenes were reinstated).

The critics were pretty much of one voice in loving the film. *The New York Times* wrote, '*American Graffiti* is a very good movie, funny, tough, unsentimental. It is full of marvelous performances from actors (especially Candy Clark, Richard Dreyfuss, and Cindy Williams) hardly known for previous screen credits.'

Trade newspaper *Variety* said, 'Without exception, all players fit perfectly into the concept and execution, and all the young principals and featured players have a bright and lengthy future. And so does Lucas.'

Graffiti was released and eventually pulled in a staggering $115 million on the modest outlay of $750,000. Universal made its money back 50-fold.

As a bonus, the movie received five nominations at the 1974 Academy Awards (the one with the streaker), including Best Editing, Best Screenplay, Best Director, Best Picture (all lost out to *The Sting*) and Best Supporting Actress (Candy Clarke, beaten by 10 year old Tatum O'Neill), though it won Golden Globes for Best Musical and Best Newcomer for Paul Le Mat.

WHO WAS THAT MASKED CASTING DIRECTOR?

The enormous success of *American Graffiti* didn't change Harrison Ford's life overnight. Where actors were singled out for praise, it was always the principals, Richard Dreyfuss and Ronny Howard who got the credit. Lucas, too, was suddenly a star. But for Ford, it was back to carpentry and the infrequent tv appearances.

Ford took a role in the cult tv show *Kung Fu*, appearing as a character called 'Harrison' in the episode 'Crossties' (season 2, 1974), a story about angry farmers battling the railroad company that wants to snatch their land.

It was Fred Roos, again, who was responsible for getting Harrison Ford his next two roles. Francis Coppola was putting together another project, the highly praised *The Conversation*. Naturally he hired Fred Roos to cast the movie. And, inevitably, Roos turned once again to Harrison Ford for one of the smaller, but hardly less vital, parts in the picture.

'I still did the odd carpentry job after *American Graffiti*,' recalls Ford. 'But before too long there was Coppola's film, *The Conversation*, which I did with Hackman. I turned up playing an evil young henchman (who works for Robert Duvall's Director character) in that movie. There was no role there until I decided to make him a homosexual.'

In an effort to make something more of his role than just another walk-on, Ford had bought a loud green silk suit for the then huge sum of $900. At the script read-through,

Coppola was astonished at Ford's outfit. 'What are you?' he asked unkindly. Ford explained his idea for the character. In 1974 gay characters would have been a risk, but Coppola was nothing if not a gambler. 'Hey, that's really good,' he told Ford and instructed production designer Dean Tavoularis to create a room for the character, by now named Martin Stett, that underlined his lifestyle.

Again an important director had listened to and agreed with Ford's ideas.

The Conversation tells the story of surveillance expert Harry Caul (Gene Hackman), who records a conversation between a young couple as they walk through San Francisco. When Harry plays the tape back in his workshop, he notices a sentence in the conversation which suggests the couple are in some kind of danger. He takes the tape to the Director (Robert Duvall) of the large corporation that hired him, but on an impulse refuses to hand the tapes over to the Director's assistant, Martin Stett (Harrison Ford). Later, while visiting a surveillance equipment exhibition, Harry runs into Stett again. The young man tries to put pressure on Harry to hand over the tapes. Harry refuses. At the same exhibition, he meets and befriends another investigator, Bernie Moran (Allen Garfield). They have a few drinks together and return to Harry's workshop for a party. Also at the party is a call-girl, Meredith (Elizabeth MacRae) with whom Harry spends some time. But when he wakes up, Harry finds that the tapes of the conversation have been stolen. He tries to contact the Director but fails. Fearing that a murder is about to be committed, he takes a room next to the one in which the young couple have arranged to meet. He breaks into the couple's room and is horrified to find that a murder *has* been committed. The Director has been killed, apparently by the couple that Harry thought were in danger. Back at his apartment, Harry is warned to keep what he knows to himself as he, too, is under surveillance. Harry searches his own apartment thoroughly for the listening device but finds nothing.

The Conversation received much praise from the critics. *Monthly Film Bulletin*'s David Wilson said, '*The Conversation* is an unqualified success, a complex, reverberating study of a man trapped by guilt ... It is a measure of that success ... that the comparison which most obviously suggests itself, *Blow-Up*, leaves Antonioni's film looking empty and inert.'

Variety said, 'A major artistic asset to the film – besides script, direction and the top performances – is supervising editor Walter Murch's sound collage and re-recording. Voices come in and out of aural focus in a superb tease.'

Vincent Canby wrote in *The New York Times*, 'The members of the supporting cast are almost as good as Mr Hackman, particularly Allen Garfield as a surveillance expert from Detroit who bugged his first phone at the age of 12 and then went on to become famous in the trade as the man who told Chrysler that Cadillac was getting rid of its fins.'

But good though Ford's performance in *The Conversation* might have been, again he went unnoticed by the critics. The one big success still eluded him.

BACK TO TELEVISION

A few months after the release of *The Conversation*, Ford turned up in an episode of the legal drama show *Petrocelli*, 'The Edge of Evil (season 1, 1974), playing Tom Brannigan. It was to be Ford's last appearance in episodic television.

Ford next had a walk-on part in the tv movie *Judgement: The Trial of Lt Calley*, a courtroom drama set in the wake of a Vietnam atrocity, directed by Stanley Kramer and based on a true incident ('I played the witness who cries,' said Ford), and a more substantial role as the eldest son of Sarah Miles's Jennifer Blackwood in the lavish tv production of *Dynasty*.

Dynasty is a sprawling tale of the fortunes of the Blackwood family and their migration to Westmore, Ohio in 1823. John Blackwood (Harris Yulin), the head of the family is a man of unbending principles whose dearest ambition it is to farm the 100 acre piece of land he has acquired. His wife, Jennifer (Sarah Miles) and his brother Matt (Stacy Keach) both feel there is more money to be made in the carriage business. Eventually, Jennifer leaves John for Matt after being accused of infidelity by her husband. But the relationship doesn't work out and Jennifer returns to John. Realising the depth of her husband's hatred for her she endeavours to build the Blackwood carriage business into an empire. Matt returns to Westmore and tries to convince John to sell the farmland to the railroad for a huge profit. Though John refuses, Jennifer's youngest son, Carver (Gerrit Graham) conspires with Matt to kill John and sell the land. After John's death, Jennifer, unaware of the conspiracy, passes over her eldest son, Mark (Harrison Ford) and appoints Matt to run the Blackwood business.

Variety complained that *Dynasty*'s 'last half hour concentrates too much on Miles's ungrateful grown-up offspring' and that it 'really encompassed too wide a time span to be handled properly in a two-hour movie.' Ford had the pretty thankless role of the 'nice son' so didn't have the material at hand an actor needs to stand out in a cast. Unsurprisingly, Ford's contributions passed unmarked by contemporary critics, and looking at the film today I can see why contemporary critics might have been unenthusiastic. Ford's acting is earnest but unshowy. I don't think Ford was bad in the role, but that his style was simply ahead of its time.

So Harrison Ford was still an acting carpenter.

However, by this time, the *American Graffiti* director George Lucas had finalised a deal with Twentieth Century-Fox to make a space adventure movie called *Star Wars*. Ford was familiar with the project, but nurtured no ambitions about being in the movie. After all, he hadn't been one of the principle players in *Graffiti* and probably felt his contribution had been minimal.

'George (Lucas) had let it be known that he wasn't going to use anybody from *American Graffiti*,' said Ford. 'Not because we'd disappointed him, but he was writing a whole new thing and needed new faces. But old Fred Roos did it again. He prevailed on George to see me after he'd seen everyone else.'

The story of how Harrison Ford ended up with the role of Han Solo is another one of those tales that Ford tells better than anyone else. He recounted it within a short interview for the London events magazine, *Time Out*.

'The reason I ran into George Lucas again was because Francis Coppola's art director inveigled me into installing a very elaborate raised panel in his studio office. Now, I knew they were casting and I thought it a bit coy to be around Francis's office, being a carpenter, during the day. So I did the work at night. Well, one day something came up and I got stuck and I had to work at the studios during the day. And, sure enough, that was the day that George Lucas was doing the casting for *Star Wars*.

'There I was, on my knees in the doorway, and in comes Francis Coppola, George Lucas, four other captains of the industry and Richard Dreyfuss. In fact, Dreyfuss came through first and made a big joke out of being my assistant. That made me feel just great. I felt about the size of a pea after they walked through. But, weeks later, when they'd tested everybody else in the world, I got the part.'

Ford is guilty of a little over-simplification here. The casting for *Star Wars* was as meticulous, at the very least, as the casting on *American Graffiti*. Lucas knew he was going to have to interview literally hundreds of young actors and young hopefuls just to find the three people to portray the key lead roles. He joined forces with another young director making his first major picture, Brian De Palma, who was looking for a teenage cast for *Carrie*. For about eight weeks, De Palma and Lucas were seeing 30-40 young actors and actresses a day. Lucas sat quietly making notes and entering the names of those who particularly impressed him on a Second Interview list. After Lucas tripped over Ford in the doorway of Coppola's office, the young filmmaker approached Ford for assistance with the video tests for the *Star Wars* auditions. The idea was that Ford, whom Lucas felt at ease with, would read the male parts for the actresses testing for the role of Princess Leia. Ford initially didn't mind doing the favour for Lucas, whom he liked, but after a time became irritated with having to read a part which he thought he would never play. According to Dale Pollock's book, *Skywalking*, it was Ford's churlishness that won him the part of Han Solo. But it's far more likely that George Lucas saw in Harrison Ford elements of the character he envisaged for Solo. Ford had a certain forthright and honest way of expressing himself that isn't a million light years away from Solo's lines in the movie.

At one stage, Lucas was considering a black actor for the role of Solo. This idea probably evolved into the character of Lando Calrissian in *The Empire Strikes Back*.

But also to be taken into consideration was Lucas's unique concept of ensemble casting. Lucas had decided on Harrison Ford, Mark Hamill and Carrie Fisher as one trio. But if any of them had been unable to take part in the film, Lucas had a reserve team waiting in the wings to step in. It was all of one group or all of the other – no mixing and matching. Lucas's second group was Christopher Walken, Will Selzer and singer Terri Nunn, who would later front the band Berlin.

In some documenting of the *Star Wars* casting story, it has been reported (admittedly by me, as well, in earlier editions of this book) that Nunn was a former Penthouse Pet. However, given that she was 15 when she auditioned for *Star Wars*, this seems unlikely on two counts. Firstly, it would have been illegal for Nunn to have modelled for *Penthouse* before the *Star Wars* casting and secondly, it's inconceivable that Lucas would have auditioned a nude model for a pivotal role in his wholesome family film. While some sources assert that Nunn did appear in *Penthouse* for February 1977 under the name of Betsy Harris, I've been unable to find any confirmation of this. Indeed, Terri Nunn herself denies it. In an interview with the online *Exclusive Magazine*, Nunn was asked about the rumour of her Penthouse appearance and replied, 'No, that one's not true! I don't know who that is, but that wouldn't even be legal. But, I have heard about this before. I haven't seen her, but people need to think about the age. It's a good story, but it's not me, sorry!' Yet even if it *were* true, it would in all likelihood place the date of the photoshoot after the *Star Wars* auditions.

'For me, at least,' said Ford about the casting of the trio he was part of, 'it was obvious what the relationship would be, simply by looking at the others. It was apparent the characters were very contemporary and the situation very simple – without meaning that in a derogatory way. It was simply straightforward, a clear human story. I mean, I didn't have to act science fiction.'

George Lucas had worked out backgrounds for all his characters. Solo had been abandoned by space gypsies at a very early age and was raised by creatures called Wookiees until he was twelve. He eventually became a cadet at the Space Academy, but was thrown out for selling exam papers to his peers. Eventually he became a smuggler, living outside the laws of the Empire. Yet at the same time, Lucas knew that his actors could add the little touches that would bring the characters to life on the screen.

'Very little time was wasted,' said Ford in the Lucas biography, *Skywalking*. 'George didn't have an authoritarian attitude like so many directors: "Kid, I've been in this business twenty-five years. Trust me." He was different. He knew the movie was based so strongly on the relationship between the three of us, he encouraged our contributions.'

It's the little contributions Ford makes to the characters he's playing that makes him such an interesting actor. Which shows that Lucas's shrewdness won out over his own 'all new faces' rule for *Star Wars*. Ford goes on to explain how he went about filling in the spaces in Solo's personality.

'George Lucas gave me a lot of freedom to change little parts of the dialogue which weren't comfortable.' Ford is being charitable here. In *Skywalking* it said that Ford's favourite way of pulling Lucas's leg during filming was to say, 'You can type this shit, George, but you sure can't say it.'

'We worked together on it,' continues Ford. 'I really like working with him.'

The part of Han Solo was the biggest chance of Ford's career to show what he could do as an actor. 'This was the first time I had a character big enough to take space instead of just filling in spaces as I did at Columbia and Universal. I could do that for the first time.'

Ford had worked with big name, heavyweight actors before, but never with such a 'legend' as Sir Alec Guinness. Most of the cast were in awe of Sir Alec and Ford was no exception.

'He gave me many sleepless nights. I'd be thinking, "I'm supposed to be in a movie with Sir Alec Guinness. He'll laugh at me just once … and I'll pack up and go home." But, of course, he never did. He's really a very kind and generous person.'

When questioned by *Ritz* magazine whether Ford was using the title 'Sir Alec' out of respect or because Guinness insisted on it, he replied with his customary tact, 'Let's just say he prefers it.'

THE CHANGING FACE OF THE MOVIES

When *Star Wars* opened in the United States on May 25th, 1977, it garnered rave reviews and within months had become the most successful movie of all time. Several critics likened Ford's performance in the Han Solo role to John Wayne's style of acting. This was news to Ford, never a movie fan himself.

'I never thought about that,' said Ford, 'until I kept seeing it mentioned in the reviews.' Besides, Ford was well aware that it would be impossible to get away with imitating other actors for very long.

'If I end up acting like John Wayne, and I know I'm acting like John Wayne, then I'm in heaps of trouble. But if I don't realise I'm acting like John Wayne, and I am, then that is simply part of my subconscious supplying something that is necessary for the role. I was never aware of doing a routine. Acting is so intensely personal that if you're not operating – totally – within your own resources, there comes a moment when you'll be stuck, you won't know who to imitate. Much better to use only your own personality and resources as a tool and keep them both sharp and well-oiled.'

Probably Ford's finest moment in *Star Wars* is when he is in the prison block of the Death Star trying to rescue the Princess. Both Solo and Luke are disguised in Imperial Storm Trooper costumes, with Chewbacca posing as their prisoner. The three dispatch the prison guards – noisily – and draw the attention of the officer in charge of the detention area. The officer calls the prison block on the intercom and demands to know what is happening. It's left to Solo to try to convince the unseen Imperial officer that all is well. Realising that his reassurances are falling on deaf ears, Solo fires his blaster into the control panel to cut off the irritating stream of questions. Solo's sense of desperation is portrayed with nervous realism and, more importantly, with humour. The scene was played that way after careful consideration by Ford, 'and done in one take. I never learned the dialogue for it because I wanted to show desperation. I told George Lucas I wanted to do it all the way through first time. I just said, "Stop me if I'm really bad." He didn't.'

One side effect of the success of *Star Wars* was that it conferred instant celebrity on the three principle players. For an actor who values his privacy, that could have been a problem for Harrison Ford. 'Fortunately, I don't have as unique a physiognomy as Carrie or Mark do, so I'm much less recognised in the streets – about which I'm very happy. That could get heavy. It happens infrequently enough, and people are usually very nice, because the film is very broadly accepted – so that's a pleasure. But when they know where we're going to be, and they're sitting outside the hotel – all these autograph people – sometimes that's a drag. But none of that really bothers me.'

Compounding the fame achieved by Ford through his appearance in *Star Wars* was all the merchandising that trailed in the wake of the movie. Suddenly, the toy shops were full of plastic Han Solo figures, jigsaws bearing Ford's features and assorted paraphernalia. And, in addition to the toys, there was the fact that just about every magazine published was finding excuses to report on the *Star Wars* phenomenon. There were novelisations of the film, comic strip adaptations by juvenile publishing giant Marvel Comics and a series of novels, unrelated to the film, starring Han Solo and his Wookiee friend Chewbacca. There have been three Han Solo novels by Brian Daley published by Sphere Books; *Han Solo at Stars' End, Han Solo and the Lost Legacy* and *Han Solo's Revenge,* and three by A.C. Crispin published by Bantam; *The Paradise Snare, The Hutt Gambit* and *Rebel Dawn.*

The other major change in Ford's life brought about by the success of *Star Wars* was the financial one.

'I believe in the work ethic,' said Ford. 'That was the middle class way I was brought up. When I was offered Han Solo, I was paid less for that than when I was a carpenter. '

That was so while he was actually working on the film. But Ford, like Carrie Fisher and Mark Hamill, later received a percentage of the film's profits. Two thirds of a percent may not sound like much, but that fraction of a point totted up a healthy $53,000 for Ford in the first three months that *Star Wars* was on release. And with Star Wars having taken a staggering $798 million worldwide to date, making it one of the highest grossing movies of all time, Ford has done quite nicely out of Lucas' little science fiction film.

'Not that money means very much in my life. But suddenly having it made it possible to move into a large house in the Hollywood Hills and equip a large workshop on the premises where I now spend all my spare time making furniture. I don't think success has changed me. Sure, I live in a big house. But I still manage to be a pretty private sort of a guy. My greatest pleasure is my work and the nearest thing I've got to a hobby is my carpentry. I don't go to parties and I'm not involved in the Hollywood scene. Who knows, maybe if I had socialised a bit more, success would have come much sooner, because in Hollywood, to succeed, you have to know the right people. By some irony, all the right people – like George Lucas and Francis Coppola – all knew me, and I didn't even have to hustle for their attention.'

And in the months that followed, while Ford was waiting for work to begin on the *Star Wars* sequel, *The Empire Strikes Back,* he didn't have to hustle for the attention of other filmmakers, either. In fact, Ford was the busiest of the *Star Wars* stars during that period.

'That could be because I made an effort to take advantage of the film offers that being in *Star Wars* gave me,' he later said. 'I think people in this industry realise that I've played, and am capable of playing, these different types of characters. I was able to do small parts once in a while due to the popularity of *Star Wars.* I've been really lucky to have *Star Wars* as a part of my life.'

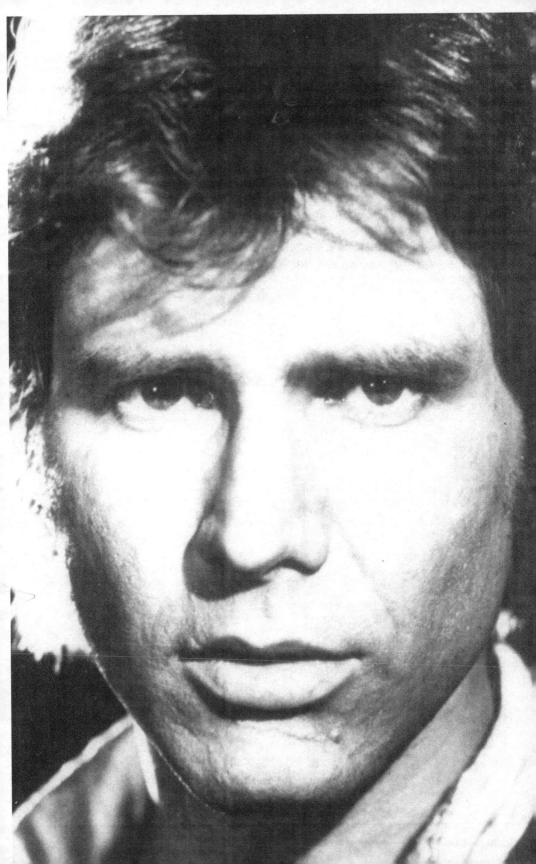

CHAPTER 3

HARRISON FORD: NEW DIRECTIONS

From Star Wars to Wars Star

'When I saw *Star Wars* before it was released, I realised the power of it as a piece of film-making, and set out deliberately to try to do something that would contrast with the character of Han Solo.' Harrison Ford

The principal photography of *Star Wars* was completed in the August of 1976. It would be nine months before the movie was dropped on an unsuspecting American public. But Harrison Ford didn't sit around and wait for success to come to him. The role in *Star Wars* was his biggest achievement in the eleven years he had been in movies. He was aware that Han Solo had been a major role in a major film. If he was to avoid the typecasting he feared would follow in the wake of *Star Wars* he had to make his move immediately. He cast around for a part that would avoid the flippant derring-do of the Solo character, and found it in a rather grim tv horror movie, *The Possessed* (1977). Starring James Farentino, the film was a cynical reworking of some of the themes from 1973's *The Exorcist*, pitting Farentino's unfrocked priest against a bunch of demons in a girls' boarding school. Ford played the cool biology teacher all the girls had a crush on.

Harrison Ford's next film role was yet another piece of space filling, which he did at the request of his old friend Fred Roos. Francis Coppola was about to begin work on his latest project, a Vietnam war tale which had been written by John Milius and had originally been slated to be directed by George Lucas as a 'mockumentary' on location in Vietnam while the conflict was in full effect. As it worked out, Lucas had stepped aside and Coppola himself ended up in the director's chair. The film was the now-legendary *Apocalypse Now*, which was shot in the Phillipines and starred Martin Sheen, Marlon Brando and Robert Duvall.

'My scene was shared with Martin Sheen,' recalls Ford. 'It wasn't a big role for me, just a nine-day cameo as a US Army Intelligence Colonel. I had my hair cut short and presented another image, Vietnam style.'

As, perhaps, a tip of the director's hat to Lucas's early involvement in the movie, Coppola had Harrison Ford's character wear a name-tag on his uniform which read 'Col G. Lucas'.

'It's just the one scene,' says Ford, 'the laundry list scene – it told the audience all they needed to know for the rest of the movie. And when George (Lucas) saw it, the scene was half-way over before he recognised me. That was exactly the way I wanted it.'

When asked by writer Tony Crawley how he would compare Lucas and Coppola as filmmakers, Ford replied, 'It's really presumptuous for an actor to get into that kind of discussion. More so for me, I'm not intellectually equipped to make such judgements. Let's see – they both have beards and glasses, and a difference in personality. I know what the differences are, but it would take me about two days to explain it. Certainly, they both allow their actors enormous freedom. Francis lets you make a choice and then moves everything to support you, to make it work for you. He's really delightful.'

But as much as Ford may have enjoyed the experience, brief as it was, on *Apocalypse Now*, it was still really only walk-on cameo. Word of Ford's performance in *Star Wars* must have been getting around, because Ford was offered a meaty supporting role in a middleweight Hollywood movie called *Heroes*.

Heroes was the film which marked the big-screen debut of Henry Winkler. Winkler had shot to fame in the phenomenally successful *Happy Days* tv series, a show based, perhaps ironically, certainly unofficially, on *American Graffiti*, and co-starring Ron Howard. Winkler had grown tired of being so irreversibly identified with 'The Fonz' and had selected *Heroes* for his escape from television. The story concerned the uncertain adventures of a returning Vietnam veteran, whose ambition it is to set up a worm farm in Nowheresville, California, and his relationships with his best pal (Harrison Ford) and his girl (Sally Field). Jeremy Paul Kagan was the director.

'I did *Heroes* for short money,' says Ford. 'It wasn't a big part, and I wasn't paid big money.'

The filming of *Heroes* was straightforward enough except for one hiccup which involved Harrison Ford and occurred before even a foot of film had run through the cameras.

'Ten days before shooting *Heroes*,' recalls Ford, 'Jeremy changed my character from a mid-Western to a Missouri farm-boy. So off I went to Missouri with a tape-recorder to learn the accent. I bummed around for about three days and went and met the actual type I was going to play – a guy interested in cars. I went into an auto-part store and told them I was a writer because if you tell them you're an actor, you spend the rest of the time talking about movies – and it also puts a certain distance between you and them.'

When it was released, *Heroes* proved not to be the cinema box-office success Henry Winkler was looking for. The film was over-long and patchy and sank without a trace.

'It was a good part,' says Ford philosophically, 'but Henry Winkler was the real star of the film.' His next role, as the American Ranger Lieutenant-Colonel Barnsby in *Force Ten From Navarone,* brought him a little closer to centre-stage.

LEARNING THE WAYS OF THE FORCE

Taking the role in *Force Ten From Navarone* was probably one of the sounder career decisions made by Harrison Ford during the period that immediately followed *Star Wars.* Although it was another supporting role, the fact that it was a major Hollywood style movie made it preferable to a leading role in a small independent production.

'It's fun to do those supporting roles, because they're good character pieces,' Ford pointed out to an interviewer. 'The problem is that they don't usually write character parts as the leads of the movies. Unfortunately, you can't always play the supporting roles because of the complicated vision that people in this industry have. Hollywood only really takes notice when you're being paid the money and given the billing that a "lead actor" gets. That's why *Force Ten from Navarone* was important for me to do. Its cast was a "package of big names" which included me.'

Force Ten from Navarone was a belated sequel to the 1961 war adventure *The Guns of Navarone* and tells how the only survivors of the first adventure, Major Mallory (here played by Robert Shaw) and Sergeant Miller (Edward Fox) are sent to Yugoslavia with Lt Col Mike Barnsby (Harrison Ford) and his squad of US Rangers to find and eliminate Nicolai Lescovar, the German spy who sabotaged the original mission and who is now posing as a Yugoslavian resistance fighter.

Ford is the first to admit that there wasn't very much in *Force Ten from Navarone* he could work on. 'Mike Barnsby was one of those macho, tough-guy parts that everyone *thought* I should be doing.' Yet, in another interview, he did talk about the character as though he respected the kind of person Barnsby was. 'He's a man of real capacity. He flies, he fights, he's got brains, but everything works against him. At the last minute he gets the Robert Shaw and James Fox characters tacked onto his mission, so there's a lot of adversity in the relationship between them, until he begins to need them and they begin to need him – a nice kind of continuity of cross purposes that become established and finally resolved. An interesting character. I think it'll work.'

When *Force Ten from Navarone* was released it wasn't well received by the critics, though *Playboy*'s Bruce Williamson gave the film a cautious thumbs-up, saying, 'Guy Hamilton builds *Force Ten* into a straightforward, man-size adventure – a nostalgic toast to the good old war years, when we unequivocally rooted for our side to win.'

The *Monthly Film Bulletin* was less charitable. 'Leadenly scripted and directed, this rather belated sequel to *The Guns of Navarone* is depressingly short on thrills and almost completely lacking in suspense.'

For me the biggest problem was the clash between ex-Bond helmer Guy Hamilton's decidedly old-fashioned movie-making style (even more so when you compare it to George Lucas' staging and direction on *Star Wars,* filmed a year or two earlier) and the very contemporary acting style of Ford, clearly ahead of his time and waiting for the rest of the movie industry to catch up with him.

In the light of the adverse criticism, Ford was given the chance to answer in a post release interview. '*Force Ten from Navarone* was an attempt, in a way, to objectify the success of *Star Wars.* It wasn't a personal success for me. It was George's movie, his success. Nonetheless, I wanted to take advantage of the chance to work. And it was a job I did for the money. And I was lost, because I didn't know what the story was about. I didn't have anything to act. There was no reason for my character being there. I had no part of the story that was important to tell. I had a hard time taking the stage with the bull that I was supposed to be doing. I can't do that, and I won't ever do that again. It wasn't a bad film. There were honest people involved making an honest effort. But it wasn't the right thing for me to do.'

HAND-OVER STREET

Harrison Ford was then moved from one World War Two tale straight into another. 'After *Force Ten* I was looking forward to doing some building alterations to my house in the Hollywood Hills when Kris Kristofferson dropped out of *Hanover Street* in England,' explains Ford. 'They asked me to come to London and take over his role at very short notice. I played an American B-52 bomber pilot stationed in wartime Britain who falls in love with an English nurse (Lesley-Anne Down) married to a British Intelligence Officer (Christopher Plummer). I enjoyed making it, but the long schedule meant it was quite some time before I saw my home again.'

Despite the fact that Ford got along well with his co-stars, Ford hadn't entirely enjoyed his involvement in the movie, and didn't talk much about the film until it was long behind him. 'I don't even like to think about *Hanover Street*,' said Ford just before the release of *Raiders of the Lost Ark*. 'The director (Peter Hyams) and I did *not* get along. I've never even seen the film.' All of which begs the question, then why appear in the movie at all? Ford had an answer for that. 'My motivation for doing *Hanover Street* was because I had never kissed a female human being on the screen before. The characters I played were totally sexless, and here was a movie that was being touted as a romance. That was a clear, obvious reason for doing it.' Then he added, 'There are a lot of other reasons, which may or may not have been the right ones for doing it.'

What Ford doesn't explain is that if he hadn't taken the role, the project would have in all likelihood have collapsed, leaving a crew of 120 jobless and the backers General Cinemas out of pocket to the tune of $7 million. Something else Ford doesn't mention is that the long separation from Mary would put a big strain on their marriage.

But for all that, the critics were less than kind about *Hanover Street*. Said *Playboy*'s Bruce Williamson, 'Ford, as a romantic leading man, is fairly stolid and one-dimensional, labouring hard to simulate the kind of casual charm that Redford, Newman and a dozen other male actors must work hard to conceal when they want to be taken seriously. Hyams gives us a pair of lovers who seldom appear to enjoy each other very much.' Uncharitable, perhaps, but cinema audiences seemed to agree on the whole and the film, taking just $3 million in the US, set no box-office records.

To be fair, while the movie plods during the romantic sequences with the gorgeous Lesley-Anne Down and a distinctly uncomfortable-looking Harrison Ford – due mostly to a complete lack of chemistry between the two – it picks up during the mission when Plummer and Ford operate behind enemy lines disguised as Nazis.

The movie gossip magazines, like *People*, were more interested in making a story out of Ford and his *Hanover Street* co-star Lesley-Ann Down being more than just co-workers. But there was more to the failure of the Fords' marriage than just idle gossip. The fact was that Mary was becoming increasing more uncomfortable with the circus that went along with Harrison's blossoming film career. Pictures of her in the post-*Star Wars* hoopla showed her on Harrison's arm, uneasy with the frenzied activities of the paparazzi around her. In was almost inevitable, in retrospect, that cracks would begin to appear in Mary and Harrison's relationship.

'I wasn't prepared,' said Ford, 'either by experience, maturity or disposition to be a good husband or good father the first time around. I wasn't easy to live with. I was bitter and cynical.'

When the separation came in 1978, Harrison and Mary kept the split amicable. Ford felt he could do no less. 'I owe everything to Mary,' he told an interviewer. 'Without her, I wouldn't be in the cinema today, because I wouldn't have accepted the role of Han Solo. When Lucas made me the offer, I hadn't been in front of a camera for three years. Mary wasn't only beautiful and kind, she gave me the confidence to accept. She pushed me back into the cinema.'

Ford voiced his regret when he said, 'The cinema separated us, and I will never forgive it for that.'

WHAT WERE THEY THINKING?

One of the post-*Star Wars* projects you'll never see mentioned in any interview with Harrison Ford is probably one of the most entertaining, for all the wrong reasons: *The Star Wars Holiday Special*.

For some reason, probably the insistence of Fox executives that the studio needed something *Star Wars* on tv during the run-up to Christmas, George Lucas okayed the making of the *Holiday Special*, then somehow managed to get most of the cast to agree to appear. And that was when Lucas wisely took a step back from this project and left Ford, Fisher, Hammill *et al* to make the best of it. Merry Christmas, guys …

It's proved nigh impossible to track down any solid information about the hows and whys of the making of this tv terror. Those who appeared in it will not even admit to its existence. Questioned about it at a science fiction convention in Australia a few years later, Lucas remarked, 'if I had the time and a sledgehammer, I would track down every bootlegged copy of that program and smash it.'

However, a little diligence and fifteen minutes searching the DVD section of eBay allowed me to buy a copy on disk. And guess what? *The Star Wars Holiday Special* is everything you've heard and more.

Far and away the worst aspect is the interminable framing interludes with Chewbacca's Wookiee family, conducted entirely in the Wookiee language (no subtitles) with the ill-considered help of character actor Art Carney and *Blazing Saddles* star Harvey Korman (in drag, no less). These sequences appear to have been shot live with multiple cameras, a common tv technique at the time, but the pace is leaden, making the scenes seem to run far longer than they actually do.

There are some *non sequitur* contributions from rock band Jefferson Starship (chosen no doubt more because of their cosmic-sounding name than for any suitability of their music) and a weird 'man's entertainment' video watched by Granpa Wookiee which features hot star of the period Diahann Carroll.

It's not all dreadful – balancing the appalling cantina sequence, with *The Golden Girls'*

Bea Arthur as the bar tender, is the moderately interesting animated sequence which introduces mercenary Boba Fett for the first time.

The grim Wookiee framing sequence is brought to its long overdue climax when Han Solo and Chewbacca show up and pitch an Imperial Stormtrooper over the balcony of the Wookiee home – then Carrie Fisher sings a song which sets a string of platitudes to the tune of the *Star Wars* theme.

Based on this and the trance-like appearances by the other *Star Wars* principle actors, you could be forgiven for thinking that Ford, Fisher and Hammill had been blackmailed into appearing in this travesty, so flat are their performances.

By the end of the treacle-like 97 minutes, you'll be ready to cheerfully strangle anyone who wishes you a Happy Life Day.

A bit of a bonus for me was the inclusion on the disk of some original Kenner toy ads from the period – no real connection to the *Star Wars Holiday Special*, though you can be sure that the audience of the show was bombarded with commercials not unlike these ...

GO WEST

Towards the end of 1978 Harrison Ford, unlike Mark Hamill and Carrie Fisher, had not signed up before *Star Wars* for all three movies, but he had agreed to appear in *The Empire Strikes Back*. Ford had negotiated with George Lucas for better terms. He also wanted to see the character of Han Solo become 'more dashing'. Lucas agreed readily to the terms, although, in the end, Ford ended up making no more than his two co-stars from the *Star Wars* sequel.

In the meantime, Ford had just time for one more movie before returning to the camp of George Lucas, *The Frisco Kid*.

The project had originally come up during the filming of *Heroes*. In his interview in *Playboy* for August 1977, Henry Winkler mentioned that he was considering an oddball buddy movie called, at that time, *No Knife*, about an immigrant Hasidic rabbi crossing America from East to West to set up a rabbinate in San Francisco, helped along the way by a bandit with a heart of gold. Although it wasn't made clear which role he was considering, it was pretty unlikely that he was considering the role of the Rabbi. What wasn't mentioned was that director Aldrich's first choice for the role – indeed the actor he had in mind while he was pulling the project together – was the legendary cowboy John Wayne. But rumour has it that an over-zealous studio exec tried to bargain with Wayne's agent over Wayne's fee, causing Wayne to drop out.

Finally, Winkler too passed up the role, though Gene Wilder, already a pretty big star with films like *Blazing Saddles*, *Young Frankenstein* and *Silver Streak* behind him, was signed for the part of Avram, the trainee rabbi.

It's not such a stretch to deduce that Winkler mentioned he was dropping out of the project during the filming of *Heroes* and suggested Ford take the Tommy Lillard role.

What is surprising is that a usually reliable director like Robert Aldrich could turn out such a turkey of a movie. Yet in the film business you're only as good as your last picture and the critics were unimpressed by such earlier Aldrich credits as *Whatever Happened to Baby Jane?* and *The Dirty Dozen*. Said one reviewer, 'Aldrich is stuck up the wrong turning he took with *The Choirboys*. Like that film, *The Frisco Kid* is based on the dangerous assumption that a number of comic episodes will add up to a comedy ... one only hopes that his itch for comedy has been well and truly scratched.' It's been suggested by some film commentators that because Aldrich fashioned the project with Wayne in mind for the Tommy Lilliard role, he was depressed and disappointed when his first choice of star dropped out and took his disappointment out on Ford.

Ford's thoughts about his involvement in the project have passed unrecorded, but *The Frisco Kid* will go down on record as the last of the films of this period that Ford should never have been involved in.

Over the next rise was Ford's return to the role that had made him a household name a few years earlier ... Han Solo.

HARRISON AND MELISSA

With the break up of his marriage to Mary, Ford had to find a new home. Not far from the residence of Fred Roos, Ford saw the house he was looking for – a well-constructed 1941 clapboard dwelling that he could work and rework until it was the perfect reflection of the American classic style that Ford had grown up with.

The other big change in Ford's life as 1978 drew to a close was his deepening friendship with Melissa Mathison. A year earlier, during the publicity tour for *Star Wars*, Ford had met up with his old friend Fred Roos who was producing *The Black Stallion* for Francis Coppola in Toronto. Also at the dinner was the screenwriter Melissa Mathison, whom Ford had met in passing in the Philippines during the shooting of *Apocalypse Now*.

Melissa had been a journalist, working for *People* magazine, then was offered a job as an assistant on *The Godfather Part II* through a family connection with the Coppolas. It was Francis Coppola who encouraged Melissa to move from journalism into screenwriting, culminating in an assignment to re-write the script for *The Black Stallion*.

Ford and Mathison were seeing each other regularly during the filming of *The Frisco Kid*. In fact, Ford had asked *Kid* producer Mace Neufeld to look at some of Mathison's work. Neufeld would come to regret not taking Ford's advice when Mathison later wrote the screenplay for *ET*, a film that went on to out-gross *Star Wars*.

CHAPTER 4

HARRISON FORD: RETURN OF THE HERO

... and back again

'I'm very cautious of the word "star". I do my job. I have
been very lucky. Now I have to figure out how to milk it
without letting it dry up.' Harrison Ford

On March 7th, 1979, the Unit Publicist of *The Empire Strikes Back* released the
following bulletin to the world's news agencies: 'American actor Harrison Ford
has reached the snow stricken pass at Finse, Norway, to start work in *The Empire
Strikes Back* in a manner to justify the claim that the show must go on.

'He arrived in the engine compartment of a snow-clearance vehicle, the only thing that
could move along the Oslo-Bergen single track railroad which avalanches and collapsed
snow tunnels have blocked.

'Ford had flown from London to Oslo to catch the train which travels a circuitous route
across some of the most hostile winter terrain in Europe. At Geilo, a sizeable ski resort 30
miles east of his destination, the train was stopped in blizzard conditions.

'The railroad had decided to return its train to Oslo. But the filmmakers needed
Harrison Ford for scenes in the morning. So they radioed the train to unload the actor
who then, by two improbable taxi rides, reached Ustaoset, just 23 miles from Finse. That
was where the snow plough found him, to bring him along the track between 50 foot high

snow drifts to Finse, which he reached at midnight.'

In retrospect, the makers of *The Empire Strikes Back* should have taken Harrison Ford's hectic arrival at the first location of the film as an omen of things to come. 'Empire went about $6 million over budget,' star Mark Hamill later said, 'and ten weeks over schedule, which drove George (Lucas) crazy because he doesn't like to see waste.' Lucas would have been particularly wary of waste on *Empire,* as it was financed with his own money, a fact he pointed out frequently to the cast and crew alike.

The script for *The Empire Strikes Back* was written by Lawrence Kasdan *after* he'd done the screenplay for *Raiders of the Lost Ark.* Kasdan explained the beginning of his involvement with the *Empire* project in the American magazine *Starlog.*

'I had absolutely no indication that my writing *Empire* was even being considered. Once I got the job I was excited because I liked *Star Wars* very much. I thought it was great art, in that *Star Wars* hooked into the archetypal images registered in our subconscious of how children perceive the world.'

Kasdan had been brought in after the death of respected science fiction and film writer Leigh Brackett, best known for her screenplays for *The Big Sleep* (1946) and *Rio Bravo* (1959). Before engaging Kasdan, George Lucas had completed a second draft, based on Brackett's first draft version. Kasdan hadn't read the complete Brackett script. 'I only skimmed it. It was sort of old fashioned and didn't really relate to *Star Wars.* George had the story very well outlined, but there were sections in his script which, when I read them, made me say to myself, "I can't believe George wrote that scene. It's terrible." I later learned that George wrote stuff like that simply so that whoever wrote the next draft would know that a scene covering approximately the same kind of material that his sequence dealt with belonged at that point in the script. My job was to take George's story and make it work through altering the dialogue and the structure. Naturally a movie is not a screenplay, but you can't make a good movie without a good script.'

FILMING EMPIRE

After the nightmare George Lucas had gone through writing and directing *Star Wars* he decided that kind of involvement in so complicated a film project was simply more than he was willing to take on. His idea was to complete a rough draft of the script for *Empire* then turn it over to a professional writer for completion and polishing up. Then, with a professionally produced screenplay, he would turn his attentions to finding a director with the experience and the enthusiasm to helm the movie. He was looking for someone he knew and could trust to remain faithful to his original vision. He finally settled on Irvin Kershner, who had been one of his film teachers during his college days at USC in California. 'I knew George and (*Empire* producer Gary) Kurtz at the University of Southern California,' Kershner confirms, 'where I took courses and also taught. Through the years I occasionally saw them, but we weren't close friends.'

Irvin Kershner, or 'Kersh' as he was called by the *Empire* crew, had started his working life as a professional musician. 'Before all this, I played violin and viola for chamber music and orchestras. I wanted to be a composer, originally, so I started with music. Then I went into art and photography. I travelled for the UN, UNESCO, for Syracuse University, for USC, for the State Department, and made hundreds of documentaries. I always did my own photography, until I began working in Hollywood. '

Kershner's film debut was with the 1958 film, *Stakeout on Dope Street*. From there he went on to direct such varied movies as *Loving* (1970), *Raid on Entebbe* (1977) and the John Carpenter scripted horror thriller *Eyes of Laura Mars (1978)*.

Kershner was brought in on the *Empire* project while Leigh Brackett was still working on her screenplay. 'She was about halfway through the script when I became involved,' said Kershner, 'and we decided to let her finish the thing before getting into meetings with her about the re-write – because I knew I'd want a re-write. So while I waited, I had discussions with George and some of the art people who were starting on the initial drawings, just sort of slowly getting started. And when she handed me the first draft, she said she was going into hospital that weekend for a check-up – and she never came out.

'So suddenly we had a first draft script on our hands and a definite start date for the picture on March 5th, 1979, which meant we'd have to get moving. So we took the script and started reading it and making a few changes – then George said, "You know, we've got to bring in a writer. Someone who is strong on dialogue and who can take on the burden of getting it whipped into shape." So we brought in Larry Kasdan, and for months we would meet at my apartment in Los Angeles and go over it section by section. He would go off and re-write a section for a few days or a week, then he'd come back and we'd go over the pages he'd done, then he'd do another section. We did a very extensive re-write but it was still basically her script.

'When we'd polished it to the point that I thought it was now workable I came over to London and began pre-production, which for the first few months consisted of making drawings. I visualised and drew up the whole film to create the flow of it, to get the feel of the sets and the actual staging of scenes and even the cutting. It had to be very precise – so precise that drawings were made before the art director began to make the sets. Then we began to incorporate how the special effects would be done and I had to keep altering the drawings accordingly.

'It took about six months producing those drawings – we ended up with a book a foot thick. I sent copies to George and to all the technicians so everyone knew what they would be doing. With this book it was possible to get the flow of the picture established, which was the most important thing of all. Because as soon as you have a picture with a lot of gadgetry, blue screens, matte shots, super-impositions, etc, it tends to become very stiff if you're not careful. The actors become as stiff as the gadgets themselves.

'That was a major problem because the whole picture is special effects. People don't realise that almost every shot has something in it that's a special effect, and about half the effects were done completely on the set. Yoda, for instance was a total special effect and all done on the set. We added nothing to him later. Then there were the mechanical effects like the water effects and the fogs – there were so many things that we created right there ... but, of course, there were many shots where I could shoot live action and then send the scene back to the studio in San Francisco for the opticals to be added. It was really a locked down situation on many of those shots. I mean, there were shots where we had to use the VistaVision camera (a special camera in which the film runs through the gate horizontally instead of vertically, giving a clearer image definition), it had to be exactly four-and-a-half feet off the ground, it had to be pointed no more than fifteen degrees up, the light had to come from the right, it had to be orange – all because of the special effects that would be added later – and then I could be free as I wanted within that frame.

'Then we reached the point where, in some shots, all I had was a completely black set and a few actors. It looked silly – nothing but a couple of lines drawn on the floor for the actors and that was *it*. I wouldn't see the finished scene for maybe six months after I shot it, then I get back a piece of film that's been married and the whole thing comes to life – it has a background and something flying around and other moving elements. It was a similar situation with some of the snow battle scenes – all I had were some men running towards me, smoke bombs, a few explosions and one man stumbling and falling in the foreground. And then the special effects team start working on it – they put in the three huge Walkers, which was a remarkable job, and then later they put in the laser blasts coming out of the Walkers, one of which hits the man I'd had fall over months before ... so it was all working backwards.'

On the set, the director would find that scenes didn't work and would have to alter carefully storyboarded sequences at the last minute. And because of these alterations he was forced to give precious shooting days over to rehearsals of the new sequences and relighting of the sets.

The animatronic puppet that played the character of Yoda also proved to be one almighty headache. 'Actually there's very little of Yoda in the picture,' Kershner told *Starburst*'s John Brosnan, 'and his scenes only took about ten days of filming, but they were very *long* days. He was monstrously difficult to work with and, on average, it took us three-and-a-half hours to shoot just two lines of his dialogue. The rehearsals took a lot of time too because we had a bank of tv monitors and three, sometimes four, technicians to manipulate Yoda. Frank Oz was coordinating it with me and we were both wearing earphones and mikes. The set was built four or five feet above the floor so we could have all kinds of mechanisms underneath Yoda ... and it took endless rehearsals because you'd start and one of Yoda's eyes would go in the wrong direction or one ear would suddenly fall down, and I'd have to say, "Up with the left ear," or "Now take the left eye and move it around to the right ... that's right, now focus it a little closer."

'Frank Oz would be watching the tv screens and I'd be watching the screens and the creature but we were the only ones who could hear what Yoda was saying. The crew and Mark Hamill heard nothing – they didn't know what was happening. Finally, we had to put a tiny earphone on Mark – a tiny miniature earphone with a very fine wire going back behind his ear so he could hear what Yoda was saying.'

Nevertheless the results were worth the bother. Yoda is a very convincing creation on the screen and the character won over the hordes of *Star Wars* fans instantly.

In the meantime, the problems that Kershner was experiencing were costing the production money. The 'standing still' budget (the money it cost to keep the production in business without shooting a single foot of film) was a staggering $100,000 a day. It was left to George Lucas to try to find the extra money from somewhere to ensure completion of the picture. Eventually he was forced to turn to 20th Century-Fox for help, something he wanted to avoid at all costs. And with the mounting financial pressures on *The Empire Strikes Back,* relationships between Irvin Kershner, George Lucas and Gary Kurtz became strained.

WORKING WELL

Yet through all this, Harrison Ford had only good things to say about Irvin Kershner. 'He was wonderful,' Ford enthused. 'He's a different kind of director. But we also had a very close relationship on the level of freedom to contribute.'

Kershner, a director sensitive to the needs and talents of his actors, encouraged every contribution Ford was willing to make.

'Occasionally, I feel very sure about the changes,' says Ford, 'like the "I love you", "I know" scene. I knew that my last speech had to be a strong character line. I convinced Kersh to give me the "I know" decision and I'm grateful he did. When George finally saw the sequence cut together, he said, "It's a laugh line. I'm not sure it belongs there. This is a serious, dramatic moment."

'I said, "I think it really works." and Kershner agreed with me. So George said, "Okay, go with it."

'From what I've seen and heard, the "I know" line really does work. It relieves a grim situation without generating laughs or diverting the drama. It also serves to make Solo's plight more poignant and memorable.'

Harrison Ford has no qualms about altering a line of dialogue that a writer might have spent months on if he feels it will improve the end result.

'Writers sometimes have to live with a script so long,' he says firmly, 'that it begins to suit them *too* well – they can't see the validity of changes.'

Lawrence Kasdan wasn't too happy with some of the changes that had been made to his script – sometimes on the very day of shooting. 'Han and Leia's relationship is not at all what I had envisaged,' Kasdan told the American magazine *Starlog*. 'I could be the only person who feels this way, but I thought their romance had a touch of falseness about it. Han and Leia's scenes were among what I was proudest of in my script, but they hardly remained. Their being changed had a lot to do with the circumstances of filming, Kershner and the actors' feelings about doing their roles again. I was one of the people who wasn't crazy about Harrison Ford in *Empire*.'

When *The Empire Strikes Back* opened in America on May 21st, 1980, *Star Wars* fans across the country had been queuing for three days. The film recovered its cost three months after that and eventually went on to pull in nearly as much in ticket sales as the original *Star Wars* movie. Not bad for a film that caused just about everybody connected with it too many sleepless nights.

GOOD PRESS, BUT ...

The critics' reception of *The Empire Strikes Back* was only a little short of a standing ovation.

Variety wrote, 'Having already introduced their principal players, the filmmakers now have a chance to round them out, assisted again by good performances from Mark Hamill, Harrison Ford and Carrie Fisher. And even the ominous Darth Vader is fleshed with new – and surprising – motivations.'

The Washington Post thought, 'the total effect is fast and attractive and occasionally amusing. Like a good hot dog, that's something of an achievement in a field where unpalatable junk is the rule.'

The San Francisco Chronicle said, 'The emotional landscape of *The Empire Strikes Back* is the richest in the *Star Wars* trilogy. Every character is more developed, more familiar, more quirky in this movie. Han, the smart-aleck, now is in a full-court press to woo Princess Leia, and his repeated mocking of her "royal highnessness" goads her into a classic mating ritual of teases and glances – and wet kisses.'

Yet some did point out that the ending of the film was no ending at all and smacked of the same kind of thinking behind the cliff-hanging endings of the old Saturday morning serials – a cheap shot to get the audiences back for the third part of the trilogy. Harrison Ford backed the filmmakers' decision in the face of such comments and answered them smoothly.

'I have no real defence for that argument,' he admitted, 'but what obligation is there to tie up every question with an equal answer? The cliff-hanger is because the trilogy was really constructed in the classic form of a three-act play. Naturally, there are going to be questions in the second act which have to be resolved in the third. I guess it really depends on what you go to a movie for. I figure there was at least eleven dollars worth of entertainment in *Empire*. So if you paid four bucks and didn't get an ending, you're still seven dollars ahead of the game.'

Audiences agreed and voted with their cash. *Empire* was safely the biggest earner of 1980 and its worldwide box-office of almost $534 million means that it's the 39th highest grossing movie of all time.

The Academy nominated the movie in the categories for Best Art Direction and Best Score and awarded *The Empire Strikes Back* the Oscar for Best Sound, as well as a Special Achievement Oscar for the Special Effects.

The accusations that *Empire* was too serial-like could have been an omen of Ford's next project. Though he didn't know it at the time, Harrison Ford would go on to star in George Lucas's homage to those same Saturday morning serials in the brilliant 1930s-style adventure movie, *Raiders of the Lost Ark*.

CHAPTER 5

HARRISON FORD: MATINEE IDOL

From the Stars to Star

'Harrison Ford is more than just an actor playing a role in *Raiders of the Lost Ark*. He was involved in a lot of the decision-making about the movie as we went along. And this wasn't by contract, it was because I sensed an exceptional story mind and a very smart person and called on him time and time again.' Steven Spielberg, director of *Raiders of the Lost Ark*

T he little film that George Lucas and Steven Spielberg decided to make together is growing by the minute. Shooting begins of *Raiders of the Lost Ark* on May 15th, 1980 at George's happy hunting ground of Elstree Studios – and already, before a single shot is completed, they have four sequels in the planning stages,' was how British fantasy film magazine *Starburst* announced the start of work Lucas' follow-up to the *Star Wars* saga in February, 1980. The report gave Lawrence Kasdan as the script writer, Frank Marshall as producer, but no hint as to the cast.

Before long, rumours were circulating that *Raiders of the Lost Ark* was not a new project at all, but the third part of the *Star Wars* saga. Said *Empire Strikes Back* producer Gary Kurtz of that idea, 'I can categorically deny that. It's not science fiction at all. It's a Thirties action adventure type story about a search for a lost treasure. A typical Clark Gable, soldier-of-fortune kind of movie.'

No more news issued from the Elstree set of *Raiders* until the movie opened in America on May 25th and at London's Empire cinema on July 30th, 1981.

FROM THE SANDS OF HAWAII TO THE SANDS OF THE SAHARA

The tale of *Raiders*' genesis was reported both in Dale Pollock's *Skywalking* (the George Lucas biography) and in Tony Crawley's *The Steven Spielberg Story*. Both books told of Lucas's retreat to the Hawaian beaches to forget the horrors of making *Star Wars,* and of Spielberg's joining him there with the news that *Star Wars* had been a monumental hit. Over a sandcastle, the world's two most successful filmmakers hatched a plot to make a movie that would mix the mythic qualities of the occult and the derring-do of the Saturday matinee serials and out-Bond Bond in the process. The co-author of the original story of *Raiders,* Philip Kaufman, was originally slated to direct, but when he dropped out of the project, Spielberg stepped in.

At this stage, the project still had no writer. Until Spielberg introduced a young Chicago advertising copywriter, Lawrence Kasdan to Lucas. Spielberg had read a screenplay by Kasdan called *Continental Divide* and was trying to acquire it to produce for himself.

'When Spielberg first read it,' said Kasdan, 'he told my agent, "I'm doing a movie with George Lucas and I think this guy would be great to write it. Would it be all right if I showed George *Continental Divide?*" And we, of course, agreed. Then I came in and met George – he had read the script and liked it – and at that first meeting, George hired me to write *Raiders.'*

Lucas, Spielberg and Kasdan spent a week thrashing out the basic plot of *Raiders.* These sessions were preserved for posterity on tape and at the end of the week Kasdan went off to write the first draft script.

'I left those meetings feeling I was in pretty good shape and then sat down and realised, Uh-oh, this is going to be hard!' said Kasdan. And hard it was, at least hard enough to keep the young writer occupied for a full six months.

Finally, Kasdan took the finished script in to show Lucas. What happened next came as something of a shock. The scriptwriter working on *Empire,* Leigh Brackett, had died suddenly. Lucas desperately needed a writer to take over. Could Kasdan handle it? 'But you haven't even read *Raiders,* yet,' protested Kasdan. Lucas only smiled. He was following his instincts – which were rarely wrong.

Meanwhile Spielberg had read Kasdan's *Raiders* script and was delighted. 'Larry didn't stick with our story outline one hundred percent,' commented Spielberg, 'A lot of the movie is Larry's own original ideas, his characters. George provided the initial vision, the story and the structure of the movie. Then George and I together provided key scenes throughout the film. And Larry essentially did all the characters and tied the story together, made the story work from just a bare outline, and gave it colour and some direction.'

With the script in the safe hands of Lawrence Kasdan, Lucas and Spielberg could turn their attention to who was to play the key role of Indiana Jones.

The auditions for the movie were to be held at Lucasfilm's West Coast offices. 'We wanted an unknown, originally – a total unknown. Conceitedly, George and I wanted to make a star out of Johnny the Construction Worker from Malibu. We couldn't find a construction worker in Malibu, so we began looking at more substantial people in the film industry.'

Both Lucas and Spielberg had a picture in their mind's eye as to the kind of hero they were looking for. Lucas saw Jones as a scruffy playboy, the kind of adventurer who, on duty, dressed like Humphrey Bogart in *Treasure of the Sierra Madre*. Spielberg's Jones was more of a grizzled alcoholic, gruffly romantic and ruggedly handsome.

Lucas and Spielberg then approached well-known Marvel Comics artist Jim Steranko to produce some concept paintings to nail down a visual appearance of the character of Indiana Jones and his world. Steranko came back with four paintings, which defined the appearance of Indy, from the fedora hat, which Steranko had added unbidden, to the leather jacket which Lucas had asked for and the Sam Brown webbing, again Steranko's addition. Lucas and Spielberg were so impressed with the artist's work that they asked him to produce a further fifty paintings, one for each major scene in the movie. But the catch was that the artist would only have fifty days, a deadline that would be gruelling, to say the least. Steranko, not wanting to turn in sub-standard, rushed work, declined the assignment.

The filmmakers' first choice for the role was TV actor Tom Selleck. Selleck was enthusiastic but aware that the new pilot he was working on, *Magnum P.I.*, might turn into a full series for CBS television. CBS didn't seem to be in much of a hurry to take up the option for the first series of the show. 'The show had sat there and nobody wanted it. And the option was about to lapse,' recalled Lucas. Itching to get on with *Raiders*, Lucas contacted *Magnum* production company Universal with a request that Selleck be released from his contract. But while Universal were agreeable, CBS were suddenly alerted that the two biggest names in Hollywood were interested in 'their' star for a movie and instantly picked up Selleck's contract for *Magnum P.I.* So Lucas and Spielberg still had no lead actor for *Raiders*.

'We were stuck,' said Spielberg. 'We had three weeks left to cast the part of Indiana Jones, and there was nobody close. Then I saw *The Empire Strikes Back* and I realised Harrison Ford *is* Indiana Jones. I called George Lucas and said, "He's right under our noses!" George said, "I know who you're going to say!" I said, "Who?" and he said, "Harrison Ford! Let's get him." And we did!'

According to *Skywalking*, Harrison Ford had read the script for *Raiders* shortly after Kasdan had finished it but had remained cool towards the project. 'They could find me if they wanted to,' Ford is quoted as saying. Nevertheless Ford must have known that the part was perfect for him. 'It was clearly the most dominant single character in any of George's films,' said Ford, 'quite in variance with his theories about movie stars and what they mean.'

Despite his enthusiasm for the project, one aspect of *Raiders* bothered Ford. 'My only immediate reservation about playing Indiana Jones,' said Ford, 'was that in the script the character was a little bit like Han Solo. Steven Spielberg and I wanted to make sure that the characters were spread apart. We did that by making use of the opportunities that existed in Lawrence Kasdan's screenplay.'

Time was too short for a re-write of the script. Yet Spielberg recognised in Ford a native ability with dialogue and wanted to implement some of Ford's suggestions. What happened was like a scene out of *Let's-make-a-movie* movie. 'The production was based in London,' said Ford, 'and Steve and I sat on the plane from Los Angeles and went through the script, line by line, for fourteen hours. By the time we got to Heathrow, we'd worked out the entire film.'

It's just as well that they had, for no sooner had Spielberg and Ford arrived in Britain than the entire cast and crew were whisked off to La Rochelle in France to spend the first five days of the movie's shooting schedule filming the submarine hijack of the Bantu Wind. It was during these five days that Ford was to get his first taste of the stunts he would be required to perform in the course of portraying Indiana Jones. 'Swimming to the submarine didn't involve danger,' said Ford, 'it only involved discomfort.' The worst was yet to come.

Star Wars had put the phrase 'special effects' into everyone's mouth. Suddenly, after *Star Wars* opened, reviews were peppered with the words. It was as though George Lucas had invented the concept all by himself. With *Raiders,* Lucas was to elevate another previously ignored movie art to star status. Stunts.

Much was made, at the time, of the fact that Harrison Ford did many of his own stunts for the film. 'Hell,' he quipped, 'if I hadn't done some of the stunts in *Raiders,* I wouldn't have been seen in the movie at all.' Yet strangely Ford is no kind of keep fit freak. 'People always ask me how I keep in shape. Every time the question comes up, I can manage to sneer. It's a common enough question, considering *Raiders.* And I say, being in movies is enough exercise for me.'

In reality, Ford was lucky enough to have some of the best stuntmen and stunt directors in the business working with him. Stuntmen are always used for the most dangerous 'gags' for the simple reason that if the star of the film were to hurt himself and hold up shooting, hundreds of thousands of dollars would be wasted.

'There were some very capable stuntmen doing some of the action bits, but I probably did a good deal more action stunts than an actor normally would do. That was important because we wanted to have our fights always be character fights, instead of just having whatever spectacular event a stuntman could come up with. Indiana Jones fights in a certain way, which Steven (Spielberg) let the stuntmen and me choreograph. Some of Indy's battles are incredible. "How can Indy possibly do all this?" We had to take the edge off that with a bit of humour and at the same time not make fun of the material. So Indiana Jones had to be a character with a sense of humour. It's Indy's way of looking at life that makes our fights unique!'

Glen Randall was the stunt co-ordinator on *Raiders.* Says Randall, 'They talk about the dangers stuntmen go through, wrecking cars and airplanes, but I think the stunt that gets the most people hurt in this industry is the simple fight routine. When you throw a punch, you're throwing it with all the force you'd normally use to hit someone, but you're missing them by inches. There are a lot of stuntmen who just cringe when they find out they've got to do a fight with an actor who's not had a lot of experience doing them – 'cos nine times out of ten, they're going to get hit!'

One of the most spectacular thrills in *Raiders* is in the opening sequence when Indy races the giant rolling boulder for the exit in the Temple. It was Ford himself outracing the rock. 'Looked a little scared that scene, didn't I? I'd have to have been crazy not to be. It wasn't a *real* boulder, but it wasn't cardboard, either. It took 800 pounds of plaster to make it roll right. And if I had tripped, I could have been in big trouble. The director thought at first we ought to use a stuntman - but I thought I could do it and Glen Randall, our stunt coordinator, agreed. We all felt the more action scenes I could personally do, the easier it would be for the audience to identify with and believe in the character. But if I didn't trust the stunt guys who were manning the safety devices and looking out for me, I never would have done it. No way!' The scene was shot from five different angles, twice from each angle. 'So Harrison had to race the rock ten times,' said Spielberg. 'He won ten times and beat the odds. He was lucky. And I was an idiot for letting him try!'

Indy's escape from the Well of Souls provided an opportunity to the filmmakers for a really spectacular stunt. In an effort to break a hole through the wall of his prison, Indy topples a huge statue of a jackal god and rides it as it falls, a tip of the hat, perhaps, to Slim Pickens' riding the Atom Bomb to his last round-up in *Dr Strangelove*. Harrison Ford, intrepid but not stupid, knew the time to step aside for professional stunt double Martin Grace.

As Glen Randall explained, 'The Jackal was 28, maybe 29, feet high. Plaster of Paris but still incredibly heavy. And we put big hydraulic rams on one leg and hinged it at the bottom so we knew exactly the plane it was going to fall in. It could only fall one way, if everything went right. We had a huge breakaway wall for it to fall through.'

But for all the planning, something went wrong as the stunt was filmed. If you watch closely during this scene in the movie, you'll see 'Indy' lose his footing for an instant as the statue begins to topple. 'Yes, it went too soon,' agreed Martin Grace. 'And that's when you have to think very fast. I was actually still hanging down when it started going. I should have been actually on my position … Stunt people are usually very fast thinking people. In situations like that you have to think very fast and get it together. We've got sort of lightning reflexes, very sharp minds and that's a great combination to come up with the goods.' Grace emerged unscathed.

With Ford doing so many of his own gags, it's no surprise that he had a couple of near misses himself.

'There's a scene where I run through the jungle,' Ford told an American magazine, 'swing on a vine, let go the vine, fall into the river, grab onto the pontoon of a seaplane that's taxi-ing, get onto the wing and climb into the cockpit as it was taking off – and the plane crashed on take-off. '

Of course Ford wasn't hurt. But it does show that no matter how careful you are, accidents will happen.

Harrison Ford must have been on a lucky streak during the filming of *Raiders*. He had had another near miss on location in Tunisia during the shooting of the Tannis Dig sequence. Ford told the story to *Prevue*, the magazine published by *Raiders*' concept artist Jim Steranko. 'Indy has a fight which takes place in and around the propellers of a Flying Wing airplane. The engines are running full tilt and one set of wheels is chocked, so the plane's going round in circles. The bad guy is supposed to throw me down in front of the wheels and I was supposed to roll over backwards to get away from the wheels.

'All day long the technical crew was having trouble with the plane. It weighed a couple of tons, so they were powering it with low-gear, high-torque electric motors – the kind that can push through a brick wall without slowing down. They had to stay out of camera range, at the end of a cable 50 yards away.

'I still wanted to do the fight myself. I'm able to add bits of character touches to moments like these, and when the audience recognises the actor, it adds credibility to what is normally straight action stuff. We rehearsed the scene several times, then decided to shoot it.

'Everybody's ready and the take begins. I go down and start to roll away – and my foot slips, right under the rolling plane's tyre.

'Everybody was yelling, "Stop! STOP!" while the tyre crawled up my leg. Luckily the brakes worked – inches before my knee was crushed – but I was pinned to the sand.

'I'm not normally a worrier, I know they're not going to kill the main character in a twenty million dollar film. I also know Indy wouldn't look good with a peg-leg. I was a lot more careful about stunt work after that!'

And he'd have to be. Still to come was the hazardous chase in which Indy starts by leaping from a horse onto the speeding German truck that's carrying the Ark, and ends with our hero falling from the front of the truck, crawling hand over hand beneath the vehicle, then being dragged for a couple of miles down the road in the dirt before climbing up the tail board. You'd think for that Ford would insist on a stuntman. He did, and he got one ... for the long-shots. In the close-ups, there was Ford, hanging onto the rear of the truck, scraping up the gravel road on his belly. As usual, Ford was dismissive. 'It couldn't possibly be dangerous,' he said at the time, 'because I have a few more weeks shooting the picture.'

Being so closely involved in so many of the gags on *Raiders* has given Harrison Ford a stuntman's outlook as far as 'falls' are concerned. 'The stuff that always turns out to be dangerous is the stuff nobody thinks about. It's not the dangerous stunts – which you think about, protect yourself, calculate and worry about, so that you take the danger out of it – it's the stuff you *didn't* think was dangerous that sneaks upon you.'

'SNAKES. WHY DID IT HAVE TO BE SNAKES?'

Most people would think that an actor who also did so many of his own stunts, like Harrison Ford, would have enough on his plate in a film like *Raiders of the Lost Ark*. Not so. The folk who made *Raiders* knew that the more severe the trials suffered by the hero, the more the audience would be rooting for him. Also, a hero with a failing seems more vulnerable and easier to identify with for an audience. So the filmmakers gave Indiana Jones a fear of snakes and needless to say, Indy met more than just a few snakes during his adventures in *Raiders*. The Well of Souls was filled with them.

'Steven Spielberg kept wanting more and more snakes,' said Ford, 'but he had to make do with six thousand garden and grass snakes flown in from Holland, and used bits of garden hose to fill the spaces the boas and pythons couldn't.'

Fords's co-star, Karen Allen, wasn't mad about doing the scene in the Well of Souls at first. 'Harrison has on his boots and gloves, and leather clothes, and I have naked arms and nothing on my legs or feet. In the beginning it was tough, because I just couldn't stand the snakes on my feet. But I got used to them.'

Producer Frank Marshall, who shot some of the snake footage, wasn't wild about reptiles, either. 'I had to cure myself of a common phobia of snakes. But once you see other people, like a snake handler, not worry about it, then you touch one. Then I got to be real comfortable with them. Some of the shots I did were a real challenge. Snakes aren't afraid of anything, they'd even go right into the fire. So we had to invent a way to get them to stay away from the fire.'

Though most of the snakes used in the scene were harmless, the crew did use a couple of cobras, whose bite can kill, to add a little real danger for Indy.

'When we used the cobras,' recalled Howard Kazanjian, the film's co-executive producer, 'we had a hospital gurney on the set, and outside the stage we had ambulances with open doors. On the end of the gurney was an open medical kit with a hypodermic needle placed into the phial of serum from India.' This does sound like a typical piece of studio hype.

In the shot where Indy comes face-to-face with the angry cobra, it's pretty easy to see the cobra's reflection in the sheet of glass that separates them. The gurney and the hypo were probably for the unfortunates whose job it was to handle the snakes off-camera.

Harrison Ford dismisses Indy's fear of snakes with his characteristic easy smile. 'They don't bother me at all. When I was a kid, I worked in a boy scout camp as a nature councillor, I used to collect them. Used to run and catch every snake we could. And I'm amazed that that's the most frightening scene for most people.'

But, as I said, all heroes must have a failing. There is something the intrepid Ford doesn't like. 'Spiders!' he told *Movie Star* magazine. 'Not because they're creepy, but inside my house they multiply, and then their kids have kids. Ugh. All those spiders all over the place.'

One particularly gruesome scene in *Raiders* does just happen to have a few spiders in it. The scene in the Temple in Peru. But unlike the scene with the snakes, it was the spiders that had to be watched out for rather than their human co-stars. 'It's funny how people think tarantulas are so dangerous,' said producer Frank Marshall, 'when in fact they're very fragile creatures. If they fall or you drop them, they die. You have to be very careful with them. We did lose one of them one day when two got in a fight – a battle to the death.'

But for Ford, it was the snakes that had the last laugh: shortly after the opening of *Raiders,* Ford told author Tony Crawley of a strange incident. 'Back home,' said Ford, 'just the other week – you're not going to believe this – I got bitten by a damn snake in my garden!'

'I PUT AS MUCH OF MYSELF INTO THE CHARACTERS AS POSSIBLE.'

The only other thing Harrison Ford had to do in *Raiders of the Lost Ark* was portray the character of Indiana Jones. Director Steven Spielberg had nothing but praise for Ford's abilities as an actor. 'Harrison is a very original leading man,' he said. 'There's not been anybody like him for 30 or 40 years. In this film he is a remarkable combination of Errol Flynn in *The Adventures of Don Juan* and Humphrey Bogart as Fred C. Dobbs in *Treasure of the Sierra Madre.* He carries this picture wonderfully. '

Ford was well aware of what was expected of him. 'It's a question of responsibility to define the character for the audience, to make the film as good as you can.'

But he had a good ally in Steven Spielberg. 'Steve allowed a kind of collaboration that was really a lot of fun for me. I like to become really involved as much, and as long, as possible. If I had a little bit of an idea, Steve added to it, and then I added to it, and then he added to it, and it built into something we both thought was better than before ... or so stupid we both ended up rolling about on the floor with laughter.'

And, in the spirit of Indy's line in the movie, 'I'm making this up as I go,' Ford and Spielberg were making changes to the script even during actual shooting.

'My only impulse to change lines comes when the words are impossible to get out of my mouth,' said Ford. 'The process of film-making involves so many situations and personalities that it becomes a very liquid medium. The physical presence of actors and crew are concrete factors, but the script should relate to them more like a road map of probabilities than a rigid blueprint.'

The biggest change Spielberg and Ford made to the script was to delete the 'Sword vs the Whip' duel that was written as a climax to the battle in the marketplace in Cairo. In the film, Indy comes face to face with a giant of a swordsman. The swordsman performs an intricate routine with a huge scimitar. Indy, unimpressed, pulls out his revolver and shoots him. Not sporting, but efficient.

'I was in my fifth week of dysentery at the time,' recalled Ford later. 'The location was an hour and a half drive from where we stayed. I'm riding to the set at 5.30am, and I can't wait to storm up to Steven with this idea. I'd worked out we could save four whole days on this lousy location this way. Besides which, I think it was right and important, because what's more vital in the character's mind is finding Marion. He doesn't have *time* for another fight. But as is very often the case, when I suggested it to Steven – "Let's just shoot the sucker" – he said, "I just thought the same thing this morning." Sure, the idea was nothing. Putting it on film, that's the most difficult part.'

That scene also told the audience much about Indiana Jones. The world-weary expression on Indy's face as he draws his gun, sums up the character's directness. As Ford explains, 'Indy is a kind of swashbuckling hero type, but he has human frailties. He does brave things, but I wouldn't describe him as a hero. He teaches, but I wouldn't describe him as an intellectual. I wanted to avoid any elements in the role that might be too similar to Han Solo. But Indy doesn't have any fancy gadgetry keeping him at a distance from enemies and trouble. The story is set in 1936, after all, and he's right in there with just his battered trilby and a bull-whip to keep the world at bay.'

STAR!

'All I care about is good acting,' George Lucas was once quoted as saying. 'Star value is only an insurance policy for those who don't trust themselves making films.' But when *Raiders of the Lost Ark* opened in America on July 12th, 1981, that's exactly what Harrison Ford had plenty of.

'There's more excitement in the first ten minutes of *Raiders*,' said *Playboy*'s Bruce Williamson, 'than any movie I have seen all year. By the time the explosive misadventures end, any moviegoer worth his salt ought to be exhausted.'

Just about all the reviews were of the same opinion. *Raiders* was a masterpiece of popular cinema. 'Surely destined to go down in history as one of the great, fun movies,' said Britain's trade journal, *Screen International.*

'*Raiders* represents Spielberg's best work in years, a return to the briskness and coherence that have been missing since *Jaws*,' said *Time* magazine.

At the press screening I attended in 1981, the opening twelve minutes received a standing ovation from the several hundred jaded film hacks in attendance. Now *that's* a reaction.

The film's reception at the box-office was nothing short of exuberant, which came as no great surprise, ending up as the highest earning movie of 1981. Its position in the all-time box-office hit list is just as impressive, with the film at the 40th position earning a US gross of over $242 million.

At the 1981 Academy Awards, *Raiders* was nominated in the categories Best Music, Best Cinematography, Best Director and Best Picture, and won for Best Sound, Best Special Effects, Best Art Direction and Best Editing. The film also earned Ben Burtt and Richard Anderson a Special Oscar for Achievement in Sound Effects Editing.

Ford himself was happy about his involvement in the film and the end result.

'*Raiders* is really about movies,' he explained. 'It is intricately designed as a tribute to the craft. I'm quite in awe of the film, and the way it was accomplished. Steven set out to make an epic film, technically complex, on a short schedule. He finished twelve days early and under budget. He didn't waste any time in retakes. Steve was very fast and efficient, and that's the way I like to work.'

Yet his experience on *Raiders* did leave Ford with one cautionary thought 'I occasionally wonder how much longer I can perform in heavy action roles,' he told an interviewer. 'Working in sub-zero blizzards and 130 degree deserts is incredibly demanding, physically. Sometimes I think the most difficult part of being in films is being cool as an airplane rolls over your leg – and acting like it doesn't hurt at all.'

As Harrison Ford's next film project drew closer, his attitude had mellowed a little 'With me,' he said, 'the last film is always the toughest. I'll soon be down on record as saying *Blade Runner* was the toughest.'

By the time Ford had finished with *Raiders* in late 1980 and returned to his home in Benedict Canyon, Melissa had moved in with him and the tabloids were inexplicably in another feeding frenzy. One of the first guests they welcomed as a couple was British film director Ridley Scott who was courting Ford for the lead in his next picture, a science fiction detective yarn based on the Philip K. Dick novel *Do Androids Dream of Electric Sheep?*

CHAPTER 6

HARRISON FORD: ACTOR

From Artisan to Artist

'Harrison has an immense understanding of the entire
movie-making process. You can't fool him. He always
knows exactly what is happening. His contributions were
tremendous, on a story level as well as to his own character. He brought many ideas to me. In fact, it got bloody
embarrassing. They were so good there was no way I could
wriggle out of using them.' Ridley Scott, director of Blade
Runner

The release of *Blade Runner* in May, 1982 (September, 1982 in Britain) marked a
definite attempt by Harrison Ford to change his image. The fan-following built up by
such light entertainment vehicles as the *Star Wars* pictures and *Raiders of the Lost
Ark* were puzzled by the singular lack of humour in Ford's performance. So much so that
they stayed away in droves. *Blade Runner* was not initially a commercial success.

But *Blade Runner* was perhaps Ford's most important film up to that point. Certainly,
it was his first opportunity to sustain an *acting* performance in a starring role. The insight
and depth he brought to the character of Rick Deckard showed that Ford was capable of far
more than the wisecracking characterisations of Han Solo and Indiana Jones would lead
audiences to suspect.

More than that, the backdrop against which the drama of *Blade Runner* was played out,
although futuristic, was grittier and more realistic than the fantastic environments of Indy
and Solo.

IN THE BEGINNING WAS THE WORD.

No matter how skilled a film's performers and technicians are, unless the blueprint from which they work – the script – is tightly crafted, the final movie will suffer as a result. Most movie people agree that just about all the problems encountered during the shooting of a film can be traced back to difficulties left unresolved by the scriptwriter – yet when everything goes swimmingly, it's the director who gets all the credit.

The script of *Blade Runner* was based, loosely, on the novel *Do Androids Dream of Electric Sheep* by respected science fiction author, the late Philip K. Dick, who died tragically on March 2nd, 1982, shortly before the completed film of *Blade Runner* was released.

The need for the script to be 'right' is so universally recognised by filmmakers that it often takes longer to produce a screenplay that everyone is satisfied with than it does to shoot the actual film. *Blade Runner* is no exception. Work began on the transfer of Dick's story to the screen almost a decade before the film was released.

'It all began years ago,' Dick told *Starlog.* 'Martin Scorsese and Jay Cocks were both interested in *Androids,* but they didn't option (purchase the film rights to) it. That was the first movie interest in any property (story) of mine. Then later, Herb Jaffe optioned it and Robert Jaffe did a screenplay back about 1973. The screenplay was sent to me and it was so crude that I didn't understand that it was actually the shooting script. I thought it was a rough. I wrote to them and asked if they would like me to do the shooting script, at which point, Robert Jaffe flew down here to Orange County. I said to him then that it was so bad that I wanted to know if he wanted me to beat him up there at the airport or wait until we got to my apartment.'

The Jaffes made little progress with their attempts to put *Do Androids Dream of Electric Sheep* on the big screen. But the Jaffes weren't the only film folk interested in the project. Some time in 1974, Hampton Fancher approached Dick with a view to obtaining the film rights to the novel, but as the rights still rested with the Jaffes, Dick was unenthusiastic. Then, in 1977, the Jaffes let their option on the film rights lapse and within a year, Fancher and his partner Brian Kelly found themselves in possession of the movie rights for Dick's novel.

Kelly approached Michael Deeley, Oscar winning producer of *The Deer Hunter* with a view to raising finance for further development, but the reception was cool. Deeley felt that there would be too many problems involved in translating Dick's complicated story to the big screen. Nevertheless, Kelly and Fancher persevered. Fancher produced an eight-page outline for the film which so impressed Deeley that he encouraged the partners to come up with a full script. 'I hadn't ever intended to write the screenplay myself,' Fancher recalled, 'but I was convinced that this was the only way to get the project off the ground.'

'Lord knows,' commented Dick, perhaps uncharitably, 'I didn't think much of his screenplay.' But despite Dick's reservations, Kelly and Fancher took their script to Deeley once again. 'He loved it,' said Fancher.

Deeley began to hawk the script around the production companies in Film City. 'People were interested,' said Fancher, 'but they wanted changes. They'd want a happy ending or they'd want something else changed. It was pretty precarious there for a while. I think there were about four or five drafts written before Ridley Scott came into it. When Ridley came in that sort of wrapped it up because of the *Alien* reputation. That's what it needed for the studio to get down to business with it.'

On the strength of Ridley Scott's participation, Michael Deeley had put together a deal with Filmways. At this point the title of the project had changed from *Do Androids Dream of Electric Sheep* to *The Android*.

At the time Scott was approached to direct *Blade Runner,* he was scheduled to helm Dino De Laurentis' multi-million dollar adaptation of the best-selling series of *Dune* novels by Frank Herbert. But delays in the production made it possible for Scott to squeeze *Blade Runner* in before beginning work on *Dune*. (For the record, *Dune* was later filmed by the team of director David Lynch and cinematographer Freddie Francis).

What was it about the script that convinced Ridley Scott to take on the project? 'What appealed to me, having just done *Alien* which was very interesting, was the involvement in just developing that future environment further. I love that whole process, almost as much as any other part of movie making. I just didn't want to step off onto ordinary ground again. What I felt was great about the script was that it was dealing with the near future. It had to be a familiar city, which it is. A lot of aspects of that city are familiar right now. In fact, a lot of people who will see the film, will experience that kind of future themselves. I also liked the aspect that there was a real character in there, rather than a two-dimensional cardboard character, which happens too often with science fiction films. Because the film is usually dominated by a monster or event the characters do, essentially, take second place.'

After Ridley Scott was signed to direct, a major revision of the script, by now called *Dangerous Days,* began. Initially, Fancher was resistant to some of the changes proposed. And as a co-owner of the project, Fancher was in a position to dig his heels in. But pressure to alter portions of the script became so great that Fancher realised the only way out of the situation was to bring in another writer.

Enter: David Peoples.

As Fancher remarked later, 'I was surprised when I got Peoples' script. Those things that Ridley had wanted that I thought couldn't be integrated into the script had been rendered by Peoples in ways that were original, tight and admirable. I really liked it. But we never actually collaborated. He came in on very short notice and he had a lot of work to do, but he did it very fast and very well.'

Peoples had been brought into the project during November 1980. Shooting was still several months away. 'I read the script,' said Peoples, 'and immediately felt that it was so good that I was disappointed, because when they came to have a meeting I told them I couldn't make it any better. It was a terrific script. I don't know which ones Phil Dick read that he didn't like, but certainly the one I read was absolutely brilliant. And that was the one I worked from to make the changes Ridley wanted, to make it more his vision.'

Throughout this process of re-writing, Ridley Scott kept a watchful eye on the developing script. Another title change was instigated.

'The final title actually came from an obscure science fiction paperback (by Alan Nourse),' Ivor Powell, the associate producer told me. 'This paperback had something to do with doctors in the future, when doctors and medicines are banned. There are all these illegal doctors who go out to administer medical help to the sick, and the people who supply them with instruments when they run out are called blade runners. Hampton Fancher gave that name to Deckard in his script as a code-name. I'm not sure whether it was Hampton or Ridley who came up with the idea of calling the film *Blade Runner.*'

Dutifully, the filmmakers bought the rights to Alan Nourse's *Blade Runner* novel, only to discover that there was another book of that name by William Burroughs. Originally Nourse's novel was to be filmed and Burroughs had been hired to adapt the script. But when the movie fell through, Burroughs had his version of the story novelised and published in book form. *Blade Runner*'s producers were forced to purchase the rights to that version of the story, too.

In the meantime, David Peoples was running into problems. During his revision of the script many of the sets and vehicles were either under construction or already built.

'One time I changed a scene,' said Peoples, 'and somebody said, "Jesus, you wrote the ambulance out!" I said, "So what?" and they said, "Well, it's already built."'

Peoples gives full credit to Ridley Scott as the true architect of *Blade Runner*. 'If anybody was authoring it at this stage it was Ridley. He was dominating, supervising and caring about what went on here. Then, down the line, Harrison Ford and Rutger Hauer made some really nice contributions in the way of dialogue. I would sometimes be writing a scene that Ridley would be shooting the following week, and twice I guess, I was writing stuff that was going to be shot that day.'

THE CASTING

Harrison Ford's involvement in *Blade Runner* goes back further than that of David Peoples. 'They first asked me about *Blade Runner*,' said Harrison Ford, 'when I was doing ... hmm, *Empire*, I guess – I have such a bad memory. They were going to make it in London at that point in their plans and I said, "Well, thank you very much, gentlemen, but I don't want to work in London any more. I want to go home." Five of my last eight films have been made in London. When they came back to me, it turned out that they couldn't put it together in London for some reason.' That reason was intertwined with the collapse of Filmways and the involvement of Tandem Productions and The Ladd Company.

However, according to the book *Harrison Ford: Reluctant Hero*, Scott had approached Ford during the filming of *Empire* in 1978, not about *Blade Runner*, but about *Alien*, to play the role of Captain Dallas. Ford turned it down as he didn't want to play another space pilot and the role went to Tom Skerrit. Scott's approach to Ford about *Blade Runner* was during the filming of *Raiders* in 1980.

I asked Ivor Powell to explain the ins and outs of the move from London to LA. 'After getting Filmways in as the major and the distributor, the next problem was how to shoot the film. Despite all the location scouting we did, there was no one place that had the concentration of architecture that was right. As always, with a film like *Blade Runner*, it comes down to how you are going to crack the script, how you're actually going to make it work, how the logistics are going to work and how they are going to work within a price. The budget was gradually being pushed up and Filmways, I guess, were being carried screamingly along with it, and though we were unaware of it at the time, they were having tremendous cash-flow problems. They believed in the project, but I don't think they had the money for a twenty million dollar movie. The budget had gone from about twelve or thirteen million dollars, which was totally impractical, right up to twenty million plus. Finally, Filmways collapsed and Michael Deeley, very cleverly I think, turned the film around to Tandem Productions (the company of Jerry Perenchio and Bud Yorkin) and The Ladd Company in a very short space of time, though we went through a terrible hiatus where we were trying to hold the crew together. The directors' strike was looming for later that year. We knew if we didn't start the movie by a certain date, we would never start at all. It was one of those pictures that you *knew* that if it didn't get made then, it would never get made at all. It wasn't every director's cup of tea. Finally, the cash-flow started and we got off. We had, at that time, attempted to do a budget. I'd done a quick budget, which had come in at seventeen or eighteen million dollars, if we were making the picture in England. But if we'd made the move to England, it would have been too late to beat the director's strike, which ironically never happened anyway. So for that, and some other reasons, we made the movie there, at the Burbank Studios.'

With the production base re-located to Hollywood, Harrison Ford once more became available for the leading role as Rick Deckard, blade runner. But for many of Ford's fans, *Blade Runner* was a radical departure from the kind of film that had endeared their hero to them. Ford was following his oft-stated intention to avoid type-casting and ensure that each of his roles was sufficiently different from the last.

Ford was finally signed for *Blade Runner* while the finishing touches were being put on *Raiders of the Lost Ark*. And, as with *Raiders,* Ford was not the filmmakers' first choice for Deckard. I asked Ivor Powell why Harrison Ford had been picked for the role. 'By popular demand, really,' said Powell. *Raiders of the Lost Ark* hadn't come out then, so we didn't know if it was going to do well. At one time, we were even talking to Dustin Hoffman, and that would have been a totally different picture. Dustin is not a macho character and he asked Ridley, "Why the hell do you want me to play this macho character?"

'Ridley was searching for more than just a superficial, macho film,' continued Powell. 'He wanted a real character in there, and Dustin, as I understand it, put forward some wonderful ideas. But it wasn't the film we were talking about making. Finally, I think it just came down to the fact that Harrison fitted the bill.'

Ridley Scott also told me that, as far as he was concerned, Harrison Ford was the man for the job. 'He has a very unusual quality that shines through in two pictures, *The Conversation* and *Apocalypse Now*. It's a strange, slightly sinister, side. Very low-key and sombre. Almost a different Harrison Ford. Very dangerous. It fitted the nature of both Deckard and the film very well. The only other actor we saw for the part was Dustin Hoffman. He was looking for a different kind of movie. But, god knows, I'd like to work with Hoffman some day. After things fell through, we went straight to Harrison. He'd been under consideration from the beginning.'

And at the beginning, Ford seemed pleased to be involved in the project. 'I'm preparing to start work on *Blade Runner,*' he told an American fan magazine, shortly before *Raiders* opened. 'I'm sure I was considered for the film as a result of *Star Wars,* just as Ridley (Scott) proved his capabilities in this genre with *Alien*.

'I can't complain so far. *Star Wars, Empire, Raiders* and *Blade Runner* are classy, high-quality melodramas, not pot-boilers. They all contain currents of intelligence and morality, and are handled with taste. I'm looking forward to *Blade Runner*. I think I can give it an aspect that will set it apart from *Raiders* or *Star Wars* or anything else I've done.'

And while on a trip to Britain to promote *Raiders of the Lost Ark,* Ford had apparently brought his enthusiasm for *Blade Runner* with him. As he told the British magazine, *Films,* '*Blade Runner* is an important step towards more serious roles. And I think it will be a very commercial film because of its unique vision. But I was serious about it because of the people involved and was happy to find out that Ridley was interested in developing the density of the characters as well. I felt that we could work together to present a character who was interesting and very different to anything else I've done until now.'

Ford and Scott laboured long and hard to achieve something they could be proud of. 'We have a lot of discussions about scenes,' said Ford during filming, 'but not about motivation. I don't ask him what my motivations are and he doesn't ask me what they are. The discussions are usually about practical matters – what we're trying to get out of a scene, what the obligations are on him as master of the story and me as the character. Then we look for common ground to accomplish the story points and the character points at the same time. And sometimes that's done without any discussion at all, and sometimes we discuss all hell out of it!'

This process was underlined by Ridley Scott. 'There is always a period of rehearsals before the film, and I at least try to get a couple of weeks for casting and reading through the script. I usually take a certain amount of time and tell the actors about the overall film, not just about their particular parts. It's usually a lengthy process, but then it is worth it because they know how they sit, how they figure within the overall piece. It is very important that they understand the entire thing.'

Ford was also aware that the characters must be clearly defined before the first foot of film ran through the camera. 'Ultimately it is the actor who has to perform the act and commit it to film. So, while a director's job is incredibly complicated and difficult, there are elements that are never resolved – how a prop should work, whether the character carries his gun here or carries it there. These may be simple little details, but they are only decided when somebody gets a strong attitude about things and begins to form a point of view. The character Deckard does finally. He begins to develop a point of view about the circumstances around him.'

Yet for all this there seemed to be a fundamental difference between Deckard as Ridley Scott saw him and the character as envisaged by Ford. Scott's Deckard was apparent to the director as far back as the Hampton Fancher versions of the script. 'It started to emerge for me,' said Scott, 'that Deckard was a kind of Philip Marlowe character, which is an obvious comparison. Harrison figured he should go for utter reality, almost like de Niro's Travis Bickle in *Taxi Driver*.' Ford himself saw Deckard as, '... a reluctant detective who dresses like a middle-aged Elvis Costello. He's a skilled investigator, an expert in his field, but he's a little out of practice when the movie opens. He's lost his motor drive. Exterminating people, even non-human ones, is not something he likes to do, and he's not comfortable with authority. He's very tough, but he's no match for a top-of-the-line replicant.'

Tough though Deckard may have been, he didn't seem to be quite tough enough to resist the aspect of Chandler-esque pastiche that was creeping into the movie. Under Scott's direction, *Blade Runner* seemed to be taking shape as a kind of homage to the great black-and-white noir movies of the Forties. As the film's director of photography, Jordan Cronenweath, told *American Cinematographer*, 'Ridley felt the style of photography in *Citizen Kane* (1940) most closely approached the look he wanted for *Blade Runner*. This included, among other things, high contrast, unusual camera angles and the use of shafts of light.' All the film lacked at this stage was a punchy voice-over narration delivered in the kind of lazy drawl made famous by Humphrey Bogart. 'The generation of the idea of a voice-over came very quickly,' said Scott. 'Eventually a screenplay was written with a voice-over very much in mind.' Ford wasn't happy at the prospect of a voice-over narration, but for the time being kept his counsel. There was still the problem of being able to satisfy the requirements of the script without compromising his own goals and principles.

'My object,' Ford told an American fan magazine, 'every time out of the gate is to contrast the public's last known impression of me. So, with *Blade Runner,* I'm working against *Raiders of the Lost Ark.* They originally wanted Deckard to wear a big felt hat. I told them I had just finished wearing one in *Raiders,* so we changed that.'

Despite evidence to the contrary, Ford felt that the science fiction content of *Blade Runner* was minimal. 'I wouldn't call *Blade Runner* science fiction,' he said, 'because it's much different from the public's conception of sf-based on movies they've seen in the past.' Granted, but *Star Wars* was actually less worthy of the tag Science Fiction than *Blade Runner.* 'There are special effects in it,' he continued, 'but they're kind of throwaways. From a technical point of view, *Blade Runner* is not an effects film, but I'm sure Doug (Trumbull)'s work will add a great deal to the story.'

And even at this early stage, Ford was aware of the film's noir potential. As he told the reporter of *Movie Guide,* '*Blade Runner* is a big city detective story, the kind Raymond Chandler might have written, but it takes place in the future. It's realistic and gritty and takes place entirely on Earth.'

Still, for all the confusion over what *Blade Runner* and Deckard were all about, Ford was enjoying working with Scott. At least for the time being. 'Ridley's very particular and demanding in all elements of the production. I knew he was a great visual stylist, but I was glad to find depth and subtlety of character.'

THE FILMING

The filming of *Blade Runner* finally got under way on March 9, 1981, after a year of preproduction planning and an additional fourteen weeks of constructing and dressing sets. The project was already running three months behind schedule.

Actual locations, both in the United States and in Europe, had been considered by the film's producer, Michael Deeley. But finally, the idea of location filming had proved both impractible and undesirable. The production team were happy to settle for shooting the exteriors on the Warner Brothers New York street set, which had been used for such earlier detective yarns as *The Maltese Falcon* (1941) and *The Big Sleep* (1946) as well as more recent fare like 1982's *Annie.*

Industrial designer Syd Mead and *Blade Runner*'s production designer Lawrence Paull had been hard at work for twelve months creating the backdrop against which the drama would be played. The cast had been assembled and carefully coached in the lore of *Blade Runner.* The on-set smoke machine was switched on. The real work could begin.

Most of the action in the movie takes place at night. This meant the cast and crew knuckling down to a gruelling, hours-of-darkness shooting schedule. Lunch was called at midnight and the 'day's' work ended at four or five in the morning. Scott and his key cast and crew members had to survive on an average of four hours of sleep a night, which prevented the kind of family atmosphere Ford had been used to on the Lucas films.

Unlike Lucas, who delegated many of his responsibilities as a filmmaker, Scott preferred to be personally involved in every aspect of the process. Reports filtered through to the trade publications that Ford and Scott weren't getting along. These reports hinted that Ford was unhappy with Scott's attention to the mechanics of film-making, a fascination that ran to the extent of Scott operating his own camera during key scenes, a charge Ford denied. 'It was no big bone of contention between us,' said Ford. 'I don't think he ever got around that problem. He just learned to accommodate the reality. Ridley was able to shoot a few things he really wanted to. And he's very good. Especially with the hand-held camera. I think there's quite a few shots in the film with Scott operating his hand-held camera. He likes to watch the performance through the lens. As an actor, I'm glad he wasn't able to do that all the time. I think it's better to have his attention on other things. He knows that's the way I feel. I think that when a director is looking through the camera, he's watching the edges to be sure where everything is. I want a director to be helping me with a whole scene, the performance. It's not that this isn't possible, or that Ridley hasn't done it before ... and very well.'

Ford kept himself pretty much to himself during the seventeen weeks of shooting. His co-star Sean Young would have welcomed more collaboration between them. 'I think Harrison is probably an all-or-nothing type of person and he can't really relate to other cast members full out, because he feels he might become too wrapped up, and by being friendlier with the crew, he can avoid that whole mess.'

Rutger Hauer was less open in his views on working with Ford. 'I only had two moments in the film with Ford,' he said. 'I didn't work that long with him, but he was fine. Our scenes were very clearly written in the script. I didn't feel there was a problem of communication because we didn't have to talk about it. It was just a matter of doing it without getting hurt.'

As was his custom on his other films, Ford did most of his own stunts for *Blade Runner*. One memorable scene had him clinging precariously to a ledge, hundreds of storeys above the teeming streets.

'We were using a 65mm Mitchell camera,' explained effects man David Dryer, 'which weighed about 75 pounds. With that kind of weight cantilevered out over Ford there was always the chance that the camera would break a casting and come right down on him. So we rigged a special plate and support to get the camera actually looking back down on itself.'

It was Rutger Hauer's job to haul Ford up onto the roof. 'Harrison didn't want to fall down that twenty foot drop, or whatever it was. So he was hanging there, with a wire for support, but it was still kind of tough to get him up.'

But Ford was dismissive of the danger involved. 'That shot where I'm hanging from the girder ... well, god knows, I'm not hanging 30 storeys above the ground there. Not only am I not hanging from the girder, I've got a safety belt on and a wire that's got me clipped to the bottom of the girder ... and I'm *acting* like I'm hanging from a girder, from the contortion of my face, the sweat of my brow. That's all acting ... wonderful acting!' But on a more serious note Ford is careful to draw a clear distinction between what he does and 'real' stunts. 'What I've done in *Raiders of the Lost Ark* and *Blade Runner* is "physical acting". Stunts are falling off a tall building or crashing a car. Something you're silly enough to think isn't going to hurt the next day.'

Meanwhile, rumours abounded that Ford had drastically altered his appearance for the movie, one American newspaper even claiming Ford played Deckard with a shaved head. 'The crewcut was my idea,' said Ford. 'And I had to talk Ridley into it, because he was afraid that it might make me less ... gorgeous. The haircut couldn't be done unless Ridley was there. It took about four hours to get it. With long pauses for consideration by Ridley.'

My ambition was always to get it right down. Real short. I wanted to give the impression of a character who has given upon himself, was unconscious of his appearance and had lost, to a large degree, that ego that keeps us all doing things like combing our hair, brushing our teeth and all of that. I thought it was important to suggest that and change my appearance in some way. I think it's more interesting for an audience, even if they know right away who it is. They don't have the same expectation of you if you don't look the same. It gives you a foot forward.

'And one of the other things that drives me nuts when doing a four month shooting schedule is when someone is fiddling with your hair between every shot. I just can't stand that. It just drives me nuts. If I could have short hair on every film ... I mean, some of my best friends are hairdressers, but it does drive me nuts. The first thing I do after a film where I have long hair is cut it all off.'

The beard was also Ford's idea. 'The first day of *Blade Runner*, I'm shaved. When the events begin to take over my life, it hardly seems a proper time to shave ... when things are going the way they are in *Blade Runner*, there doesn't seem time for a bath and a shave. I think that kind of detail goes to make up the character. I try not to lose sight of those little things.'

By this time, Ford had had a chance to think through Deckard's relationship with Rachael. 'It's clear that Deckard doesn't think very much about women at all,' he told the author of *Blade Runner* souvenir magazine. 'He's the type of guy that would see them occasionally but not have any use for them around the house. He has a wife and child but they seem to have gone in search of a better life. Deckard acknowledges on Rachael's first appearance that she is attractive. But then she becomes a puzzle and, when he figures out she is a replicant, he seems to have no further use for her. He sees Rachael as a zero. But her display of emotion, even though he knows it's false, implanted, pulls him out of his despair. As he begins to become involved with her, he is forced to confront what is really going on around him.'

THE RELEASE

Director Ridley Scott called 'cut!' for the last time on *Blade Runner* during the second week of July, 1981. The production was already over-schedule and over-budget. The filmmakers busied themselves with such vital post-production activities as editing, dubbing and adding the excellent Vangelis music. The following January, the first of the *Blade Runner* trailers was released in America. It featured scenes from the movie under the music of the Inkspots, enhancing the idea of *Blade Runner* as a 1940s pastiche.

A rough cut of the film previewed in Denver, Colorado. The feedback from that screening indicated the fans were unhappy with the abrupt ending of Deckard and Rachael stepping into the lift and the doors slamming shut behind them.

'Fortunately, we had also shot an alternative ending, with Deckard and Rachael leaving the city together in a Spinner, heading towards the unpolluted Northwest,' said Scott. Also at this stage, there was no Harrison Ford voice-over to explain the more ambiguous scenes in the film. I was lucky enough to see this version at an early preview in London around March, 1982, and feel this 'first draft' to be far superior to both the theatrical release cut and the later 'Director's Cut' released on VHS video.

When the film came out on June 25, 1982 in America, the 1940s look and the laconic (some would say, 'bored') narration was singled out by the critics as the chief target for attack. Ford was a little defensive about such comments. 'I thought it had the makings of a very original film,' he said. 'It was no ambition of mine to play the character like a Forties Bogart figure, but it was always on Ridley's mind. It was always my hope that there wouldn't be a voice-over, that we wouldn't need one. I thought the character needed to be a representation of a certain type of physical environment, the result of that kind of life. The voice-over was always Ridley's idea, from the beginning.'

Scott was a little more philosophical. 'We never addressed the problem of the voice-over early enough,' he told me. 'I wanted the voice-over from the beginning. The screenplay was written with a voice-over.' But that wasn't the voice-over that appeared in the finished film. And Scott was far from happy with the end result. 'The voice-over is an essential part of the Marlowe-type character of Deckard and also to a degree helps clarification. One of the most interesting aspects of *Apocalypse Now* was the voice-over. It was incredible. I think Coppola went on for nearly six months trying to get that right. I think, with hindsight, I would have re-done the voice-over in *Blade Runner,* and I think Harrison would as well.'

As it turned out, the final narration was no masterpiece and it jarred against the other aspects of the production. Of particular note was the corny speech over the scene in which replicant Roy Batty dies. Ford's tired voice proclaims. 'I don't know why he saved my life. Maybe in those last moments he loved life more than he ever had before. Not just his life. Anybody's life. My life. All he'd wanted were the same answers the rest of us want. Where do I come from? Where am I going? How long have it got? All I could do was sit there and watch him die.' Raymond Chandler it's not.

Almost predictably, the reviews weren't good.

Playboy's Bruce Williamson thought *Blade Runner* was a 'major disappointment' despite 'smashing production values and fine actors' and summed up the movie saying, 'by the time Ford and Hauer face off for their climactic showdown, *Blade Runner* had grown dull – a simple case of Philip Marlowe meets Frankenstein.'

The British trade publication *Screen International* felt 'the special effects dominate the film while the plot and characters fade into the background,' and pointed out that 'in spite of his voice-over ironies, Rick Deckard is no Philip Marlowe.'

The American trade bible *Variety* said that 'Ford's frequent inertia mutes the detective angle of the story which is couched in some hard-boiled Chandleresque narration and in the long run proves to be the weakest aspect of the pic.'

Some critics believed that the level of violence in *Blade Runner* was more explicit than was necessary. Ford countered this in his usual eloquent style. 'There's a really unfortunate and ill-advised attitude to the violence in the film. I am conscious of violence in a film. I abhor it when it is used for the sake of itself. I was anxious to make sure this character represented the abhorrence of violence. And he does. He wanted to get out of the police force because he couldn't stand the killing. After every incident of having to kill someone, the character's revulsion is clear. And, ironically, he is not killing human beings. That's what the thematic backbone of the film is. They're not really human beings. And yet, his empathy with something that looks like a human being – which is later to lead him into a romance with a machine affects him.'

In spite of the negative criticism of the film, Ford's performance was praised. Scriptwriter David Peoples was enthusiastic about Ford's portrayal of Rick Deckard. 'Harrison is an absolutely magnificent actor,' he commented. 'He's amazing. He's like the great old guys. He becomes Deckard. I mean, you don't see him act like Deckard, he *is* Deckard and Deckard is different from Han Solo and entirely different from Indiana Jones. In *Blade Runner* he's a seething guy with a lot inside him. He's a guy who's got a lot of problems, who's holding a lot in, and Harrison does it brilliantly.'

Science fiction author and friend of Philip K. Dick's, Norman Spinrad was more restrained about Ford's performance. 'Harrison Ford is fine in the rather undemanding role of Deckard,' a comment that seems to me to be sniffy and dismissive.

In my view *Blade Runner* remains probably the most literate science fiction film ever made. Ford's performance is a masterpiece of understatement and contributed mightily to the film's artistic success. Ford himself has spoken critically of his involvement in the film, stating that he's very unhappy with Ridley Scott's later revelations that Deckard was always intended to be a replicant. However, I never felt that Deckard was any kind of replicant, just that the momentary doubt about his own humanity the character experiences is enough to finally convince Deckard that replicants are worth no less than human beings.

Yet *Blade Runner* was an extremely important step in Ford's career. It was his first opportunity to show what he could do as a serious actor. It was becoming obvious that Ford was a far better actor than his *Star Wars* and *Raiders* vehicles allowed audiences to see. But further expeditions into the area of serious acting would have to wait. Already the date for the beginning of principal photography of the third part of the *Star Wars* saga was approaching. It was almost time for Ford to return to the worlds of robots and rayguns as Han Solo in *Return of the Jedi*. But not before he'd rested up a while. 'It would take an Act of Congress to get me to work before *Jedi*,' he said, 'I haven't had six months with the kids for a long time.'

But Ford would be back at work quicker than he expected. Melissa had been around on set much of the time during the filming of *Raiders*, working with Spielberg on the script for *E.T.* During the filming of *E.T.*, Spielberg had Melissa work with the child actors, rehearsing their scenes. It was inevitable that Ford would end up with a role in the movie. Spielberg also persuaded Melissa to play the part of the nurse who takes the "drunk" Elliot to the principal (played by Ford). As with most of the other adults in the film, their faces would not be seen. But nervous Melissa's hands trembled so badly during her scene she pleaded with Spielberg to scrap the footage. So not for the first time in his career one of Ford's performances was consigned to the cutting room floor.

CHAPTER 7

HARRISON FORD: CONTRACT PLAYER NO MORE

From 'Get me Harrison Ford' to 'Get me a Harrison Ford type!'

'Harrison Ford is a pure cinema actor, there is nothing theatrical about him – it's just him. He doesn't mind it his shirt's out or his hair's ruffled or his profile isn't beautifully lit. What matters is what he's doing.' Richard Marquand, director of *Return of the Jedi*

The close of *The Empire Strikes Back* left Han Solo (Harrison Ford) sleeping the sleep of the living dead, frozen in a block of carbonite and on his way to the palace of Jabba the Hutt, an alien criminal mastermind, to suffer the penalty for dumping a cargo of illegal spices belonging to Jabba. Some of the more imaginative *Star Wars* fans put this fact together with the knowledge that Harrison Ford had only signed for one *Star Wars* picture at a time and began to circulate rumours that neither Ford nor Solo would be appearing in the third *Star Wars* film, *Return of the Jedi*.

But shortly after the release of *Raiders of the Lost Ark*, Harrison Ford went on record in the American magazine *Starlog* to put paid to such wild speculation. 'If I hadn't been able to do some of my other movies I might have felt differently about doing *Return of the Jedi*. As it stands, I'm delighted to be coming back. Han, Luke and Princess Leia were created to tell this story, so I'm glad to be in on the third act.'

Yet, just how Han Solo would return was a closely guarded secret. Nobody involved with the production would talk without the express permission of *Star Wars* creator

George Lucas. Then Lucas himself broke the silence in a pre-*Return* interview – though he was giving nothing away. 'The original (*Star Wars*) idea kind of got segmented, and the fact that the story is a fairy tale got lost, especially in the beginning, because the science fiction took over. I think that *Return* for better or worse, is going to put the whole thing in perspective.'

FINDING MR WRITE

Originally, George Lucas had intended to tell the story of Luke Skywalker's struggle against the Empire in just one film. But as he completed the first draft of the tale, he realised that he had far too much story to fit into one two-hour movie. So he simply cut the story in two and continued to work on the first half. Before long it became apparent to Lucas that even two feature films would be too little screen time to tell the story in and three films would be needed.

Though Lucas wrote and directed *Star Wars: A New Hope*, the tremendous success of the film meant that Lucas's energies were divided between running Lucasfilm and overseeing the flood of merchandising which followed in the Star-wake, as well as supervising preparations for future Lucasfilm movie projects. In short, there was no way Lucas could write or direct any more *Star Wars* films ... even if he wanted to.

For *Empire Strikes Back*, Lucas had hired Lawrence Kasdan to craft the screenplay and Irvin Kershner to direct. With *Return of the Jedi*, he resolved to use a new writer/director team.

Yet, well-laid plans, particularly in the movie business, have a habit of going awry. The October 1981 issue of *Starlog* magazine carried a story under the title *of Kasdan Gets Revenge* (*Revenge of the Jedi* was the shooting title for *Return of the Jedi* and Fox even went to the trouble of printing teaser posters bearing that title – I know because I was given one by someone at Fox at the time).

'It's a big surprise to me that I'm writing *Revenge of the Jedi*,' said Kasdan. 'George Lucas called me on the phone and asked me to do the script as a favour to him. I told George that I hadn't planned on doing any more 'just writing' on films.' He said, "Aw, come on. I've done it. Paul Schrader did it for Martin Scorcese. What difference does it make?"

'I'm doing the script because I feel I owe George a lot. Besides, I like working with him. There's also a certain satisfaction in finishing the trilogy. Additionally, writing *Jedi* will be very rewarding financially. '

George Lucas had, as with *The Empire Strikes Back*, roughed out the plot of the movie first, embracing the main story-points and character developments. He was looking to Kasdan to bring pacing and humour to the final script. Kasdan, Lucas and director, Richard Marquand, spent a solid week discussing the thrust of the story and settling any differences of opinion they had as to the direction *Return of the Jedi* should take. From there on it became Kasdan's baby.

'*Revenge of the Jedi*'s basic thrust is to wrap up the trilogy's story,' Kasdan revealed in the same interview. 'You can assume that *Jedi*'s structure will be like that of *Star Wars* and *Empire*, cutting back and forth. You could probably guess which of the characters will be returning. There will also be some new characters.'

Because of the suddenness of Lucas's request, Kasdan was left with little time in which to complete his assignment. 'It's a similar situation to the terrible time problem we had on *Empire*, but I think this time I'll have a much freer hand, because the *Jedi* screenplay George gave me isn't nearly as far along as *Empire*'s was.'

THE HAND ON THE HELM

The search for the man to direct *Jedi* was every bit as exhaustive as Lucas's original *Star Wars* casting sessions had been. Lucas started out with a list of literally hundreds of British and American directors who could, conceivably, direct the third part of the trilogy. Lucas's first choice was Steven Spielberg, who had to turn the offer down because of the threatened Director's Guild strike. Another director in the frame was David Cronenberg, who probably would have made a *very* interesting Star Wars movie ...

After cutting away others who couldn't do the film because of scheduling, prior commitments and lack of enthusiasm, the list fell to just two names, one of which was Richard Marquand whose previous credits included a horror movie called *The Legacy* and the war-time adventure movie *Eye of the Needle*.

'George Lucas told me he wanted a director who could work fast, somebody – possibly from television – who could think on his feet, improvise quickly, and work with actors. Finally – and I think this is the most important thing – somebody who could work with him,' said Richard Marquand. 'Finally, there were only two of us left in the running. This was about April or May of 1981.'

Though most people associated with *Return of the Jedi* have been reluctant to discuss who didn't get through the selection process, Mark Hamill did let it slip in an interview that Marquand's rival for the job was David Lynch, director of *The Elephant Man*.

'David decided he didn't want to do a George Lucas movie,' explained Hamill, 'Because he felt he couldn't be constantly answering to another producer. George didn't want to restrict somebody that original, so they came to an amiable parting of the ways. Ironically, David left to make *Dune* for Dino De Laurentiis.'

With Marquand selected to helm *Return of the Jedi*, preproduction work got underway with a vengeance. Marquand was far more than a puppet director, and had a healthy input into the way the movie would shape up as a kind of punch-line to the first two films.

'I had a whole plan of the way I wanted to present each character, each new character,' Marquand told me in February 1983, 'to make *Jedi* slightly different from the other films. *Empire* ends in a kind of explosion – everyone's going off in different directions. I thought it would be nice if we opened *Jedi* with a tremendous sense of mystery. A 'where is everybody?' sort of feeling. We know that Vader and the Emperor are really on the Rebel's tails after *Empire*, which ended on a kind of dark note. I thought it would be nice to pick up on that. All the heroes are scattered to the four corners of the Galaxy and then I could bring in each one in an interesting way. George liked that idea. Larry (Kasdan) picked up on it and turned it into something terrific. Then I was talking about killing off one of the major characters. George wouldn't have that.'

This almost certainly would have been the Han Solo character. As Ford revealed in a later interview, 'I thought it would give the myth some body. Solo really had no place to go. He's got no papa, he's got no mama, he's got no story. But that was the one thing I was unable to convince George of.'

Richard Marquand's next step was to get together with the principal actors and hash out how the main characters would develop in the film.

'"You know this character. Tell me what this character's got to offer in terms of the public and the box-office and the story," I said. I discovered some nice things about the characters, which we were able to inject into the film.'

Marquand has nothing but praise for Hamill, Fisher and Ford. 'Carrie Fisher has made no secret of the fact that she's this sort of boy in girl's clothing,' Marquand told me, 'who marches up and down and shouts at everybody. She felt her character could do with a bit of development. And that happened to coincide exactly with my feelings. In the last movie, the Princess became such a bitch, she really was a drag. I was sure there was a lot more depth there we could use. And more comedy, too. Turn her into more of a woman. So I worked with Carrie on that. She's a very sexy, attractive lady and in this film we'll get to find that out.

'Mark's character, Luke Skywalker, is the one that develops through the whole series. That's the area of jeopardy. Will Luke move towards the Dark Side of the Force? He does; you see the darkening as he is led in this direction.

'Billy Dee Williams had all sorts of ideas about Lando Calrissian. His past, and where he had come from, the kind of skills he had. We realise that he was the first owner of the Millennium Falcon. We didn't really get to know him in *Empire*, we just learned to distrust him.

'Harrison Ford's great, he really is. He's a very professional actor. A man who is now quite a major box office star. He gets on with it. Doesn't suffer fools gladly. If you don't know what you're going to do on the day, he gets a little confused and upset. But he's terrific as an ally, someone who understands the craft of being a movie actor.'

MAKING MOVIES

By January 11 1982, the *Return of the Jedi* cast and crew were safely ensconced in EMI's Elstree Studios just outside London, and shooting began. The production was using all nine sound-stages. Sets were put up and torn down with alarming speed as the juggernaut movie careened through its paces. Down came the gate of Jabba's Palace, up went the Death Star docking bay. *Jedi* technicians built an impressive redwood forest inside one hangar-like sound stage, then built the Ewok village among the trees.

Studio shooting forged ahead at break-neck speed and was completed in an amazing 78 days. From there, Marquand and his team flew to America and spent the next eight weeks filming the Tatooine scenes in the blazing heat of the Arizona desert. The Endor scenes were shot in the cooler redwood forests of Northern California.

In an effort to keep the curious at bay, and the prices of the local shop-keepers down, the Arizona filming was conducted under a cover title of *Blue Harvest* – 'Horror Beyond Imagination' said the crew's tee-shirts. 'Is that what the film's about?' asked somebody of George Lucas, 'No,' he replied wryly, 'that's the *making* of the movie.'

Marquand explained his directing technique to the American magazine *Prevue* in an interview published just before the release of *Jedi*. He admitted that he rehearsed the actors, 'but not in their moves. I like to show them the sets, give them an idea of the action and go through the script with them very carefully. I can't stand it when an actor walks on the set saying he cannot deliver a line that a writer, a producer and a director spent eight months working on. I won't have it.'

Yet Harrison Ford is well-known in movie circles for the amount of input he likes to have into the script. Marquand was aware of this preference and had no criticism of Ford in this area. If Ford wanted dialogue changes, Marquand was prepared to accommodate him because, 'he'll have good reasons and he'll say it a week before shooting. He'll explain why, and you'll either agree, in which case you'll go to the producer and the other actors and express his points, or you'll explain why the line is there. If you can explain it to him, he'll do it because he's a professional.'

Overall, Marquand's aim was to create 'real relationships and real action that stem from real emotions.' He was wary, rightly so, of allowing the dazzling special effects to take control of the film. But if he needed aid or advice, he felt secure in the knowledge that George Lucas would always be on hand to help him out.

'Having George Lucas as an executive producer on this film is like directing *King Lear* with Shakespeare in the next room!' said Marquand.

Lucas himself had sufficient confidence in his *Star Wars* movies to put his money where his mouth is. Unlike other major movie productions, which borrow money from wherever they can get it, then insure their borrowings like crazy in case the film flops, Lucas was using his personal fortune to finance *Jedi*.

'I decided,' said Lucas, 'I had the most faith in my own films. I'm using my profits to make more films.'

And Lucas's secret was to incorporate into his movies something that most contemporary filmmakers forget. 'One of the most important things is to create an emotion in the audience,' says Lucas. 'The movie can be funny, sad or scary, but there has to be an emotion. It has to make you feel good or laugh or jump out of your seat.' Whether Lucas had injected enough emotion into *Jedi* would be left to the critics and, more importantly, the audiences to decide.

In the meantime, Ford had taken time out between the completion of principle photography on *Jedi* and the film's release to go house hunting. Sun Valley, Idaho was considered but abandoned as it was already full of Hollywood ex-pats. Harrison and Melissa then looked at Wyoming and settled on the town of Jackson Hole, where they were shown an 800 acre property. Ford had found his paradise.

RELEASE OF THE JEDI

It's unlikely that George Lucas was *really* worried that *Jedi* would turn out to be a clinker. The film opened on the traditional date of May 25th, 1983 in America, followed by the British release on June 2nd, 1983. Although the reviews were, in the main, favourable, a few harder-to-please folk managed to find fault with the film.

'Taken on its own terms,' ventured *Time* magazine, '*Return of the Jedi* is a brilliant, imaginative piece of film-making.' *Time* then went on to say that *Jedi* sacrificed the human element for its fascination with dazzling special effects, a familiar complaint of the up-market magazines of the *Star Wars* films. 'The other flaw,' said *Time*, 'is the ending: in all three films, Lucas has almost entirely avoided the rank sentimentality to which his story is vulnerable. In the final minutes of *Jedi*, he succumbs, however, and ends his trilogy with one of the corniest conclusions in recent years.'

Playboy's Bruce Williamson thought that *Jedi* was, 'another rousing entertainment in George Lucas's nine-part epic derived from *Star Wars* ... in its script, *Return of the Jedi* falls a bit short of its predecessors and director Richard Marquand doesn't quite have Lucas's magic touch ... Lucas continues to make movie-going the kind of innocent, awe-struck pleasure it used to be when we were all light-years younger.'

It should be explained that when this review was written, Lucas had intended producing a trilogy of *Star Wars* films that came after *A New Hope*, *Empire* and *Jedi* as well as the trilogy that later preceded them. Those plans now appear to have been abandoned.

Variety, the trade paper of American show business, seemed to fall into line with the criticisms that *Time* had made. 'Lucas and Co have perfected the technical magic where anything and everything – no matter how bizarre – is believable ... the human and dramatic dimensions have been sorely sacrificed ... Harrison Ford, who was such an essential element of the first two outings is present more in body than in spirit this time, given little to do but react to special effects.'

I thought that *Return of the Jedi* was certainly the least successful of the three Star Wars movies, artistically. Its worst failing was that it fell into the same trap as *Indiana Jones and the Temple of Doom* – the filmmakers loaded it to excess with similar elements from its predessessors to the point where the overall effect was one of overkill. While there are some great sequences in the movie – notably the battle on Jabba's barge and the chase on the speeder bikes through the forest of Endor – there are elements that simply jar. The Ewoks are probably my least favourite Star Wars characters ever and Jabba the Hutt's gremlin-like pet Salacious Crumb is excedingly annoying though not, I suspect, in the way the filmmakers intended. It was as though Lucas was trying – none-too-successfully – to cater to the kiddie market.

Audiences either didn't read the reviews, or didn't care what they said anyway. The film was safely into profit inside three months and, as the end of 1983 rolled round, *Jedi* was the number one grossing film of the year and nineteenth of the list of the top US box-office hits of all time earning a staggering $309 million. Worldwide, the gross was an even more impressive $572 million, $40 million more than *Empire* ...

The Academy nominated *Jedi* for four awards, in the categories Best Sound Effects Editing, Best Sound, Best Art Direction and Best Score, and awarded a Special Oscar to Richard Edlund, Dennis Muren, Ken Ralston and Phil Tippet for Achievement in Special Effects.

Harrison Ford was not surprised that George Lucas had been proved right again and that most of the critics were out of touch with what the audiences wanted. 'People want fairy tales in their lives,' he told *Time* magazine. 'I'm lucky enough to provide them. There is no difference between doing this kind of film and playing King Lear. The actor's job is exactly the same: dress up and pretend.'

THE LAST ACT OF HAN SOLO

As it turned out, *Return of the Jedi* marked the final instalment in the *Star Wars* saga. It also marked the last screen appearances of Luke Skywalker, Princess Leia and Han Solo. Other stories in the epic tale would tell of the Clone Wars and the rise of the Empire in the first trilogy (filmed as *The Phantom Menace*, *Attack of the Clones* and *Revenge of the Sith*), while the story of the rebuilding of the Galactic Democracy was to be told in the abandoned final trio of movies. Harrison Ford was not entirely unhappy that his stint as an interstellar star was over. 'The story that Han Solo was part of,' explained Ford to

Starburst's Tony Crawley, 'which is "The Adventures of Luke Skywalker", in my guise of best friend is over. The story completes itself in this third film. I had a great time on *Jedi*. I'm glad I did it. I'm glad I did all three of them. But as well, I'm glad ... I don't ... have to do any more. After *Jedi*, the saga goes back in time, so Solo's not in the next three. There will be nine films in all. Just three for Solo. I assume they will not replace me with another person to play Solo ...'

Perhaps if George Lucas changes his mind and does decide to film the final three movies of the originally-planned nine part story, he can convince Ford to return to the role of Solo as a kind of elder statesman of the *Star Wars* universe. It may even appeal to Ford's sense of humour to do it.

CHAPTER 8

HARRISON FORD: INDIANA JONES IS BACK!

From Box Office Draw to Box Office Phenomenon

'Playing Indy is just a fun thing to do.' Harrison Ford

Every time a big, successful movie looms over the cinematic horizon, you can bet, sure as sunrise, that the same relentless movie-making machinery will grind into motion.

The first stage of this process is that every bozo with a budget in Film City, USA will think he can reproduce the elements that made the original the success it was. Within months, a flood of dismal, copycat movies will be jostling for space on screens around the world. Then, the makers of the film that started it all will begin work on a sequel – if only to show the rip-off merchants how it should be done.

Which is exactly what happened with *Raiders of the Lost Ark*.

In rapid succession, film-goers were forced to suffer *High Road to China* (ironically starring George Lucas' first choice for Indiana Jones, Tom Selleck), *Invaders of the Lost Gold* (actually just an Italian horror movie *Horror Safari* opportunistically retitled), *Hunters of the Golden Cobra*, a kind of spaghetti *Raiders* starring ex-model David Warbeck and directed by Italian hack-meister Antonio Marghereti, and *Treasure of the Four*

Crowns, another cheesey Italian effort, this time in 3D. Then, in early 1983, the American screen trade paper *Variety* announced that work had begun on the follow-up to *Raiders of the Lost Ark*.

INDIANA JONES AND THE TEMPLE OF ... WHAT?

'Steven Spielberg is helming *Indiana Jones and the Temple of Doom* on location in Sri Lanka (with lensing in Hong Kong and London's Elstree Studios to follow) for Lucasfilm Ltd and Paramount, with Harrison Ford reprising his title role characterisation first seen in *Raiders of the Lost Ark* and Douglas Slocombe back as cinematographer, Kate Capshaw, who had roles in *A Little Sex* and the current sci-fier *Dreamscape* is Ford's new leading lady.' All of which must have come as something of a surprise to certain American fan magazines which were getting excited about a *Raiders* sequel called '*Indiana Jones and the Temple of Death*'.

Other than that, information was hard to come by. Not that Ford would have put talking to the press very high on his list of priorities anyway. He had married Melissa Mathison on March 14, 1983, a short time after obtaining his final divorce from Mary and mere weeks before beginning work on *Indiana Jones*.

What was known was that Lawrence Kasdan, busy with directing his latest film, *The Big Chill*, had passed on the scripting chores. Lucas had turned to his old friends Gloria Katz and Willard Huyck, who had worked wonders with Lucas' original draft of *American Graffiti*.

George Lucas himself had hinted at the contents of further *Indiana Jones* films around the time *Raiders* was released and confessed that Indy was his personal favourite of the characters he had created. 'If I could be a dream figure, I'd be Indy,' He told American magazine *Rolling Stone*. 'It's not just that I'm interested in archeology or anthropology; a lot of that got into *Star Wars* too. It's just that Indy can do anything. He's a lot of Thirties heroes put together. He's this renegade archeologist and adventurer, but he's also a college professor, and he's got this Cary Grant side, too. In some stories, we'll see him in top hat and tails. We don't want to make him Superman – he's just open to all possibilities. *Raiders* will be the most action oriented of the *Indiana Jones* movies – the others should deal more with the Occult.'

Lucas had no problems convincing director Steven Spielberg to re-sign on the dotted line. 'I'd hate to let it slip through my fingers into some one else's hands,' said Spielberg. 'I'll certainly not be involved in the third or the fourth one, but I really want to do the follow-up, because the story is even more spectacular than *Raiders*.'

Harrison Ford was also expressing his pleasure at the prospect of appearing in *Indiana Jones and the Temple of Doom*. 'Of course I'm doing the second *Raiders* film,' he said. 'With great pleasure. And for the first time, I think, in the history of sequels and good directors, Steven Spielberg is going to direct it. So this is very exciting for me. It was one of the best working relationship experiences of my life working with Steven.'

Pleased as he was, Ford was a little disturbed to hear from *Starburst*'s Tony Crawley that there were a total of five *Indiana Jones* films on the Lucasfilm launching pad, in varying stages of development. After completing filming on *Return of the Jedi*, the actor said, 'Actually, I'm only committed to one film at the moment. That's another *Indiana Jones* film. I had hoped to have a year off between the end of *Jedi* and the beginning of the next

Indy film. Five (*Indiana Jones* films) is okay with me. I mean I really enjoy working on them. And I really enjoy the character very much. And certainly I couldn't hope for better company than Lucas and Spielberg. But having done one, I don't think I'd do four more of anything. They must be talking to Roger Moore ... one at a time for me!'

THE WRITE STUFF

Though they were newcomers to the *Indiana Jones* series, script-writers Willard Huyck and Gloria Katz were no strangers to Lucasfilm Ltd. They had written the screenplay for Lucas' first big hit, *American Graffiti*, succeeding in producing a workable script where others, including Lucas, had failed.

Huyck and Katz, a husband and wife team, had met at University in California, worked together at Francis Coppola's studio where they first encountered Lucas and went on to write *Graffiti* (1973), *Lucky Lady* (1975) and *French Postcards* (1979).

The writers were first contacted about writing *Temple of Doom* in February, 1982. 'We flew up to George's house with Steven Spielberg and spent four days there,' said Huyck. 'In the first hour, George told us what he had in mind. Essentially, the story started in Shanghai and had Indy get into a situation in which his plane crashes. Then he's asked by villagers to recover a sacred stone. That's the basic outline we were given and we started building from there.'

The events in *Temple of Doom* take place a year before those in *Raiders*. Consequently, the new script called for a completely new cast of supporting characters, notably Short Round, Indy's child companion and 'bodyguard' and Willie Scott, a nightclub singer.

'We sat around trying to come up with names for the new characters,' explains Huyck, 'and we said that since George named Indiana Jones after his dog, Steven Spielberg and us should be able to name the characters after our dogs. So Steve named Willie after his dog and we named Short Round after ours. But our dog is named after a Korean child in the Sam Fuller movie *The Steel Helmet* (1951).'

'Short Round really came out of the notion that George wanted a child in the movie,' adds Katz. 'He wanted a girl, but we didn't like that idea too much, and Steve didn't feel comfortable with it, either. So we thought of the idea of Short Round and then of his character. How he participated in the script developed out of the story conferences.'

The script went through three full drafts on its way to completion, with pauses for less major rewrites along the way. The first draft took Huyck and Katz six weeks, 'because we wanted to get something we could talk about immediately,' says Huyck. The second draft took another six weeks, with the third draft being completed in a breakneck four weeks of work. From there, the writers were called away to attend to their next project, *Best Defense,* though throughout the period of shooting on *Temple of Doom,* they were continually called upon by Steven Spielberg for polishing on the final draft.

FINE TUNING

With the script out of the way, the production crew could turn their attention to the casting of both the supporting actors and the locations. In the September of 1982, the 'line' producer of *Temple of Doom*, Robert Watts, set off for Asia with the movie's production designer, Elliot Scott.

'First we went to Hong Kong,' said Watts, 'looking for locations for the Chinese sequence. Hong Kong was too modern and we had to rule it out. From there we went to Macao, which hasn't been developed as much as Hong Kong, and we found locations that would do for Shanghai. Then we went to India, where the bulk of the movie is supposed to take place, and we found most of the locations we wanted. The only problem was that they were miles apart.

'Carrying on to Sri Lanka, we found, to our surprise, that we could get almost everything we wanted in the environs of one town, Kandy, with the exception of the Maharajah's Palace.'

It was decided to base the production location at Kandy with only three days set aside for filming the Palace sequences on mainland India. Then Watts ran into hurdles. The Indian Government has rigid policies concerning the making of movies within its borders. A number of changes to the script were asked for. Too many for Lucasfilms' liking.

'George Lucas had very clear ideas on how the film should be,' said Watts. 'It is an adventure and the things that happen couldn't possibly happen in real life. But the film, if it is to work, has to have the look and feel of reality. We were prepared to go so far to meet the Indian Authorities' demands, but to have gone the whole way would have robbed the film of that element. In the end we decided it wasn't worth it, least of all for three days shooting, and we closed our Bombay office.'

To get around the problem of being denied the necessary location, the filmmakers decided to build the Palace on the backlot at Elstree Studios and use matte paintings – a special effects technique to incorporate realistic artwork into live action footage – for the long shots.

Watts' next objective was to take care of casting the actors. 'The film has a very small cast,' said Watts, 'though this is not always apparent because there are always lots of people on the screen. In fact, I would say that it is possibly the smallest and most difficult casting I've ever worked on.'

That Harrison Ford would appear as Indy was never in dispute. But finding the right actor to portray Short Round caused all concerned headaches.

'We had open casting calls in New York, Vancouver, London – anywhere with a substantial Chinese community,' explained Watts, 'and out of hundreds of boys there was only one who was really suitable.'

Ke Huy Quan was discovered during casting sessions in Los Angeles. A Vietnamese refugee, his English was good, but not so polished as to sound like a native American.

For the key role of villain Mola Ram, Indian star Amrish Puri was cast. 'The only trouble was,' said Watts, 'that being such a popular actor in India, he was working on eighteen films at once. Scheduling him was a nightmare!'

The casting of Kate Capshaw for the part of Willie Scott was a lot more straightforward. Capshaw had been introduced to the character of Indiana Jones when she was dragged, under protest, to see *Raiders of the Lost Ark* in 1981. 'I went, very petulent and sulky,' admitted Capshaw, 'and stayed that way for about two minutes! When I came out, I would have been a great advertisement for going to see that movie.'

A couple of years later, Kate Capshaw's agent just happened to be out jogging with one of the casting directors on *Temple of Doom* ... and the rest is history. 'Every director has a gut feeling for who a character is, what their special qualities are. They don't know who has "got it", but they'll know it when they see it. Steven felt I had it when he met me.'

With *Indiana Jones and the Temple of Doom* the plan was to set it apart from *Raiders*, with Indy himself as the only linking factor. This was underlined in the filmmakers' approach to the character of Willie Scott. Kate Capshaw was at pains to make Willie as different from Karen Allen's Marion Ravenwood as she could. Where Marion was tom-boyish, Willie was feminine, Where Marion was tough and capable – up to a point – Willie was nervous and flappable.

'Willie has led this pampered life,' explained Capshaw, 'and feels that's what's due to her – to be cared for and looked after. She meets Indiana Jones, a person unlike anyone she has ever been involved with, and ends up going off with him. In the course of their adventures, all of her earlier life is stripped away from her and Willie must fall back on her own resources. She discovers that she is a strong woman and a very gutsy lady.'

The screen writers Huyck and Katz don't necessarily share Capshaw's vision of Willie. Their intention was to depict Willie as an ordinary person caught up in extraordinary situations, whose first reaction to the assorted plights she finds herself in is to crack up, not an attribute that Huyck particularly admired; 'I never really cared for the character very much in the first place,' he said. 'But we felt that she was reacting realistically to the kind of things Indiana Jones goes through ... the kind of situations where, since she's not so tough – as few people would be in those situations – she'd scream.'

I thought that this take on the film's female lead was its biggest liability. Willie did little more than scream throughout the whole picture, and ended up as little more than a typical 'damsel in distress', but that kind of talk tends to upset Gloria Katz.

'People have very mixed feelings about Willie,' said Katz. 'I'm a little offended by the idea of a macho woman. I think that's a woman as conceived by men. I don't think that's a woman that necessarily, realistically exists. When you're covered in insects, your instinct is to scream! So I think Willie represents the audience's realistic point of view, what they would be like if they were thrown out into the jungle. True, it's not a brave, strong woman but it's a different kind of woman and, I think, a more realistic one.'

WHEN THE SHOOTING STARTS

Filming on *Indiana Jones and the Temple of Doom* began on 18th April 1983 on location in Sri Lanka and in Macao. When the Chinese sequence was safely in the can, the Macao unit joined the crew in Kandy and, with the two crews working side by side, the location work was wrapped in three weeks. From that lush setting, the cast and crew came back to earth with a bump, spending the next twelve weeks toiling through the British summer at EMI's Elstree Studios at Borehamwood, just outside London. Additional location scenes were filmed in Northern California in the United States, where Hamilton Air Force Base stood in for Shanghai Airport and the Tuolomne River played the part of the Ganges. Principal photography finished on September 8 1983 without incident, barring one mishap, though the special effects work would continue up until March 1984.

Like *Raiders* before it *Indiana Jones and the Temple of Doom* is packed to overflowing with complex and dangerous stunt work. The 'one mishap' very nearly shuttered production on the movie when Harrison Ford fell from an elephant and aggravated an old back injury – with a third of the picture still to be completed! Ford was jetted back to Los Angeles to undergo emergency laser surgery and filming was halted while the star recuperated. When he returned to the set, he found the most strenuous stunts – including his battle with the henchmen of Mola Ram and his climactic fight on the rickety rope bridge – were still before him. Fortunately for Ford, his doctors had patched him up perfectly and filming resumed without a hitch. Ford, as usual, was dismissive about the incident.

'I'm now as fit as a fiddle,' he said, 'but I could never have done it without Vic Armstrong. Guys like Vic are invisible. They never get any credit. Nobody ever interviews them.'

Armstrong had worked with Ford several times before, on *Raiders of the Lost Ark*, *Blade Runner* and *Return of the Jedi*, doubling for Ford when the going got too rough. Armstrong was philosophical about Fords remarks.

'We have to be invisible,' he conceded, 'if people are going to believe in the film.'

Maybe 'invisible' isn't the right word, for Armstrong bears a striking resemblance to Harrison Ford. While working on the set of *Raiders*, so many people mistook Armstrong for Ford that it came to be something of a running gag. But there's more to doubling for an actor than just physical resemblance. Of Ford, Armstrong said, 'He's a natural athlete and he wants to do it all. I say to him, "H, we can't afford to get you smashed up in this scene because we've got a whole crew that needs to make a living." And he says, "Yeah, you're right," and does the scene anyway. He could have made a great stunt man himself.'

THAT'S A WRAP!

When Steven Spielberg called 'Cut!' for the last time on 8th September 1983, it's unlikely that he would have realised just how literally that order could be taken. As with *Raiders*, certain scenes had been cut from the screenplay before and during shooting, obviously with Spielberg's blessing, but when *Temple of Doom* was presented to the censors, the word 'cut' began to take on sinister overtones.

On the plus side, the scenes that had been excised from *Raiders* had been modified and incorporated into *Temple of Doom*.

'The idea of the plane crash and then jumping out of the door in a life raft had, at one time, been in the original,' confirmed Huyck.

'The other thing was the mine car,' added Katz. 'George had thought of the mine car race for *Raiders*. But I don't know how it was written or what happened to it. He wanted a roller coaster ride.' And he got one!

There is a chance, then, that scenes cut from *Temple of Doom* might well find their way into some future *Indiana Jones* movie. Like the scene in which Kate Capshaw, as Willie, was to wrestle a boa constrictor.

'We had a snake scene that Kate wouldn't do,' explained Huyck. 'They had a boa constrictor and they had trained it. For weeks in advance, she had been trying to psyche herself up for this. She said she touched it and, the first time, it sort of ... undulated. And she thought she was going to die. She started sweating. Then they tried to put it on her shoulders to show her what it would be like, and she just freaked out. Steven (Spielberg) was sort of ashen and said, "That's all right."'

'It was a very funny scene,' added Katz, 'because there she is, being strangled by a snake, and Indy is just helplessly standing there!'

'So they didn't do it,' continued Huyck. 'Kate just couldn't do it. That's when Steve said, "Okay, if you're not going to do this, there's no way you're not going to do the bug scene."'

Another cut, involving the child Maharajah, ended up causing the film to be a little less clear than it should have been. It comes as something of a surprise to audiences to discover, late in the film, that the young monarch is under the control of the Thuggees. A couple of explanatory scenes had been written, but had never been filmed. During the banquet sequence, the prime minister Chattar Lal is seen talking to the shadowy figure of Mola Ram in the gardens outside the Palace. Later, Indy is teaching the young Maharajah how to use his whip. When the child comes to try it himself, he gets it wrong and hurts himself. Short Round laughs and a scuffle follows. During the scrap, Short Round sees the Maharajah's eyes glow red, and understands something weird is going on. Presumably these scenes were taken out, sacrificing clarity for pace, as the dinner sequence was long in itself.

A far different kettle of cuts was the chunk of *Temple of Doom* hacked out by overzealous censors in their never-ending quest to protect those who share their sensitive dispositions, but not their incorruptibility. The film was given a PG rating for its American release and immediately came under fire from journalists and parents' associations across the country.

'The movie,' said *The New York Times*, 'in addition to being endearingly disgusting, is violent in ways that may scare the wits out of some young patrons.'

Parents who had taken their young children to early preview screenings said their offspring were particularly disturbed by the scene in which Mola Ram tears the still-beating heart from the chest of a living sacrifice victim and the victim's subsequent immersion in boiling lava. The PG rating was called into question in some quarters, and the distributing company, Paramount, added a warning line to the newspaper ads, which read: 'This film may be too intense for younger children'.

In the UK the British Board of Film Censors took a harder line. Numerous changes were requested from Paramount before the BBFC would grant the picture the desired PG rating. Secretary of the Board, James Ferman, felt that the US version of the movie couldn't even get a fifteen rating under the British system. To obtain a fifteen, the scene in which 'the slow burning of a man in absolute agony' is shown would have to go. Faced with the threat of an eighteen certificate, Paramount decided to make cuts to the British release print. Yet, even in this toned down version, the film drew some flak for its violence. The late Alexander Walker, admittedly not noted for his tolerance towards youth-oriented movies, dismissed the picture as 'Indiana Jones meets the Marquis de Sade.'

Harrison Ford took such criticisms in his stride. 'This is a completely moral tale,' said the actor, 'and in order to have a moral resolve, evil must be seen to inflict pain. The end of the movie is proof or the viability of goodness.'

Still, in spite of all the fuss, *Indiana Jones and the Temple of Doom* was yet another in a long line of box office records for George Lucas, Steven Spielberg and Harrison Ford. No matter what the critics and the censors thought, the cinema-going public gave the movie the best vote of confidence they knew how. Between them, they spent enough ticket money to propel *Temple of Doom* to the top end of the movie charts for 1984, putting it in the number three slot, just a whisker behind *Ghostbusters* and *Beverley Hills Cop* in the battle for the number one slot and raising it to number 88 in the all-time box-office champs list with a take of almost $180 million in the US and $333 million worldwide. In addition, the American Academy nominated the film in the category of Best Score and awarded the movie an Oscar for Best Special Effects. And no one can argue with that kind of success.

And while the critics and the audiences were chewing over *Temple of Doom*, Ford was moving onto another of his 'small time' films, *Witness*. 'It's a calculated departure.' states Ford. 'This movie is the story of an Amish woman and a Philadelphia cop and the intelligence of the script gives me some wonderful cloth to cut.'

And despite their earlier denials, Spielberg announced in the early part of 1984 that he *would* be directing the third *Indiana Jones* film, and Ford, too, had been signed for the project. 'Playing Indy,' said Ford, 'is just a fun thing to do!'

CHAPTER 9

HARRISON FORD: ACADEMY AWARD NOMINEE

From Star to Actor

'My ambition was to play real people in *Star Wars* and *Raiders*. Doing *Witness* didn't feel any different from doing any other movie.' Harrison Ford

With all the box-office kudos Ford had earned for himself via the list of hugely successful films he'd appeared in over an eight-year period, it was time to do some art for arts' sake. Though I'd be the last to criticise the entertainment value of movies like the *Star Wars* and *Indiana Jones* series, Ford had made it clear that the high hopes he'd had for his role in *Blade Runner* hadn't turned out as expected and that he was looking for a part that would move him away from the rousing action films he'd been appearing in since his career had moved into high gear. When the script for *Witness* by Earl Wallace and Bill Kelley came to Ford's attention, the role of John Book seemed to fit the bill perfectly.

'The material,' said Ford later, 'represented a unique opportunity, I had not seen this movie-script before. Eighty-five percent of the scripts I read I know where they came from. This was a literate script for adults. I *saw* a movie when I read it. On paper, *Witness* looked real. More than that, it had something to say.

'Unlike many films that get made these days, it has a moral context, a moral point of view. It derives power and impulse from that and it derives also emotional value that the audience can experience along with the characters. There's an emotional relationship to goodness here, not just a visceral relationship to seeing something violent and horrible on screen.'

For these reasons, Ford agreed to appear in the Paramount project, the film was immediately greenlit. and the search for a director began. Ford had cannily insisted on director-approval when he signed on and selected Australian Peter Weir on the strength of the director's work on *The Year of Living Dangerously* (1982). Weir was already under contract to make a film version of Paul Theroux's best-selling novel *The Mosquito Coast* and was in the final stages of negotiating with Jack Nicholson's people, but 'when that failed to come together, Paramount sent him *Witness*,' says Ford, 'He responded to it almost immediately.'

When *Mosquito Coast* fell through, 'I said to my agent, "Get me a green-light picture",' said Peter Weir in 1999. 'I wanted to do a film like in the old studio days. So he sent me three scripts which were green-lit. One of them was *Witness*.' After meeting with Ford, Weir signed on.

CAN I GET A WITNESS?

Though *Witness* is on the surface part cop thriller and part clash-of-culture comedy-drama, the heart of the tale is the impossible love between city cop John Book and Amish widow Rachel Lapp. As such, the film is full of sensitively drawn character vignettes and is very light on running and shooting.

The film is shot in a painterly style by cinematographer John Seale, who went on to photograph *The English Patient* (1996), for which he won the Oscar, and *Cold Mountain* (2003). 'During pre-production in Philadelphia,' said Seale, 'there was an exhibition of Dutch genre painters, 17th Century, beautiful domestic scenes, strong light coming in from the side with one half of the person's face lit and the other falling into shadow. There was an early scene in the film where Daniel walks up to the group of mourners gathered around Rachel and expresses his sympathy. That wide shot with the group on the right and Daniel on the left is to me just like one of those Dutch paintings.'

To the untutored eye, the leap from the Art of Star Wars to the Art of the Flemish masters might seem like a huge one. Not to Harrison Ford. He maintains that John Book is not a departure from his other characters, just an extension. 'Some people say, "Well, *Witness* is real acting. It's great you're getting a chance to play a real person." In fact, my ambition was to play real people in *Star Wars* and *Raiders*. Doing this movie didn't feel any different to me from doing any other movie. The process is the same. It was regular acting.'

Irvin Kershner, director of *The Empire Strikes Back*, said of Ford, 'He is constantly looking for the authentic moment.' *Witness* is crammed with such moments.

For the first time since *Heroes*, Ford researched some background for his character and approached his task in his usual meticulous way, spending time with Philadelphia's homicide squad. 'I went on a couple of things with them, but the action wasn't as informing as a lot of the tension I saw. I learned as much from sitting around and having a cup of coffee with those guys. But they spend most of their time connecting and reconnecting various complicated relationships, following up on mundane details, deciding what's important and what's not.' These guys are people under pressure, and the attitude in your head and the wildness in your eyes can make a deep impression at just the right moment.'

Witness opened to rapturous reviews on Febraury 8, 1985. 'Harrison Ford has never been as good,' said the *London Evening Standard*. 'Serious, vulnerable, likeable. What is this man doing wasting his time in the juvenile junk of the Spielberg-Lucas cartoon world?' they added, a little unkindly. 'On this showing, Eastwood and Redford should hearing him coming up behind.' *The Daily Telegraph* said, 'No actor I can think of has lately transmitted sheer manliness so well and so gently as Harrison Ford.'

Business was brisk with the film earning back more than a third of its $12 million budget during the first weekend and it went on to take $65.5 million at the US box office, which isn't a bad return on investment.

Even better, *Witness* was taken seriously by the Academy of Motion Picture Arts and Sciences and was nominated in no fewer than eight categories. It lost out on the Best Original Score, Best Art Direction, Best Cinematography, Best Director and Best Picture awards to *Out of Africa*. Ford himself lost the Best Actor Award to William Hurt in *Kiss of the Spider Woman*, though *Witness* did win for Best Screenplay and Best Editing. Ford was also nominated in the Best Actor category of the Golden Globes, but lost out on that to Jon Voigt in *Runaway Train*, a movie that isn't as well remembered or as satisfying as *Witness*.

Ford's nominations for Best Actor were significant and showed that he'd made a big step towards being accepted as a Serious Actor. His next film looked as though it might give him another crack at that.

TOILING IN THE TROPICS

The commercial, critical and Oscar success director Peter Weir and Harrison Ford had enjoyed with *Witness* was very likely what persuaded the money-men to give them the budget to make *Mosquito Coast*. I'm not one to speculate on such stuff, but I think it's telling that before *Witness*, Weir was already under contract to direct *Mosquito Coast* with Jack Nicholson when the deal fell apart. Is it possible Ford agreed to do *Mosquito Coast* if Weir would first direct *Witness*? Will we ever know?

In any case, if Ford really had designs on being considered a serious actor ('It's always been my ambition to be a – quote – serious actor'), he'd have to be severely lacking in judgement not to jump at the chance to appear in a film adaptation of the Theroux novel as directed by a gifted creator like Peter Weir.

Ford had proved his potential in *Witness*, but while the part was emotionally complex, he was still portraying an action hero. As the obsessive Allie Fox in *The Mosquito Coast*, based on Paul Theroux's novel, he portrayed an altogether different kind of character.

'Both Peter Weir and I thought we shouldn't be slavish to the book,' said Ford. 'We needed a different Allie Fox. In the book Fox is crazy from the beginning. If audiences thought that he were crazy, they'd give up on him.'

Ford's agent Pat McQueeney wasn't enthusiastic about Ford doing the role. 'The audience thinks you're a hero,' she told Ford at the time. 'They aren't going to want you to be this mean guy who drags these people through the jungle.'

But Ford wasn't to be diverted. 'Allie is a complicated person,' he said in a later interview, 'and it's a complicated job for the audience to figure him out. He's a good father and a bad father. He's a monster, a clown, a fool, a genius. It was necessary always to preserve enough compassion for him so the audience could understand why he does the things he does.'

Finally, it was the quality of the writing, by screenwriting maestro Paul Schrader, that convinced Ford to not take McQueeney's advice. 'It's mostly about love,' the actor stated. 'Fox is a love junkie of one kind or another. He requires respect and admiration from his family and everyone he meets and he bullies his family into going along with everything. He carries the seeds of destruction within him.'

But Ford is film-savvy enough to realize all the great writing in the world is no good unless there's some way for the audience to connect with the hero of the story. 'We wanted a lot of the edgy feeling of the book still to be preserved; we didn't want to abandon the balls of it,' he says, 'because it's not necessary for him to be entirely likable as long as the audience can understand what he's about. You're always saying, "I know what he's talking about here," but then it's "He's going too far. Jesus Christ!" Part of his irresistible charm is that he's willing to go further than anybody in the audience would have gone, he's got to outstrip them emotionally. And they've got to be by turns delighted and frightened by where he's going.'

In the event, with Ford's agreement in the bag, producer Jerome Hellman went to friend Saul Zaentz for advice. Zaentz read the script and offered to finance the project himself. With the money in place, Weir pressed on to cast the two other crucial roles. For the part of Mother, Weir auditioned dozens of actresses, but it was apparent the moment she walked through the door that Helen Mirren was perfect. "The number of implications that come off her appearance speak the words that aren't written in the script,' said Weir, 'giving us the information that would take a long time to be written.'

The equally crucial role of Allie's son Charlie eventually went to River Phoenix. 'Diane Crittenden, the casting director, said, "there's a boy on this tape, he's terrific, only he's fifteen".' Weir initially though Phoenix too old for the role, 'but finally, I said, "What the hell does it matter how old he is? He looks like Harrison's son." And I cast him.'

The cast and crew then decamped for Belize where the Central American state stood in for 'La Mosquitia'. Conditions were harsh, the heat oppressive, though Weir tried to keep morale high by bringing in a range of conveniences for the cast and crew including VCRs, computers and even a cappuccino machine. Nonetheless, Ford rented a 120 foot air-conditioned boat which he moored near the location so Melisssa would have somewhere to work on her script for the tv movie, *Son of the Morning Star.*

Whether it was the influence of the trying conditions under which principal photography took place or whether it was because there genuinely is a bit of Allie Fox in Ford's temperament, some observers swear that Ford started to act like Allie off camera as well as on. During the earlier location scouting, Ford told author Theroux, 'Get a cargo plane. One of those C-130s. Fill it up with a prefab house in lots of sections, all the plumbing, all the wires, maybe a helicopter too. Drop the whole thing into Belize in one package and bolt it together.' Theroux could only admire the ease with which Ford switched into Allie Fox mode. 'Without any apparent effort, he'd turned into Allie,' said Theroux. 'The beaky cap, the flapping shirt, the pushed back hair, the I-know-best eyes and the gently maniacal voice explaining his brilliant plan.'

But the other side of Ford hadn't entirely gone away. As usual, he bonded better with the crew than he did with the cast. Between shots he'd pitch in and help the crew shift boxes or take on any other manual labour that was going. 'I'd rather help than stand around and wait for them to do it themselves,' stated Ford. 'If I can't stand in front of a camera until all that crap gets moved to the other side of the river, I grab a box. To everyone's absolute amazement and amusement. I'm just used to being part of a working group of people. The collar around my neck is blue.'

When *The Mosquito Coast* opened at the end of November in 1986, the reviews were a little mixed, perhaps reflecting the unfocussed nature of the tale being told. Said Roger Ebert of the *Chicago Sun-Times*, 'Fox is played in *The Mosquito Coast* by Harrison Ford, and it is one of the ironies of the movie that he does very good work. Ford gives us a character who has tunnel vision, who is uncaring toward his family or anyone else, who is totally lacking in a sense of humour, who is egocentric to the point of madness. It is a brilliant performance – so effective, indeed, that we can hardly stand to spend two hours in the company of this consummate jerk.' *The Washington Post* thought that '*The Mosquito Coast* is the worst kind of failure – a near miss that's sometimes great,' though trade paper *Variety* made reference to Ford's 'stunning performance'.

Audiences, too, seemed to be in two minds about the film and domestically it grossed just over $14 million against a budget of $25 million. Once more, it seemed as though Ford's Han Solo and Indiana Jones fame conspired to keep audiences from seeing what was probably his best acting performance to date. However, I wouldn't say that *The Mosquito Coast* is an easy film to watch. It's terrific, gruelling and sometimes mesmerising, but I'm not sure that it's what I would call entertaining. And I'm not sure I could sit through it again.

Ford, too, was too film-savvy to be blind to the reasons for its modest performance. 'It's the only film I have done that hasn't made its money back,' he later said. 'I'm still glad I did it. If there was a fault with the film, it was that it didn't fully enough embrace the language of the book. It may have more properly been a literary rather than a cinematic exercise. But I think it's full of powerful emotions.'

The Golden Globes committee seemed to agree that Ford had done a good job with the role and nominated him once more in the Best Actor category, though it Bob Hoskins who took home the award for his work in *Mona Lisa*.

MODERATELY DISTURBED

After the demanding histrionics of Allie Fox, Harrison Ford returned to more familiar territory with the Hitchcock-style thriller *Frantic* for exiled director Roman Polanski. The film would be shot in Paris and it was this, along with Polanski's impressive body of work, that brought Ford on board.

'In the beginning,' said Polanski, 'we did not know what our leading character would be like and we were very concerned about this, though we realised that he should be "All-American". When Melissa Matheson came to Paris with her husband Harrison Ford, we mentioned *Frantic*. Harrison was tremendously enthusiastic. Confident of his agreement, we carried on writing, imagining Walker to be like Harrison and drawing on certain aspects of his behaviour.'

Polanski's *Chinatown* collaborator Robert Towne had an uncredited hand in developing the screenplay. 'Robert gave the script a final polish and provided us with some good ideas for dialogue,' said Polanski. But in the end, not much of Towne's work appears in the finished film. 'Unfortunately I had to cut some of these passages that at first I thought indispensable. The more progress I made with the editing, the more necessary it seemed to strip down the story in order to maintain the tension.'

Ford displayed his customary attention to detail in researching the role. 'I talked with the French cardiologist who indirectly was the inspiration for Richard Walker. I attended heart valve transplants and I chatted with the surgeons. These men had few characteristics in common and it became clear to me that there is no typical surgeon.' But Ford did glean one thing about these doctors. 'Heart surgeons are among the elite of the doctor world. I found a certain elegance or vanity of gesture that was common to these guys. Lots of hand movements. I already gesture enough with my hands, so that wasn't a challenge.'

Polanski and Ford had the deepest respect for each other's ability as filmmakers. 'Harrison is a great professional,' said the director. 'On the set he is the model of patience and tenacity. At the end of the tenth take of the scene in the shower I was amazed by how chilled and strained he was looking. "What's the matter?" I asked. "The water's cold," he replied. He had been standing for half an hour under an icy stream of water. I wanted to stop everything, but he insisted on carrying on to the end and did five more takes without faltering.'

Ford worked well with his co-star Emmanuelle Seigner as well. 'He helped Emmanuelle a great deal,' commented Polanski. 'They had an immediate affinity.'

Seigner concurs, 'I don't know how I would have done it without Harrison's help and his immense generosity. At the beginning I was very intimidated. I was afraid he would overwhelm me. In fact the opposite happened. He helped me to act. I only had to look at him to act properly, because no one can be bad opposite him.'

'I respect and admire Polanski's talent immensely,' said Ford. 'I had come across his work briefly in 1969 and had seen most of his films – *Repulsion*, *Rosemary's Baby* and *Chinatown*. But above all it was the screenplay of *Frantic* that appealed to me. The character of Richard Walker was not like anything I had acted and I became involved in it from the first time I read it.'

Polanski spent a great deal of time in preparation and rehearsals. 'Sometimes he asked us to play a scene ten times before deciding the position of the cameras, the close-ups. His direction adapts very subtly to the way the actors play their roles, their movements, the intensity they display. When Roman feels we are ready, he moves on very quickly and sometimes he films the rehearsals directly.'

Though no disciple of the Method School of acting, Ford found that the relentless downbeat of Walker's mood was something that was hard to shake once off-set. 'The frustration and anger I had to create had a serious residual effect on me. I took it home with me every night in a way I never had before. I usually get that out of my system, but this one was unremitting, relentless. My wife often found me in the same frustrated mood as my character, a mood I thought I'd been able to drop.'

That mood had been apparent to the critics, as well, when *Frantic* opened in the US on February 26, 1988. Commented London's *Evening Standard*, 'Ford plays it straight rather than frantic, but a shade too muted to please the Indiana Jones fans.'

TV Guide's comment, 'Harrison Ford, outstanding as an American innocent abroad, moves persuasively from complacency to confusion, rage, and paranoid desperation in a performance comparable to James Stewart's best work for Hitchcock,' was probably more generous than the film deserved.

While Ford turns in a solid performance and Seigner has a commanding presence in her fourth (not debut, as some sources claim) film role, the two leads are let down by a script that begins intriguingly but settles down into a standard thriller that is reminiscent of, but below the standard of, 1950s Hitchcock.

The movie didn't set the box office alight, either, taking just $18 million in the US. Ford wasn't fazed and commented, 'I always knew the title was a mistake. The script never had a frantic pace. I told Polanski we should call it "Moderately Disturbed". He was not amused.' The star was already in preparation for a new film where his would be more of a supporting role than a starring one.

FORD GOES ROM-COM

The Kevin Wade script for what would later become *Working Girl*, was brought to Harrison Ford's attention as early as 1986 by his manager, Patricia McQueeney. She had wanted him to do romantic comedies but was thwarted by an inability to find a quality script. Ford was initially resistant, seeing the project as, 'a girl's movie'. McQueeney continued to work on Ford and eventually he agreed to throw his hat in the ring. McQueeney called the producer Larry Mark who told her they were about to sign Alec Baldwin as the male lead. But at the prospect of being able to bring Ford into the cast, the producers had a rethink and cast Baldwin as Melanie Griffiths' faithless blue collar boyfriend Mick instead, giving the meatier role of Jack Trainer to Ford. The changearound didn't seem to upset Baldwin too much. 'The minute Harrison Ford shows up, you drop everything and sign up Harrison,' he told the press later.

There was actually a little more to it than that, as producer Douglas Wick, explained. 'We wanted a guy who looked like he could be a winner on Wall Street, but who also had that look of burnout around the fringes. Harrison has that funny softness and warmth that goes against the grain of his personality.'

There was one bit of business in the script that indicated some reworking to accomodate the casting of Ford – the story of how Jack Trainer acquired the scar on his chin. At first Trainer claims a guy pulled a knife on him, then he relents and tells Tess 'the truth' – 'I was nineteen and I thought it'd be cool to have a pierced ear,' says Trainer. 'My girlfriend stuck the needle through and I heard this pop and fainted and hit my chin on the toilet.'

Ford had almost worked with director Mike Nichols many years earlier when he was called back a second time while auditioning for the part of Ben Braddock in *The Graduate*. Nichols had been a protege of Columbia's Head of New Talent Walter Beakel during Ford's stint as a contract player there in the mid to late Sixties.

Working Girl was an attempt to evoke the sort of films made by Carole Lombard or Jean Arthur during the 1930s, but brought up to date. Though Ford's part was expanded to give him more screen time, the movie is really about Melanie Griffiths' character, Tess McGill, and how she's driven to desperate measures to establish herself as a credible player in the corporate world dominated by appalling characters like Sigourney Weaver's Katharine Parker. Ford's part was still a supporting role as Griffith's love interest, an executive for another company who helps Griffith's character broker an important merger while her boss is laid up after a skiing accident.

After the film opened in the US on December 20, 1988, Roger Ebert of the *Chicago Sun-Times* liked *Working Girl* a lot and said of the actors, 'If [Griffith] is subtle, so is

Ford, an actor whose steadiness goes along with a sort of ruminating passion. When he's in love with a woman, he doesn't grab her; he just seems to ponder her a lot. Weaver and Ford provide the indispensable frame within which the Griffith character can be seen to change.'

The *Washington Post* also liked what they saw and remarked, 'Ford, looking exhausted and mussed, is something of an amiable love prop as Jack. But there are still a few tines in this rake, a bit of Indiana Jones in the three-piece suit.'

Overall it's a pretty good romantic comedy, and it probably suited Ford as an interesting diversion before he put on the battered fedora again – but it's a minor entry in the Ford resume.

The public seemed to like the movie well enough, shelling out an estimated $130 million at the worldwide box office against an original budget of $28 million – which Twentieth Century Fox must have been pleased with.

The Hollywood Foreign Press Association were also pretty impressed with the film because although Ford wasn't recognised, it still carried away the Golden Globe for Best Picture for 1988. It also took Awards for Melanie Griffith for Best Actress in a Musical or Comedy and for Sigourney Weaver as Best Supporting Actress. And Carly Simon's song "Let the River Run", heard during the opening shots of commuters disembarking from New York's Staten Island ferry, took not only a Golden Globe, but also an Academy Award and a Grammy. The movie garnered a clutch of Oscar nominations as well, earning nods for Melanie Griffith (Best Actress), Sigourney Weaver and Joan Cusick (Best Supporting Actress), Mike Nichols (Best Director) and Best Picture. All the nominees lost out to other performers, but it was still a very impressive achievement, and did Ford no harm at all to be associated with such an artistically successful film.

INDIANA JONES RIDES AGAIN

Ford was tight-lipped about how the third *Indiana Jones* film was shaping up, except to say that shooting was due to start in January 1988. 'There's little else I can tell you about it.' However, he was hinting that it wouldn't carry the same tone of darkness as *Indiana Jones and the Temple of Doom*. More somber and violent than its megabucks predecessor, *Temple of Doom* had been criticised for its violence and horror. Ford has never been one to offer criticism of his own films or his co-workers, but in the runup to *Last Crusade*, there was a sense that he wasn't 100% happy with the content of *Doom*. 'This sort of falls into that private area of how you deal with the people that you work with, and I don't want to go over any of that,' he said. 'But if I had agreed totally with everything that they had done, we could talk about it, but I don't, and so I can't. Still,' he added, 'you hate to see Spielberg miss an opportunity to give you pleasure.'

Asked about how he felt about taking on another *Indiana Jones* film, Ford replied cryptically, 'I'm just an ordinary 42-year-old creaky bag of bones and I have to work out to get in shape for a film.'

CHAPTER 10

HARRISON FORD: CRACKING THE WHIP

From Actor to Action Hero

'I think Steven and I get along about as well as a director and an actor can.' Harrison Ford

It had been four years since the last Indiana Jones movie, *Indiana Jones and the Temple of Doom*, a movie that had not enjoyed the same critical reception as its illustrious predecessor. There was a sense at Lucasfilm that if they were going to make another *Raiders* picture then they shouldn't make the same mistakes they had with *Temple of Doom*.

George Lucas's initial idea was to have Indy go on a quest for the Holy Grail. But this was vetoed by Steven Spielberg. 'I didn't like the idea of the Holy Grail at first, because I'd always associated it with *Monty Python* and couldn't really relate it to any present day myth,' said Spielberg. 'The Grail legend was interesting to me symbolically because it represented the search for oneself, but making a movie about it seemed too esoteric for this genre.'

In trying to write a story about the Grail, Lucas himself floundered. 'The Ark of the Covenant was supposedly a real artifact, whereas the Grail – or at least the story surrounding it – is more of a myth,' said Lucas. 'As a result my initial ideas were very metaphysical and the Grail was difficult to define.'

So the filmmakers jettisoned the Grail and engaged Chris Columbus to write a script about the Monkey King of Chinese legend set in Africa. 'Chris writes brilliant comedy,' Spielberg revealed to *Cinefex* magazine, 'and his script was very humorous. It was upbeat and was full of the same nostalgia tapped into in *Raiders*. So in that sense, Chris was right on the money. But I don't think any of us wanted to go to Africa for four months.'

After the Columbus script was shelved, Lucas came up with the notion that drinking from the Grail could confer immortality. But Spielberg was looking for more. 'I didn't want Indy on a headlong pursuit without a subplot that was almost stronger than the actual quest itself. So I came up with the father-son story because the Grail is symbolic of finding the truth in one's life, the truth we are always looking for, consciously or unconsciously. For me that was represented by Indy and Henry meeting. In this context the Grail made sense to me. They actually go after the Holy Grail, but their quest is symbolic of their search for each other. Once I could look upon the Grail twofold – as a physical antiquity from religious history and as a symbolic metaphor for self-illumination – then it became interesting to me.'

With the basic story in place, first Menno Meyjes (who'd worked with Spielberg on *The Color Purple* and *Empire of the Sun*) and later Jeffrey Boam (who'd scripted the Spielberg produced *Innerspace*) were hired to produce a script.

Spielberg, Lucas and Ford spent a great deal of time with writer Boam, hammering out five drafts of a storyline which would be more in keeping with the first movie in the series and introduced Indiana's father, Dr Henry Jones, as well as offering audiences a glimpse of Indy as a teenager.

LAST CRUSADE ... BUT ONE?

Filming on *Indiana Jones and the Last Crusade* began in a dry river bed in Spain in May 1988 with Indy chasing a Nazi tank on horseback and making the leap from the horse to the tank in mid-gallop. Though Ford likes to do as much of the 'physical acting' as possible, rendering stunt double Vic Armstrong's job almost unnecessary, Armstrong was asked to double for Ford for this sequence.

'Harrison's participation in the stunts is what makes them so exciting and enjoyable to moviegoers,' said Armstrong. 'It enables characterisation in the context of the stunt. In some action films, stunts and acting never come together.'

Spielberg agreed. 'Some of the best character nuances of Indy's personality come during an action sequence,' he said. 'An expression after a punch, a shrug after a gag. It's part of the same panache.'

In another scene, Indy is supposed to leap from a ledge, knock a baddie off his horse, jump on the horse and gallop away. Ford thought he could do the action himself, though Armstrong was concerned. 'The only way I could dissuade him was to drag him to one side and say that if he did stunts he would do me out of money. Harrison was horrified and said, "Sorry, Vic, I just didn't realise. Of course, I'll shut up".'

But the day-to-day risks in appearing in action films has never bothered Ford. 'I know in making these movies I'm going to get dirty, bruised and bumped around a lot.' he says, 'It's what distinguishes an Indiana Jones film from another adventure film. You sit there in the theatre and you know I'm doing it.'

Indiana Jones and the Last Crusade was a difficult and demanding for more than just its stunts. Not only did the crew travel to more locations than the previous two *Raiders* movies combined, but the physical conditions they had to endure were trying. Especially hard was the sequence where the adult Indy battles the original thief of the Cross of Coronado on a freighter supposedly just off the coast of Portugal. In reality the scene was filmed in the water tank at Elstree Studios just outside London. A section of deck was built on gimbals to create the appropriate rocking motion and there were wind machines and tanks dumping hundreds of gallons of water onto the actors. 'Scenes like this are actually more difficult to do than dangerous stunts,' commented George Lucas, 'because with stunts you take so many precautions to make sure no one gets killed. But storm scenes like those on the boat you can't really control. Everyone was getting battered around.'

Spielberg elaborated, 'It was the coldest summer in London's history, so the water was ice-cold. When we came to work in the morning, all of us got into our raincoats – except Harrison who couldn't wear anything but his fighting clothes. Nobody wanted to be under water for three days, and after *Jaws*, I hate water, anyway.'

A far bigger problem than the discomforts of filming in water tanks was finding an actor impressive enough to play the father of Indiana Jones. The filmmakers' first thought had been to make Dr Henry Jones an eccentric, gnome-like English gentleman, more librarian than adventurer. But Steven Spielberg had other ideas. He'd originally signed on for the *Indiana Jones* films because George Lucas had promised him something 'better than Bond'. So Spielberg figured that if Indy was inspired by James Bond, why not get the original and best screen Bond in to play Indy's father? Perhaps surprisingly, Connery was enthusiastic about the idea, but wanted to have some input into Dr Jones Sr's character and even persuaded British playwright Tom Stoppard to polish and expand his character's dialogue. 'I wanted to base my character on a Sir Richard Burton idea,' said Connery, 'someone who would have been quite indifferent to his son growing up and would have gone off and not been heard of for six months and think nothing of it, not feel guilty at all. That's quite un-American, of course, and I think that shocked Lucas and Spielberg in a way.'

'It was the same with the sexual mores,' continued Connery. 'I wanted my character to have had a relationship with the girl before Indiana even got there and that was a no-no immediately. I asked them why. It's been written before, you know. Some of the old Greeks were ahead of you in that.' In the end, Connery's idea made it into the finished film. When Boam was later asked if he really believed that the older Dr Jones would have already slept with his son's love interest, he replied, 'No way ... but Sean Connery would!'

When the film opened, it was apparent that everyone was excited at the prospect of seeing Harrison Ford and Sean Connery play two generations of the Jones family. If director Spielberg had been worried about a clash of egos between the two actors, he needn't have been. The pair bonded immediately and had nothing but praise for each other.

At first Ford had been sceptical about the casting. Connery was just 58 when he was chosen. 'My first reaction was, "He's not old enough." Then I realised *I'm* too old.' At forty-six Ford was playing a thirty-five year old character. In the event, Ford was worrying unnecessarily. Connery was completely believable as Indy's dad and the on-screen banter between the two would be one of the film's greatest assets. Certainly, Connery seemed to enjoy working with Ford.

'The nice thing about *Indiana Jones* is the humour,' said Connery, 'and the fact that it's back to an older age. I'm always looking for the humour in a situation and Harrison Ford has a nice sly sense of humour.'

When asked by the LucasFilm Fan Club how he'd enjoyed working with Connery, Ford was effusive in his praise. It was, he said, 'a great pleasure. Sean is such a terribly experienced actor and that makes it interesting to work with him. He's an awfully nice guy, too! I've enjoyed knowing him as well as working with him.' Ford later elaborate on their 'father-son' relationship, 'I think it gave me the opportunity to how much I'm like my own father. All those things that drive me crazy about my own father have started showing up in my personality.'

'I didn't know quite how it would work,' confessed Spielberg, 'but there was the most wonderful chemistry between the two of them. It's a little like the Newman/Redford chemistry in *Butch Cassidy* and *The Sting*. It's a real sparkle of screen magic.'

The two were so relaxed working together that they took to playing practical jokes on each other to try to get the other to break up on camera. 'The biggest thrill,' said Spielberg, 'was putting Harrison and Sean in a two-shot, calling "Action!" and trying not to ruin the take by laughing.'

While shooting their scenes on the Zeppelin, Connery in his tweeds and Ford in his leather jacket were both sweltering. Connery took care of that by taking off his trousers, since he would be sitting at a table and only filmed from the waist up. Ford blinked, then took his pants off too and sat down to continue the scene.

INTRODUCING ... JONES JUNIOR

The audience would also be given the chance to see Indiana as a teenager, and who better for the role than Harrison Ford's screen son from *Mosquito Coast*, River Phoenix? So successful was Phoenix's portrayal of the hero's teenage self that the idea evolved into a tv series, *The Young Indiana Jones Chronicles*, though Sean Patrick Flanery would play the title role in the show.

Some vital back-story involving the young Indy would be revealed in the movie's opening sequence which featured his run-in with the mysterious figure Indy would later model himself on. This character, named 'Fedora' in the movie's credits, was identified as Abner Ravenwood in the script, the unseen late father of Marion Ravenwood from *Raiders of the Lost Ark*. From a story point of view this makes a great deal of sense, as it's obvious that two people ostensibly in the same line of work would come to know each other eventually. My guess is that the filmmakers played down this connection for fear of confusing the three or four people who hadn't seen *Raiders*. Lucas and Spielberg also threw in another explanation of Ford's famous chin-scar, by having Young Indy try to crack a whip, only to nick himself in the chin, and had the teenager trapped in a wagon full of snakes to account for his later irrational fear of the reptiles.

For this sequence, the last section of the movie to be shot, Harrison Ford was on-set alongside Spielberg, coaching River Phoenix through his performance to ensure he played the part of young Indy to perfection. 'I wanted to make sure he got the moves right,' said Ford.

'I had Harrison there every day,' Spielberg elaborated. 'He pretty much directed River, helping him with his line readings and gestures, and talking with him about how Indy would move, which made my job a lot easier.'

Leading lady Alison Doody, who plays Dr Jones Sr's traitorous assistant Dr Elsa Schneider, also gave Ford much credit for helping her through the film. 'Working with Harrison was such a pleasure. He's a great man to work with. He helped me a great deal in my scenes. He would talk scenes through. And if I had a problem at all, he was always there and willing to try and sort it out.' In the scene in which Elsa had to kiss Indy, Doody was a little uncomfortable with the idea, but Ford eased her embarrassment by puckering up, making kissy-sounds and calling, 'Alison, I'm ready!' However, in an interview in the *Daily Mail*, Doody claimed that kissing Ford was no big deal. 'It was like kissing the back of my hand,' she claimed. 'And it was the same for Harrison, too.'

Ford was also happy to be reunited with Spielberg. 'It's always been fun to work with Steven,' remarked Ford. 'I enjoy his inventiveness and sense of humor. I think we get along about as well as a director and an actor can. Our ideas are frequently very consistent and we seem to spark each other with ideas. He's so sure of his skills technically that it makes things go rather quickly, which is a pleasure in this business.'

And predictably, Spielberg had nothing but praise for his star. 'He's more like Humphrey Bogart every day, but better looking,' Spielberg said. 'I think when Harrison moves into his late fifties, the way Sean Connery has, he's going to really fall into those Clark Gable/ Humphrey Bogart roles. I think the older he gets, the better he's going to get and he's never going to lose his popularity.'

Less fun was the scene in the sewers under Venice where Indy and Elsa share the space with thousands of rats driven mad by a raging fire. The scene used a large number of mechanical rats and two thousand real ones, specially bred for the task. The idea was that captivity-bred rats should theoretically be free of the kinds of infections found in their wild cousins. But this didn't stop a number of the more squeamish crew members disappearing off the set. 'Same thing with the snakes,' complained Spielberg, 'We lost half the crew on the first movie and we lost three-quarters of the crew with the bugs.'

The choice of rats for this film's 'yuck' factor didn't seem to bother Ford much. Asked which were the most repugnant, *Raiders'* snakes, *Temple*'s bugs or *Crusade*'s rats, Ford responded, 'They're all the same to me. The only hard thing is keeping them on the set. You tend to lose a lot of snakes, roaches and rats.' But he admitted, 'it was the rat droppings and the water that made it the most uncomfortable.'

Incidentally, it was the inclusion of the rodent scene that caused actress Amanda Redmond to turn down the role of Elsa, as she couldn't bear to be in the scene with live rats.

Indiana Jones and the Last Crusade was a box-office and critical smash. On the opening weekend of May 24, 1989, the picture took $29.4 million at 2,327 US screens, eventually racking up $197 million in ticket sales in the US and more than that again in worldwide take, ranking it 42nd in the list of all-time world-wide box-office champs.

The London *Evening Standard* praised the film and said, 'Ford and Connery are the film's heartbeat. They keep the blood pumping round veins of inventiveness that might have varicosed in less loving hands than Steven Spielberg's. They make it a joy to keep up with the Joneses.'

'The Harrison Ford-Sean Connery father-and-son team gives *Last Crusade* unexpected emotional depth,' said *Variety*, 'reminding us that real film magic is not in special effects … This is a film of which Lucas and Spielberg and their collaborators long will be proud.'

'Mr Ford's role is more diffuse than it was in *Raiders* or in the overactive, gruesome sequel, *Indiana Jones and the Temple of Doom*,' offered *The New York Times*. 'He swerves among action, sentiment and cartoonish lines like, "Nazis! I hate those guys!" In Venice, he has a brief, James Bondish fling with his father's former assistant, just after he tells her: "Leave me alone! I don't like fast women!" But Mr Ford accommodates each shift, for this role fits him as perfectly as the fedora that gives him his 1930s heroic look.'

If, as some have suggested, Spielberg's chief reason for taking on a third Indiana Jones film was to banish the bad taste left by the reception of *Temple of Doom*, then he succeeded in his aim. For me, *Last Crusade* is a serviceable enough adventure elevated mightily by the sparkling on-screen chemistry between Ford and Connery. The film's biggest liability was the character of Elsa Schneider, who fell somewhere between the tomboyish-ness of Marion Ravenwood and the girliness of Willie Scott – but was as memorable as neither.

Sean Connery was nominated for a Best Supporting Actor gong at the Golden Globes, and though Globe nominations are often repeated at the Oscars, *Last Crusade* was nominated for just three Academy Awards, Best Soundtrack, Best Sound and Best Special Effects, winning only in the latter category.

NEVER SAY NEVER AGAIN

The shot of the four old friends riding off into the sunset at the end of *Indiana Jones and the Last Crusade* was meant, I believe, to reinforce the subtext of the film's title. In 1989, the main authors of Indy were all saying that there were done with the character. Emphatically. With finality.

'I don't foresee there being another one,' George Lucas said. 'Anything is possible, but I've run out of ideas. I've had a great time making the *Indiana Jones* films, but now it's time to move on. I would just as soon do other things.'

During the publicity tours for *Indiana Jones and the Last Crusade*, Ford was giving the same message to the press. When asked by a hapless journo if Indy was hanging up his bullwhip, his reply seemed unequivocal. 'Read my lips. Bye-bye Indiana! Look, nobody's got any intention of doing another. We set out to do three films if we could all agree on the sum and substance of them. Now George says that he doesn't want to make another one, Steven says that he's completely off the case and I'm happy enough to let it go also.'

Only Spielberg seemed sorry to see the back of Indiana Jones. 'I'm really going to miss working with Harrison as Indy,' said Spielberg. 'I look forward to working with him in other sorts of roles but I'll really miss sitting with him in that hat and that jacket with all the sweat and the dirty khaki shirt and the boots and the bullwhip and the pouch and the sidearm and the five-day stubble – and most of all, I'll miss his sense of humour. Working with Harrison as Indy was kind of like working with Fred C. Dobbs from *Treasure of the Sierra Madre* for eight years – and I'm going to miss that very much.'

CHAPTER 11

HARRISON FORD: CROSS-GENRE STAR

From Criminal to Victim to Spy

'I guess I finally began to understand that people felt they owned me in a way. I understand acting is a service occupation. I've never misunderstood that. But my occupation is assistant storyteller. It is not icon.' Harrison Ford

Following his first efforts to break away from his action hero persona with movies like *Witness* and *Mosquito Coast*, it seemed as though Harrison Ford returned to the safe waters of Indiana Jones to regroup and gather his thoughts. Because once *Last Crusade* was over, Ford once more made a series of films that appeared to demonstrate to audiences that the man was more than just a running, jumping stunt star. And what a varied series of movies these were, culminating in the start of a new Harrison Ford franchise as he brought to life the definitive Jack Ryan, lead character of Tom Clancy's best-selling military intelligence novels.

But first, Ford was going to take up a position on the other side of the law and play Rusty Sabich, a morally ambiguous public prosecutor who finds himself on trial for the murder of his mistress, in *Presumed Innocent*.

'I was interested in the character and his dilemma,' Ford told *US* magazine in 1990, 'but the difficulty was that the novel had been written in a first-person narrative form. And that worked well in the book, but there was no way that could be made to work in a film.'

As well, we had the difficult job of disguising "whodunit" in a dramatic way. I think that is a real intellectual challenge. Happily, we had a director who's up to that sort of thing – incredibly tenacious about going after the values that he wanted.'

It also helped that Ford was able to identify with the character of Rusty Sabich. 'Well, we come from the same geographical background. I was raised in the Midwest. I found it very easy to connect with him. He's a guy who has a very strong moral attitude, who nonetheless finds himself drawn into a compulsive love affair. I can especially understand is the depth of the conflict that this caused him.'

The novel on which *Presumed Innocent* is based appears to be set in Chicago, Ford's hometown, though author Scott Turow is careful not to identify the story's setting. The film's producers settled on Detroit for their location shooting, reasoning that the city wouldn't be too well-known to general audiences. Ford, with his usual meticulousness, spent two weeks hanging around with the folks at the Prosecutor's Office in Detroit. 'They gave us incredible cooperation,' said Ford. 'Everyone we worked with was so intelligent and so very willing to help.'

Once the Detroit locations wrapped, the production moved to the Astoria Studios in New York for all the interior office and court room settings, with the town of Allendale, just outside New York, doubling for the Sabich family neighbourhood.

When *Presumed Innocent* opened on July 27, 1990, it was up against blockbusters like *Home Alone*, *Ghost* and *Pretty Woman*. Reviews were mixed. *The New Yorker* called it a 'dreary ponderous spectacle that turns an exciting game into a two-hour, slow-motion replay,' though they did single out Raul Julia's performance as a career best and admitted that Ford's role was probably unplayable, observing that, Ford had to 'drain himself of personality and maintain a tense, repressed, impenetrable expression throughout the picture.'

The London *Evening Standard's* Alexander Walker wasn't much kinder, writing, '*Presumed Innocent* is coloured by such misanthropy. It is all the better for that, though film goers used to the bright lights and pacey chat of *LA Law* may feel the moral weather is oppressively overcast – particularly by Ford who registers worry like a speak your weight machine.'

The *Daily Mail* was more generous, calling the movie 'The thinking man's thriller' and observing that the film is 'high-calorie stuff, richer than your average format puzzle or shoot-first saga. There are abundant little touches of care and thought.'

To be fair to Ford, the negative comments are unnecessarily harsh. The essence of *Presumed Innocent* is to keep the audience guessing as to whether Sabich is guilty or not. This left Ford having to play the character – who knows the truth – in such a way as to keep from giving anything away to the audience. It's a difficult path for any actor to tred, so the fact that Ford kept us guessing right till the end is a tribute to how well he handled such a challenging task. And despite Ford's generosity to his director, Alan Pakula could have given his star an easier ride with the script and the direction. It is a flawed movie, but the blame goes to Pakula for that, not to Ford.

Ford had his own thoughts about the reception of *Presumed Innocent*. 'Nearly every article and review had some reference to my haircut,' said Ford in a 1992 interview in *Entertainment Weekly*. 'That was the one time I was absolutely befuddled. I guess I finally began to understand that people felt they owned me in a way. I understand this is a service occupation. I've never misunderstood that. But my occupation is assistant storyteller.

It is not icon. And they were saying this is not what we want our icon to look like. And I was saying, "Well, what about the f---ing story? Do you understand that this is part of storytelling? Not about a f---ing haircut?"'

For all that, *Presumed Innocent* still managed to take $86,303,188 at the US box-office, raking in an a respectable $221,300,000 worldwide, which makes you wonder if the newspaper critics are on quite the same page as the audiences.

Ford's next role would garner as much unmerited sniffiness from the film critics as this one, considering the pedigree of the filmmakers involved ...

PLAYING THE VICTIM

The project *Regarding Henry* began when 23 year old JJ Abrams (currently enjoying enormous success with tv's *Fringe*) managed to get producer Steve Rudin to read his screenplay. Rudin showed the script to Harrison Ford who agreed to play the lead role. 'I had a strong emotional response to the script,' said Ford. 'Emotion is what really hooks me, what keeps me involved in a story. Henry was different from any other character I'd played before. Most people have a level of protection from their own emotions and an awareness of the effect their emotions might have on other people. Henry doesn't have that sophistication after his accident. He's unable to censor himself.'

Ford took the script (and his enthusiasm) to director Mike Nichols, whom he'd worked with on *Working Girl*. 'Jeffrey Abrams' screenplay was about something I'd never seen dealt with,' said Nichols, 'something that happens in life that we rarely hear anyone talk about; for all the searching for happiness we do, we tend not to notice that it's catastrophe that re-orders our lives in wonderful ways. There's something about cutting loose everything and starting again after a catastrophe that somehow tells you the most about what is real life, especially family life. *Regarding Henry* is a movie about paring everything down to what is real life – love and family. Jeffrey told this story in a way that's surprisingly funny and very moving.'

Producer Rudin had good things to say about Abrams' writing as well. 'It was startling to discover that so young a writer could achieve a story of such emotional complexity, intimacy and detail.'

But living up to these expectations wasn't easy for Abrams. 'The hardest thing about writing this script was that basically the villain was Henry, at least during the first half of the film. In plotting it, I had to figure out how to make it work dramatically for the villain to actually become the hero. But I love the thought that you can do something wrong and then years later you can go back and make it right, like Henry does. That's something I do believe: there's hope for even the smallest regrets. A lot of people feel that if something is done, it's done, but I think you can always go back and correct yourself, change things for the better.'

As with all his roles, Ford spent a few weeks researching the behaviour of patients like Henry. 'I didn't want Henry to be childlike,' said Ford. 'I wanted him to be naïve, slower than he was before. I wanted him to be slightly disadvantaged in terms of being able to keep up with the speed and complexity of events. Although Henry is disadvantaged by his accident, what he's been able to come away with balances out what he's suffered. His relationship with his family is really to me what is most meaningful about this whole experience. He starts out as a guy whose family life is grim at best, and who suddenly becomes an appropriate, interested father and husband who needs his family, who's learned to love again. And that's the core of it, I think.'

Location shooting began in and around New York in September 1990 and lasted about six weeks. Then the production moved to Paramount Studios in Los Angeles to film the interiors. The production team assembled a strong supporting cast, lead by Annette Benning as Henry's devoted wife and Mikki Allen as their 12 year-old daughter. Bill Nunn steals all his scenes as the tough-talking physiotherapist Bradley who gets Henry to walk and talk again after his horrific injuries and there's efficient, restrained performances from Bruce Altman and Rebecca Miller as Henry's legal partners. Look quickly for John Leguizamo as the gunman that shoots Henry and an incredibly young-looking Jeffrey Abrams as the delivery boy who drops off vegetables at the Turner apartment.

Ford's research for his role as Henry was probably the most extensive he'd ever conducted. He read just about every book on brain trauma he could get his hands on and made many visits to a rehabilitation clinic, sitting in on therapy sessions and closely questioning neurosurgeons. 'It got very emotional at times,' recalled Ford, 'watching patients with appalling disabilities who, after a period of depression, realise that there is light at the end of the tunnel.'

Ford also met a lawyer, a graduate of Princeton, who had the same type of injuries as Henry. 'This man gave us access to his private life,' said Ford, 'and he gave me the most faith in the correctness of the choices we made in creating this character. He told us we were right on the mark and that's all I needed to know.' To help him keep track of where Henry was in the recuperative cycle during the out-of-sequence filming of the story, Ford would refer to a set of index cards he'd made up with notes on how capable Henry should be at various points in the recovery cycle. Which is typical of Ford's thoroughness ...

Regarding Henry opened in the US on July 10, 1991 to less than enthusiastic reviews. '*Henry* is just another variation on the body-swap trend that surfaced a few years ago – *Big, Vice Versa*,' commented *New Statesman*, 'and which reflects the American tendency to go all gooey over the idea of childhood as a state of perfect innocence that can never be revisited. It never occurs to anyone that the problem with most adults is that they never stopped being children.' Admittedly, that's a great line and an extremely valid point, but it has no place in a review of *Regarding Henry*, because Henry doesn't revert to a childlike state. He doesn't play with toys or run around with his arms outstretched making airplane noises. His mind is wiped clean and he reverts to an innocent state. Big difference.

About Ford's performance, *Statesman* went on to add, 'Ford is a terrific screen presence in the Gary Cooper mould: great at straight reaction and all the varying degrees of understatement that make performing in genre pictures, such as thrillers and action-adventures, look a lot easier than it probably is. But despite his diligent role research, he is not a method performer *a la* Hoffman or De Niro, and *Regarding Henry* requires just that sort of *tour de force*.' Which is nonsense, really. An actor friend of mine, Andy Lucas, once told me that Hoffman had the easy task in *Rain Man*. Far more difficult was Tom Cruise's role, having to be effective in the shadow of Hoffman's '*tour de force*'. 'Flashy acting is easy,' Andy told me. 'Underacting is really, really difficult.'

Rolling Stone liked the movie better, offering, 'Though the role invites overkill, Ford, an effectively recessive actor (*Witness, Presumed Innocent*), handles Henry's drooling, stuttering and bewilderment with admirable restraint. But the script is a stacked deck. A man who can no longer recognize his family must get to know them again. In the process of being reawakened to the joys of sex, marriage, fatherhood and love, Henry must reject false values and, egads, find himself.'

The almost universal negative reception of *Regarding Henry* is puzzling. The script is a remarkable achievement, regardless of Jeffrey Abrams' age when he wrote it. Mike Nichols directs with his usual sincerity and attention to detail. The supporting players all deliver sterling performances and Ford himself is a model of restraint where other, lesser actors would have resorted to gurning and drooling to convey Henry's condition to audiences. And despite a couple of cheesy scenes and plot twists – nice Henry buying the puppy for his daughter and the revelation that both Henry and Sarah had both had affairs before Henry's shooting – the film treads a careful line of the right side of soap opera and even has a couple of genuinely moving scenes. Not sure what film the critics were watching in 1991, but it wasn't the movie I saw.

The box-office reception was weaker than *Presumed Innocent*, pulling in a modest $43 million in the US. But Harrison Ford had a plan to stem this decline. He would join a new movie franchise and play Jack Ryan, the hero of a series of military intelligence novels by best-seller Tom Clancy.

A DIFFERENT KIND OF ACTION

The first movie made from a Tom Clancy Jack Ryan novel was *The Hunt for Red October*, which had cast Alec Baldwin in the Ryan role. Interestingly, Paramount had approached Ford then with the idea of him playing Jack Ryan, but he turned them down. He would, he said at the time, consider playing the part of Russian sub commander Ramius, as he felt that was the more interesting role, but in the event backed away from that too. 'I said, "Submarine movies, uh-uh,"' joked Ford later, laughing. 'That's how smart I was.' Of course the film was made with Sean Connery playing Ryan's nemesis, Marko Ramius. So though Ford had beaten Baldwin to the role of Jack Trainer in *Working Girl*, Baldwin was the first to play Jack Ryan on screen. I've often wondered if *Red October* might have been an even more interesting film if it had reunited the Jones boys just a year after the actors' triumphant teaming in *Last Crusade*.

The fact is that neither *Presumed Innocent* nor *Regarding Henry* had been big critical successes, though the earlier film had performed respectably at the box-office. Harrison Ford is one of the most intelligent actors around and with the Jack Ryan movies, he saw a chance to move back in the direction of Indiana Jones without signing up for an all-out fantasy/action franchise.

In an interview with one of the British broadsheets, Ford elaborated on why he chose to sign up for three Jack Ryan films.

'You find yourself always being drawn back to your origins. Sure, you can expand your repertoire in any direction. You can do comedy. You can do serious drama. You can do everything that isn't comic book. But in the end people always have a pre-formulated picture of your first success story. And for me, that was Indiana Jones.

'I don't want to do that sort of thing again. But what I would like to pursue are stories involving more complex heroics. I liked the character of Rick Deckard in *Blade Runner*, and I liked John Book in *Witness*. They were very human-type heroes, and the fascination of those characters, as opposed to Indiana Jones, is that they really can be hurt.

'I haven't done a thriller in a while and though I don't believe that this is a conventional thriller by any means, I think it's very traditional in its approach. I like things which are simply constructed, because it prevents any kind of false grandeur being built around it.

'Also I think there's much depth to the character of Jack Ryan, and I think that he will be continually interesting in that the dilemmas he finds himself in will be rich stuff for myself or any other actor. The characters that wear out are the ones like Han Solo, who don't have much to say. They have an attitude, but not much more than that.'

One of the toughest scenes to shoot was the final boat chase across Chesepeake Bay. Preview audiences had reacted badly to the originally-filmed ending with Ryan and Miller fighting hand-to-hand on some rocks, with Miller eventually falling into the sea and drowning. So a new ending, with a speedboat chase, was hastily written. Clancy reacted angrily to the changes and went on record with the press about his dissatisfaction with the revisions to his original story. Only the intervention of studio head Brandon Tartikoff seemed to mollify Clancy and the writer once again came on-side and endorsed the movie.

With only five days of shooting time allocated to the scene, director Philip Noyce decided to film the sequence in Paramount's specially-built sunken car park, where Charlton Heston had parted the Red Sea and Spock had conversed with whales. With the cars removed, the space was filled with water. An elaborate sprinkler system was constructed to provide rainfall and huge sheets of silk were hung to diffuse the light. Two 20-foot speedboats, four wind machines and a brace of wave machines were added to the mix and everything as ready to go.

'This is old-time moviemaking,' said producer Mace Neufeld of the set-up. 'Until you get it going, you don't know how it's going to work.'

Director Noyce was a little daunted himself. 'I thought this was my Waterloo,' he confessed. 'The wind machines broke. The special-effects guys in the water got hypothermia. And Harrison bumped his head. All I could see were a couple of boats driving around in a swimming pool.'

For take after take, Harrison Ford, drenched to the skin, wrestled with the wheel of a speedboat mounted on hydraulic gimbals, while FX technicians spayed him with fire hoses. How does an actor cope under this kind of stress? Apparently, with some difficulty. Said Ford, 'If I can't open my eyes because the wind machines are too high and the raindrops too big, then I have to say, "Guys, I can't open my eyes." If I can't open my eyes, I can't fucking act. I can't tell the story.'

But after several difficult nights, Noyce did get the story told. 'It was a desperate experiment, but we finally got some footage we were happy with. When it looked like the boats weren't going fast enough, we discovered we could perform some sleight of hand by just moving the water past them.'

Patriot Games opened in the US on June 5, 1992, and on September 25 the same year in the UK, eventually pulling in $178 million in tickets sales worldwide. The press seemed to like the film, too. *The Sunday Times* said, 'Ford is something rare among modern stars: he is prepared to subjugate his personality to the persona of the part. Thus he doesn't come on board with the baggage of a Schwarzenegger or a Stallone, instead he pulls on the costume offered and builds the part from the page.'

Roger Ebert of the *Chicago Sun-Times* praised Ford's contribution but had reservations about the ending. 'Harrison Ford once again demonstrates what a solid, convincing actor he is, and there's good supporting work from Anne Archer, Thora Birch as the Ryans' precocious daughter, and the irreplaceable James Fox as a British cabinet minister. But at the end, when a character is leaping into a burning speedboat in choppy seas, I wondered if this was exactly what Tom Clancy had in mind.'

The Washington Post commented, 'Ford doesn't do anything new here; he's pretty much Indiana Jones in a suit. But his star performance is almost enough to make the picture worth watching. The movie's final scenes deliver on the promised confrontation between Ryan and Miller, and Noyce does a serviceable job with the climactic action sequences.'

I was already a big fan of the Jack Ryan books, so for me it was the best possible outcome to have Ford play the part in the film franchise. And if Ford makes a suitably intense, though thoughtful, Jack Ryan my only minor niggle would be that the filmmakers fell into the trap of beefing up the action to suit their perception of what Harrison Ford action movie star should be doing. I don't recall the book's Jack Ryan as being quite so gung-ho.

RUN, HARRISON, RUN

Ford's next project was to be a movie version of the hugely popular 1960s tv show, *The Fugitive*. The show had starred David Janssen as Richard Kimble, a man wrongly accused of murdering his wife with British actor Barry Morse as his nemesis, the relentless Lt Gerard, who chased his quarry through four seasons of must-see tv. The unprecedented final two-parter that resolved the storyline and tied up all the loose ends was watched by tv's biggest global audience for a tv drama at the time.

Harrison Ford was pretty much the first name to be signed on for *The Fugitive*. 'Harrison is the most involved actor I've ever had the privilege of working with,' said producer Arnold Kopelson. 'From his entry into the project, he's been an integral part of the production process. He has been part of many creative decisions, such as re-writing, casting, art direction, set design and costumes. He's a consummate professional and a pleasure to work with.'

The next name to join the project was Andrew Davis, who had directed Steven Seagal's best film, *Under Siege*. Davis received the Ford seal of approval: 'It seemed we'd found a director who could bring the kind of energy and excitement the project deserved. For his part, David had no intention of slavishly following the tv show. 'The movie is a modern version of a classic thriller. The challenge for me was to make it seem fresh and alive in ways that people wouldn't expect and still satisfy all of the strengths of the tv series. The main difference is that this film has a much more in-depth view of Richard Kimble and what caused him to be a man on the run.'

Ford too had some thoughts on what made Kimble run. 'When we first meet Kimble, he is a prominent vascular surgeon who has an ego and a degree of vanity. He appreciates beauty and fine things. He is happy in his work and with his life and he's doing well by doing good. Kimble is very happily married. He and Helen have a vital relationship based on trust and devotion. They depend on each other rather than on the people around them which makes her death all the more painful and makes him more driven to find the real killer.'

The key role of Kimble's hunter, Deputy US Marshall Sam Gerard (Lieutenant Gerard in the tv series) went to Tommy Lee Jones. Not looking for any underlying vendetta between the characters, Jones pointed out that Gerard 'is meant to be chasing just another fugitive.

He has no other motive than to do his job and do it well.'

Ford agreed with that, adding, 'Kimble doesn't care whether Gerard believes his innocence or not. Kimble's sole intent is to find the real bad guy, the person behind the murder.'

The filming took up 15 weeks in and around Chicago. 'It's nice coming back', said Ford at the time. 'I grew up in Chicago, went to college in Wisconsin, and came back to take summer jobs for three years. I felt this was the best possible option as a location. It's a city of neighbourhoods. We could get the grittiness, we could get the flash of the architecture, the charm of the lake. It has it all.' And as always, Ford spent his customary couple of weeks learning the little details that would make his vascular surgeon Kimble more believable by hanging around with the surgeons at the University of Chicago hospitals, making rounds and watching surgical procedures. 'I wanted to develop a medical detective story,' he said. 'What I had to do was to gather enough elements so there was a believable character development within Kimble's course of discovery towards the truth.'

To that end consultants from the Rehabilitation Institute of Chicago worked with the filmmakers to create a realistic model for the mysterious 'One-Armed Man' that Kimble believes killed his wife.

As might be expected of a Harrison Ford film, there is some degree of running and jumping. The most spectacular action set piece is the train wreck that sets Richard Kimble on his road to freedom. The filmmakers used a private railway, the Smokey Mountain Railway in North Carolina, for the staging of the crash. 'We decided early on that we would do this full scale and not in miniature,' said co-producer Peter Macgregor-Scott. 'Both (director) Andy Davis and I feel if you can do things full-size, you're much better off, because you can see the results right away.'

Ford's old friend, stunt coordinator Terry Leonard, was also on board the *Fugitive* train as Second Unit Director. 'The problem with derailing a 250,000 pound train is the risk to crew and equipment. So in anticipation of trying to outsmart what the train was going to do, I contacted a number of insurance investigators and told them what we wanted to accomplish. Because they investigate accidental derailments all the time, they were able to tell us what we could reasonably expect to happen once the train hit the bus. We were then able to position the cameras accordingly.'

So how does Ford appear to be just inches away from the explosion? 'I can't give all our secrets away,' smiled Leonard, 'but I promise it looks very realistic.'

The Fugitive opened in the US on August 6, 1993. Roger Ebert of the *Chicago Sun-Times* was again impressed with Ford's performance. 'Ford is once again the great modern movie everyman: dogged, determined, brave and not demonstrative. As an actor, nothing he does seems merely for show, and in the face of this melodramatic material he deliberately plays down, lays low, gets on with business instead of trying to exploit the drama in meaningless acting flourishes.' And went on to dub *The Fugitive*, 'one of the year's best films.'

The Washington Post loved the movie in general and Ford in particular. 'Ford makes the perfect rider for a project like this, with his hangdog-handsome everyman presence. He's one of us – but one of us at his personal best. It's great fun to ride along with him.'

While *The Fugitive* is a superior piece of thriller entertainment, the only carp that could be leveled at it is that it is a very long film ... even Ford's not inconsiderable charisma struggles to hold the attention quite that long. That said, the film does manage to revitalize a familiar and slightly old-fashioned story, and Ford deserves at least some of the credit for that.

The film took $184 million in the US, and a total of $353,900,000 worldwide making it one of Ford's most successful movies in a while and the kind of movie that studios like to sequelise. But Ford is not interested in being involved. 'I don't see how you could create a story that would be interesting to me, and would proceed from what we've done. And the studio said, "Well, you'll understand if we try, won't you?"'

Harrison Ford could take some comfort in being nominated once more for a Golden Globe, though up against Tom Hanks for his performance in the very worthy *Philadelphia*, it's not a great surprise that Ford didn't get to hold the Award aloft.

Meanwhile another blockbuster lay just over the horizon ...

CLEAR AND PRESENT DANGER

Harrison Ford reported for further Jack Ryan duty when filming began on *Clear and Present Danger* in November 1993. The first draft of the script was crafted before *Patriot Games* began shooting by *Apocalypse Now*'s John Milius, no stranger to right-wing gung-ho action epics, though usually with an intelligent twist. This version seemed to get the Clancy seal of approval. 'Tom loved it,' said Milius, an old comrade of Clancy's. 'I was very faithful to his book.' The problem there was that Jack Ryan barely appears in the first half of the story and he spends most of his time in Washington D.C. directing the actions of a crack unit of US commandoes led by the mysterious John Clarke. Something had to be done.

'There was no place for Harrison Ford in that film,' says director Phillip Noyce. 'Well, there was a place, but the audience would have rioted.' So in March 1992, Paramount hired one of *Games'* and *Hunt*'s cowriters, Donald Stewart, to put the accent on Ryan. Stewart's script – and a reported $10 million-plus payday for the star – was enough to get Ford, who was by now commiting to only one Ryan movie at a time, to do *Danger*.

Add to that the fact that *Clear and Present Danger* had a different tone to the two earlier Clancy movies. In *Danger*, there's less emphasis on action and more on the dilemma Ryan faces when torn between doing the right thing and doing what he's ordered to by the powers-that-be. This change of gear suited Harrison Ford just fine. 'I feel an obligation to expand on the role of Ryan,' said Ford. 'We were able to do that this time because we see him in such different circumstances than in *Patriot Games*, a tale of a man and his family threatened. This one has a lot more energy to it. It's a lot more intriguing story of government and corruption and one man's attempt to stand up to the system.'

But again Clancy wasn't happy. He felt that Hollywood's tinkering with his storylines was Not A Good Thing and told *The Washington Post* that Stewart's script was 'really awful'.

Clancy was even less understanding in his memos to the production team. 'First things first,' Clancy was reported to have written by *Entertainment Weekly*, 'Clear and Present Danger was the number one best-selling novel of the 1980s. One might conclude that the novel's basic story line had some quality to it. Why, then, has nearly every aspect of the book been tossed away?'

Uncharacteristically, Harrison Ford seemed to tire of Clancy's constant complaints and told *Entertainment Weekly* on the Mexico set of *Danger* in January 1993, 'I think [Clancy's criticism] did hurt the film. I don't think it should have. It's inevitable that a book changes in bringing it to the screen. It's generally accepted by those professionals that have had some experience with the process. And if one doesn't want to submit to the process, the simple expedient is not to sell your stuff.'

In all fairness to the filmmakers, the script was a work in progress, as they quickly brought in *Schindler's List*'s Steven Zaillian for another re-write, briefing him to make the script more like the book, but strengthening Jack Ryan's part in the process. Zaillian also altered the ending, having Ryan testify before Congress about America's involvement in the covert drugs war operations. Ford supported this change, saying, 'I thought we would be making insufficient entertainment if we didn't give people the satisfaction of knowing that Ryan did testify. It's hard to make an ambiguous ending to a two-hour movie.' In addition, some of Clancy's more gung-ho excesses were toned down. 'We have softened the political bias [Clancy] brings to the subject, not because we're bleeding-heart liberals, but because we wanted to divest it of some of its baggage and let it walk on its own two legs.'

As with his other films, Ford was keen to do as much of the action stuff himself as was feasible, rather than relying on doubles. Said stunt coordinator Dick Ziker, who had known Ford for years, 'He changes everything, trying to make it better. He always knows where the camera should be, where his face should be. That's why I have to use him all the time. We have a great stunt double for him, but the double never works.' During the production, Ford hung from a helicopter skid and crashed into a bus in a car going backward at 100 mph. 'He scares the shit out of me sometimes,' said Ziker. 'Harrison does the stunts. I pay the double. That's the way he wants it.'

'If you fall on the ground, it's a stunt. If you fall on a pad, it's acting,' says Ford dismissively.

With *Clear and Present Danger*, some familiar faces from *Patriot Games* returned. Most noticeable was James Earl Jones, reprising his Admiral Greer, his third appearance as the character. Also on board was Anne Archer, though unfortunately, a sub-plot involving Mrs Ryan was left on the cutting room floor.

New to the film franchise is the shadowy John Clarke, a regular co-star of the Jack Ryan books and the lead character in a couple of Clancy novels *Without Remorse* and *Rainbow Six*. In the movie he's played by Willem Dafoe, a terrific actor but not really the same physical type as the character in the novels. Clancy describes Clarke as being heavier set and I always thought of him as more of a James Gandolfini type.

The shooting of the movie didn't pass without its problems. Uncharacteristic weather in Washington D.C. and rebel action near the Mexico locations meant that the film slipped behind schedule and compromises had to be made. The original action climax had John Clarke and Jack Ryan rescuing a squad of US soldiers who've been abandoned south of the border by the American authorities. Donald Stewart flew down to Mexico to craft a new scene with a chase over and under the South American town. The Paramount Studio execs were mindful that the film was already running late and over budget and the filmmakers had to make do with a smaller scale helicopter rescue.

The film opened in the US on August 3, 1994 to better notices than *Patriot Games* received, though most felt it wasn't up to the standard of *The Fugitive*. *The Washington Post* said, 'There's a little bit of Mr Smith in Ford's Jack Ryan and there's a little bit of Capra in the techno-thriller as written and rewritten by Donald Stewart, Steven Zaillian and John Milius.'

'Its best-seller profile, action quotient and Harrison Ford as a can-do hero assure muscular late summer box office for this well-tooled entertainment ... the most interesting of the three Clancy adaptations, at least from a content point of view,' said the trade bible *Variety*.

The Los Angeles Times said, 'It reaffirms, if reaffirmation is necessary, Harrison Ford's position as the most reliable action star around.'

The worldwide gross for *Clear and Present Danger* was a very respectable $207,500,000, a bigger take than *Patriot Games*, which seems fitting as *Clear and Present Danger* was the better movie, in my view.

With the movie's promotional duties out of the way Ford was meaning to take a year off, so that he could watch the complete cycle of the seasons at his ranch. But the following month he began work on Sydney Pollack's remake of *Sabrina*, the 1954 comedy written and directed by Billy Wilder. Ford had his reasons for taking on the role played by Humphrey Bogart in the original. 'I'm always taking a year off,' he said ruefully. 'And I really mean it, and I really do try. But I didn't want to leave for a year's sabbatical with *Clear and Present Danger* as the last thing I left on the table. I've done too many grim, anxious movies lately, so I wanted to do a comedy.'

CHAPTER 12

HARRISON FORD: ROMANTIC LEAD

From Rom-Com to President and back

'Harrison Ford has this extraordinary decency in the characters he plays. He's a moral man in immoral times. He has the ability to convey a high standard of integrity into any part.' Alan Pakula, director of *The Devil's Own*

With his last few films, Harrison Ford appeared to be actively trying to shape the way the movie-going audience perceived him. For the established Ford fanbase, he made sure he appeared in a few action films, but threw in a few straight dramas for those who preferred their cinema entertainment a little more thoughtful. In the back half of the 1990s, Ford seemed to expanding this broadening of his appeal by including romantic comedies, political thrillers and even straightforward romance movies. A remake of the classic Billy Wilder movie *Sabrina* might not have seemed the natural choice for an actor like Harrison Ford, but reprising a role first played by Humphrey Bogart doesn't seem like a huge stretch given Indiana Jones' resemblance to Bogart's Fred Dobbs in *Treasure of the Sierra Madre*.

SABRINA? FAIR ENOUGH

The original *Sabrina* was made by Billy Wilder at the height of this powers, right between *Stalag 17* and *The Seven Year Itch*. With a sassy, knowing script by Samuel Taylor and the great Ernest Lehman, it's hard to imagine what the director of the remake, Sydney Pollack, thought he could bring to this version that the original lacked. Technicolor, perhaps?

The truth is that the remake came about almost by accident. Producer Steve Rudin was noodling around with a concept for a romantic comedy with screenwriter Barbara Benedek, who had written the script for *The Big Chill*. 'It was sort of a similar triangle,' Rudin recalls, 'and I said, 'It should be like *Sabrina*.' So Barbara went and watched it and said, "Why don't we just do *Sabrina*?"' After winning the blessing of Paramount chairperson Sherry Lansing (the studio also released the original), Benedek got to work. The first script was a kind of '*Sabrina* lite,' according to Rudin. 'It didn't have the depth that the script has now, but it had great jokes and it was charming. I sent it to Harrison, and together we got Sydney to do it.' Recruiting Pollack was a task. 'It took a while to talk him into it,' said Ford. 'I don't think he was sure until he could find a way of telling the story that interested him.'

'I didn't want to do a remake of Billy Wilder,' Pollack said. 'People are very unforgiving about remakes, particularly of something like *Sabrina*. So many people were so charmed by it. I said no two or three times.' Pollack also called Wilder and says he found him 'justifiably annoyed' that the studio hadn't consulted him, though Wilder had no beef with Pollack himself. 'And then I talked to Harrison,' said Pollack. 'What really changed my mind was thinking seriously about working with him – I'm a big fan of his, particularly in love stories, which he doesn't get to do very much. So then I thought, Well, what the hell, let's do it'

Ford himself had strong reasons for getting into the project. 'I wanted to do something light where I didn't have to hit anybody, or have anybody hit me.'

The filmmakers conducted a high-profile search for an actress to cast in the title role, and such famous names as Julia Roberts, Meg Ryan, Winona Ryder and even ballerina Darcy Bussell made it onto the list, but were just as quickly taken off again. In the event, the role went to the relatively unknown Brit Julia Ormond, who'd made an impression on the critics in the previous year's *Legends of the Fall* opposite Brad Pitt. Unlike Ford, who'd avoided seeing either *The Fugitive* tv show or the original Wilder *Sabrina* for fear of being influenced by what had gone before, Ormond was a fan of the original movie. 'I watched it four times before I auditioned. Then, I got the role and I've watched it three or four times since. I'm going to have to stop.'

For the supporting William Holden role in the remake, big names like Alec Baldwin (that would have been interesting), Val Kilmer and Kurt Russell were considered, but the role finally went to tv talk show host Greg Kinnear whose easy personality more than made up for his lack of acting experience.

When Rudin called Fred Westheimer at the William Morris Agency to set up a meeting with Kinnear, Westheimer said his client might not be available. Rudin was not easily dissuaded: 'I said, "Look, he's never going to get the part, so just tell him to come in"'.

'So I showed up to this meeting at Paramount,' said Kinnear. 'I did a little hyperventilating and went in and met Sydney.' Pollack told him about the part and read a few scenes with him. As Kinnear remembered it, 'He said, "Look, it's a long shot, okay? I'm not going to lie to you."'

After two taped auditions, Kinnear went on with his tv show – and didn't hear anything for three and a half months. 'At first he was sort of a mild contender,' recalled Rudin. 'Then, the more Sydney worked with him, the more he really liked him.'

Once he had the part, and Kinnear had to figure out how he was going to survive acting in a major motion picture with Indiana Jones. The first time he met the cast and crew was during wardrobe tests. Ford was already under the lights in his tuxedo, looking calm and collected, and Kinnear was told to stand next to him. 'I was just a little dazed and confused,' said Kinnear. 'I was a little nervous, and I was chewing gum.' In an attempt to strike up a conversation, he offered Ford some gum. 'It's okay isn't it?' asked Kinnear. 'To chew gum?' Ford reassured him it was. Finally, the camera is ready, a hundred voices hush, and all eyes are on the actors as Pollack calls for the camera to roll film. Once the take was done Ford wheeled on Kinnear in mock anger. 'Are you chewing gum? Sydney, I can't work with this guy!'

'It was so cruel!' said Ormond said. 'But it did kick off a relationship for the two of them. I think if he'd done that to me, I'd have probably had an apoplectic fit and left.' Kinnear stayed, and the next time they worked together, Ford took him to lunch. 'Yeah, he's quite the jokester,' said Kinnear. 'He's always had a pretty good time at my expense, I don't mind telling you.'

When asked about the story, Ford was vague. 'I sort of remember that. Well, I remember it slightly differently, I think. Oh, it doesn't matter. His version's good. He's the comedian.' Then he adds, smiling, 'He'll still have his shot at me when I do his show.'

Sabrina was released in December 1995 in the US and January 1996 in the UK to so-so business, gathering just $53 million at the world box-office against a budget of £58 million. Almost predictably, the critics weren't in a giving mood. *The Village Voice* said, 'The cine-centennial year has been just about the dullest for Hollywood movies I can remember, and Sydney Pollack's *Sabrina* is symptomatic – a soporific, superfluous recycling of a dated picture that owed whatever charm it held 40 years ago to the wan sarcasm of its writer director Billy Wilder and the strenuously doelike capering of its leading lady, Audrey Hepburn.' I think here the reviewer is more interested in showing off his effete *ennui* than actually reviewing the movie.

The Financial Times didn't like the film much either, stating, 'Harrison Ford takes the old Humphrey Bogart role and makes it seem very old indeed. As the millionaire who loses his heart to chauffeur's daughter Sabrina (Julia Ormond), while trying to steal her heart from his playboy brother, Ford acts like a matinee idol with sciatica.'

Said *The Sunday Times*, 'Ford and Ormond just don't hit it off. The scenes between them have been stretched to catch what crumbs they can and the role of Linus expanded to accommodate all sorts of stuff about post-1980s burnout and midlife crises: Ford responds with his best impression of a man with a thumping headache. I have never seen him look so seriously depressed in a film.'

The San Francisco Chronicle said, 'Despite his star power, Ford never turns Linus into someone we care about. It's the grinning Kinnear who steals the movie. When Ford does his fumbling, emotionally clumsy Gary Cooper bit, the movie flattens out.'

One ray of light came from *The San Francisco Examiner*'s Barbara Shullgasser, who said, 'Ford manages to be smart enough to appreciate *Sabrina* but still pathetic enough to dismiss her. It's a good performance, Ford's best and most lovable in years, closer to the looseness of *Working Girl* than to the over-seriousness of *Patriot Games*. He should play comedy more often.'

The odd thing is that there must have been some among the Hollywood foreign press corps who liked *Sabrina* because they nominated Ford yet again for a Golden Globe for his performance, as well as putting the film in the Best Comedy/Musical category.

The problem with *Sabrina* was that it was a remake that never should have been remade. It's tough enough for any filmmaker to take on the uphill battle of remaking a fondly remembered property of yore, but doubly difficult to try to improve on a classic made by a master director like Billy Wilder, the opinions of the *Village Voice* not withstanding. But Ford was about to step into an even more controversial film project ...

THE DETAIL'S IN THE DEVIL

'This was one of the most complex movies I have ever made,' said director Alan Pakula of Ford's next project, *The Devil's Own*. 'The subject matter is so rich because there are many different ways it can be viewed.'

If that doesn't qualify as the understatement of the last century ...

Putting Harrison Ford and Brad Pitt in a movie together seems like the dream combination. The two most pre-eminent stars of their respective generations, teamed to tell a story about loyalty and honour against a backdrop of bitter and grinding political unrest.

Ford had already worked with Pakula on *Presumed Innocent*. 'Harrison Ford has this extraordinary decency in the characters he plays,' said Pakula. 'He's a moral man in immoral times. He has the ability to convey a high standard of integrity into any part.'

This was yet another departure for Ford. Tom O'Meara is not a millionaire businessman, a highly intuitive detective nor an indestructible crime-fighter. He's an ordinary, working-class guy trying to get a job done. 'I liked this part because it was different to any I've played recently,' said Ford. 'He's a blue collar guy, a responsible family man whose world completely changes as a result of complications that arise from taking this young man into his home.'

His customary research regimen meant that Ford worked alongside the local law-enforcement guys in the run-up to filming. 'I spent quite a few nights riding with various New York police officers to get a feel for what a patrol sergeant does,' said Ford. 'It gave me a better sense of what each neighbourhood had to offer.'

Margaret Collins, who plays Tom's wife, Sheila, had no need to undertake such field research. 'It was a very comfortable role for me,' she said. 'I'm of Irish heritage, I'm a mother and my dad was a New York City policeman for 26 years. He loved his job and would always tell us stories about the things that happened when he came home. We mostly heard the funny stories. When things were really tough, he'd go out on the porch and talk with my mom.'

Brad Pitt came to the project knowing very little about the Irish situation. 'I did all the research I could,' said Pitt. 'Unfortunately, the troubles in Ireland have been going on for three hundred years and I don't think there's any way to completely understand them if you haven't grown up in them, but I travelled there several times. I read all the books and met with several people who had been involved in the struggle.'

Pitt worked with dialogue coach Brendan Gunn. 'Brendan gave me a perspective on it, but a fair perspective,' said Pitt. 'That's what I was most looking for, not a biased, angry perspective, but someone who could really sit back and say, "it's a shame, there's crimes going on on both sides" and "how can we fix it?"'

The project had been maturing for about a decade before producer Lawrence Gordon got a green light. 'It's been quite an odyssey over a period of nearly ten years,' said Gordon. 'This movie began as a pitch for which we hired screenwriter Kevin Jarre to write a script. He went off for a couple of years, then came back many months overdue with a wonderful screenplay.

'Brad Pitt committed to the story five years ago. But at that time, no studio thought he was bankable. I think most executives also shied away from the controversy of the subject matter. Harrison had always been one of Brad's favourite actors and Brad suggested we send him the script. I'd been sending Harrison every script I had for 20 years so it was to my great pleasure and surprise when he said yes to this one. We then set about finding a director and everyone agreed that Alan Pakula was the perfect guy.'

Filming began on February 5, 1996 during the snowiest New York winter on record, but all didn't go smoothly. In a later interview in *Newsweek* in January 1997, Pitt called *The Devil's Own*, 'the most irresponsible piece of film-making' he'd ever seen. He later retracted that statement and explained that, 'I wasn't being clear and didn't verify what I was saying. I put together a bunch of thoughts which led to some confusion.' This seems at odds with Pitt's reputation for fair-mindedness and his scrupulous good behaviour on every film set.

The Guardian reported in June 1997 that just days before shooting was supposed to start there was no final script. Harrison Ford had always been accustomed to running with changes being made on scripts as shooting progressed. He'd often instituted some of those changes himself. Brad Pitt wasn't so keen on this way of working.

'I think he panicked because of all the script changes,' said director Pakula. He thought we were trying to make this a totally different film, a *Patriot Games 2*. He had lost faith. But he had a contract and the studio said he had to do the film.'

Faced with a lawsuit, Pitt had to knuckle down. He went to Ford with his troubles. 'Harrison told me, "Look, we're here now, it's our only chance to do this, let's just figure it out,"' said Pitt. 'Harrison has always been one of my favourites. He comes from this place of integrity and common sense which I think was instilled in me as a kid, and it's something I always look up to when I see it. He is such a natural actor and I always say the hardest thing to do is make it look everyday.

'We didn't want to make a shit movie, we wanted something we'd be proud of, but it was trivialised and made Harrison and I out to be people hiding in trailers, which wasn't the case.'

Ford too dismissed any notion of on-set bust-ups with his co-star. 'Working with Brad was fine. In every case where we had scenes together the relationship was fine. There was no problem. The tabloids reported this battle of two egos and it was never that. As an actor, I really enjoyed working with him.'

But if you re-read what Pitt originally said and the replies Pakula and Ford made to press inquiries about problems on the set, it doesn't appear as though they're talking about the same issues. Pitt may well have retracted the statement he made and apologised under pressure from the studio, but it seemed he wasn't alone in his view of the portrayal he was required to give.

It will come as no surprise that the emotive subject matter of *The Devil's Own* pretty much blew its chances of a fair review. *The Evening Standard*'s Alexander Walker called it a 'ludicrous melodrama' and went on to say, 'You may think a film as silly as this is best ignored. But that's downgrading its obnoxious opportunism. It exploits a bloodbath that has cost thousands of lives and is dangerously active at the moment. It does so without the slightest insight into the tragedy, political or psychological, but simply fostering sympathy for romanticised terrorism and glamorising its emissaries by allowing Brad Pitt to get as many sexy kicks as he can out of ending people's lives. I'm depressed to think we allow such creatures into the country, along with their tainted product.'

Michael Medved of *The New York Post* called it, 'an eloquent apology for murderous terrorism,' and wrote, 'Brad Pitt plays the cutest, cuddliest, cold-blooded killer you've ever met – an IRA thug whose brooding, rebel-with-a-cause demeanour is supposed to suggest that he somehow feels conscience-stricken about the bodies that pile up around him. No amount of acting excellence can cover this movie's devilish attempt to rationalise and, ultimately, to glamorise the most deadly sort of political violence.'

These reviews focus entirely on the questionable premise of the movie and the apparently sympathetic handling of the terrorist character played by Pitt and largely ignore the achievements of Pitt and Ford in undeniably difficult circumstances. While I would agree with Pitt's view that the handling was irresponsible in that it appeared condone the actions of its rogue IRA protagonist, if you can get past the almost inevitably emotional response to that aspect of the film, it's still a well-crafted and well-acted piece of work and it's unfair to place blame on the actors who were under contract to play roles in a film over which they had little control once the cameras started rolling. If blame needs to be handed out, I'd be more inclined to look towards the studio executive who cared more about his $80 million investment than he did about distributing an unpopular and contentious political statement.

Inevitably the poor reviews conspired to keep the audiences away in droves. The movie managed $120 million in box office takings worldwide which doesn't add up to great business in any kind of accent.

HAIL TO THE CHIEF

It's pretty much an acknowledgement of an actor's maturity in the eyes of Hollywood when he is finally called upon, at 55, to portray the President of the United States. The role requires a certain gravitas that a younger actor – say Brad Pitt – doesn't have, even now. But Harrison Ford answered that call in 1997 when he stepped up to the plate for his first term in the terrorist thriller *Air Force One*.

Of course, being Harrison Ford, he was a bit of a kick-ass president. Not as thoughtful as Martin Sheen's turn in tv's *West Wing*. Not as stiff as Michael Douglas' portrayal in *The American President* and sadly not as goofy as the Kevin Kline version in *Dave*. But there was some movie action in the film and Ford, being Ford, avoided the use of doubles wherever possible. Which meant he was getting knocked about on a regular basis. 'Every day. No, not every day. Some days, they didn't get around to me, because they were too busy beating the shit out of each other. But I enjoy action scenes. I love being involved in the choreography of it and the storytelling through physical means. And it's fun for me to run, jump and fall.'

Fun it may have been, but Ford didn't come through the experience unscathed. 'I tore a rotator cuff in my shoulder on *Air Force One* so I'm waiting for that to heal. I hurt my shoulder over the years a number of times – you have a side you favour when you have to hit the ground and I generally land on my right shoulder. On *The Fugitive* I tore my ACL [a knee ligament] because I was running towards the camera. When we rehearsed it there had been a hole next to the camera I could run through; when we shot it somebody set a century stand in that hole and I put all my weight on my right leg to cut left to avoid it. I've given up skiing when I have a picture in the spring because I don't have an ACL in my left knee. That was run over by the flying wing in one of the Indiana Jones movies.'

But Ford is quick to underline that there's more to his role in *Air Force One* than simply beating bad guy butt. 'It's fine to be the ass-kicking President, as long as people understand that this film has very strong emotional values and is much more than just kicking ass. It's kicking ass to a moral end, and that to me is much more interesting than just kicking ass. I've never been a huge fan of action films. I think they get boring. They don't engage me as a moviegoer. What engages me is strong storytelling. And strong storytelling, most of the time, has a moral component. There's a moral contest, there's a question of human character and nature and value. That kind of a story can encourage an emotional understanding of what's going on on-screen, it seals you into the story as a moviegoer much more strongly than one kinetic event after another. That's what I look for in a film that I'm gonna do, in this general genre.'

Director Wolfgang Petersen had no doubts that Ford was the man for the role. 'We needed an actor who was believable as both the head of the country and as a tough action hero. There are only two or three stars in the world who could do that convincingly.'

For Ford, it was the quality of the story that convinced him to sign up for the project. 'When I read the material I saw in my mind's eye a film that was enormously entertaining and that had a real emotional core to it. I could relate to the emotional dilemma of the character, and I could also relate to the moral question that was being raised and answered. I think that's a very important component. I think it dignifies the whole enterprise of filmmaking, when you give it reference to something important in people's lives. There's two ways of doing it. You can co-opt an issue that's real and important and then you can give a movie solution to that problem. I think in this case, we don't offer a solution; we just offer a resolution of the conflict that we're seeing. But we don't attempt to give historic perspective for the future. But those are the reasons that I chose it. I thought that it would be a damn good summer movie! And I thought I could do an adequate job of giving the character emotional expression.'

Once he had committed to the film, Ford began to think about how the process of making the movie could be smoothed and who his co-stars would be. With typical Ford luck, he was presented with an opportunity to take care of two small problems in one go. 'I was a guest at a birthday party for President Clinton in Jackson, Wyoming, where we have a home,' said Ford. 'Glenn Close was sitting next to him at lunch. And halfway through the meal, I went over and asked if he'd be good enough to help arrange a tour of the real Air Force One – which is fairly hard to get – and I asked her if she would consider being my Vice President.'

'Glenn had to read the script and made her decision over the next couple of weeks. The President, however, agreed immediately. The next day, Wolfgang, myself, our director of photography and our art director took a tour of the plane. It helped us out enormously.'

The fact that Ford attended social functions with the incumbent President of the United States led to some speculation that Ford based his portrayal of the Chief Executive on President Clinton. Not so, said Ford. 'I didn't spend time with the President gleaning the atmosphere. No. The only time I've spent with the President has been purely privately social. I did not use the President for research.' What, not even a little bit? Surely Ford must have made a few observations. 'You don't need to be proximate to the President to glean that. I really did not use President Clinton either for inspiration or detail. There was a story that circulated somewhere that I had invited the President, that I had spent time with the President and discussed this part with him. Not at all. I'm much more interested in his story and what's going on with him. It really never occurred to me to ask him anything about this, nor did I think that would be a responsible use of his time.'

So if Ford played the President his own way, was he happy with how he performed his first time in office? 'The most important part of the film, for me, in the expression of the particularity of this president, was in that speech that he gives in the beginning of the film, and I was very concerned about how we framed that language – the rhythm and the meter of that language. The very precision of that language was critical, and the fact of the President's taking responsibility for a failure to perform was very important. The rest of it I thought came from the deference that people pay the President. There is no, I think, particular presidential behavior. So I wasn't anxious to know how Bill Clinton might play this part. I was anxious to figure out how I might play this part and use my own experience and my own emotional reserve to give expression to the ideas of this character and the ideas of this story.'

Predictably, during the publicity tours for *Air Force One*, more than one journalist asked Ford if he ever wanted to be President himself. Just as predictably, Ford's answer to that particularly dopey question was curt. 'I have no political future. I will continue to vote and be an occasional nudge, but that's as much interest as I have.'

Air Force One opened in the US during the classic summer rush on July 27, 1997 and in the UK on September 12 the same year. Critics seemed to like this movie better than Ford's last two. Roger Ebert of the *Chicago Sun-Times* wrote, 'Harrison Ford is steady and commanding as the president, even while we're asking ourselves if a middle-aged chief executive would really be better at hand-to-hand combat than his Secret Service agents.'

Rolling Stone was pleased to see Ford's return to form. 'What a relief to see this underrated actor back in gear after *Sabrina* and *The Devil's Own*, two rare flops in the Ford-canon. His wit is dry – acerbic but never campy.'

The San Francisco Chronicle found Ford's President a little unbelievable. 'As President James Marshall, Ford is beyond sincere. He is an impassioned visionary. We meet him for the first time at a Kremlin banquet in his honor, giving a speech in which he's about to implode with rage and moral fervor. "It's your turn to be afraid!" he warns terrorists, promising to send American troops to fight terrorism and tyranny everywhere it might occur.' Little did they know that ten years later, that would in reality be the incumbent President's foreign policy ...

Air Force One gave a satisfactory performance at the global box office, with total ticket sales of around $300 million against a budget of $85 million.

SIX DAYS? SEEMED LONGER

Never one to admit defeat, Harrison Ford returned to the genre of romantic comedy with his next project, *Six Days Seven Nights*. It was a genre he has mined a few times before with varying degrees of success. Most agree: *Working Girl*, good. *Sabrina*, not. This is oddly surprising, because based on his performances in films like *Star Wars* and *Raiders of the Lost Ark*, Ford has often displayed the kind of charm that led to him being compared with the old-time movie stars like Bogart and Cary Grant. So it came as a bit of a surprise that he struggled to show any kind of charm in *Sabrina*.

That didn't stop director Ivan Reitman trying to capture that same old-time appeal in *Six Days Seven Nights*. 'The film is romantic and really funny – similar to a certain type of film made in the 40s and 50s in exotic locations featuring strong people with a strong point of view and with lots of give and take between them. Magic is created by placing our heroes against very tough odds as a way of creating tension and fun. *Six Days Seven Nights* gave me the chance to do that kind of film – and the challenge was finding the correct tonal level between the two actors. I think Harrison Ford and Anne Heche pulled it off brilliantly.'

'I've always wanted to work with Harrison Ford,' continues Reitman. 'He's one of the great film actors of all time. Harrison is one of the very few legendary stars who can do action and great dramatic work equally well. You believe him in whatever part he plays – action, drama or comedy.'

Ford seemed happy enough to take another swipe at a rom-com. 'I thought the screenplay was really funny,' said Ford. 'The relationship with the character Anne played was classic, the attraction of opposites. The deserted isle provided an exotic context. I thought these elements had the potential for a very entertaining movie.'

The way Ford described his character, brought to mind Walter Eckland, the character played by Cary Grant in *Father Goose* (1964). 'Quinn is an ex-patriot American who has made a new life in Tahiti, flying cargo through the islands. He's a bit of a curmudgeon, we sense there have been some serious disappointments in his life,' said Ford. 'When the character [Robin Monroe] played by Anne Heche shows up at the airport for her journey to Makatea, she's expecting a conventional commuter flight, but that aircraft is down for maintenance and Quinn is filling in with his venerable De Havilland Beaver.'

Asked about the differences between acting drama and acting comedy, Ford replied, 'Comedy does seem to come out of character rather than being imposed as a style. I think it's a question of creating a character that has both the limitations and the qualities that cause him to be more comic than that character might otherwise be in the same story told without comic intention. And then you do, of course, a certain amount of shtick to help make it clear that's what the intention is. I don't know that I can pronounce all the comedy rules, but I think I know it when I see it.'

Anne Heche considered the film to be a career highlight. 'I was dying to do a romantic comedy. I had just come off *Wag the Dog* and I really wanted to be back in romance. I wanted to do comedy because I just love the genre. Reading the script, I knew it was right for me.

'Finding out that I would be working with Harrison Ford made me flip out,' continued Heche. 'There are some actors you put in the "I would love to work with but don't think I'll ever get the chance to" category and so I was thrilled to have the chance to work with Harrison Ford.

Filming on location in Kaua'I, Hawaii proceeded without incident.

The movie was released in the US on June 12, 1998 and in the UK on July 3, eventually taking in $165 million in worldwide box office. Not bad business for a rom-com budgeted at $70 million.

Roger Ebert allowed that, 'Ford has a nice early drunk scene where he avoids the usual cliches and gives us a man who gets thoughtful and analytical in a sloshed sort of way. Heche is plucky and has unforced charm, and does a great job of looking searchingly into Ford's eyes while he talks to her. Meanwhile, Schwimmer and Obradors provide counterpoint, mirroring in low comedy what the stars are doing at a more elevated level.' but concluded, 'If you want to see a movie that knows what to do with a man, a woman and an island, see John Huston's *Heaven Knows, Mr Allison*, in which Robert Mitchum and Deborah Kerr create atmosphere where Ford and Heche create only weather.'

Ebert has a point. I think Heche was miscast and looked way too young, at 29, to play a love interest to Harrison Ford, who looked all of his 56 years, probably intentionally as his character was supposed to be a crusty curmudgeon. Perhaps a more sophisticated, mature actress would have worked better – Rene Rousseau, maybe. Or Kristin Scott Thomas, who was – ironically – to have played the part of Robin in *Six Days Seven Nights*, but lost out on the role to Heche. Ford struggled heroically with an insipid script which didn't give him a wide enough range of acting to do and once more ended up relying on his natural charm to carry the picture. I would have been more interested in seeing the story of Quinn's relationship with the fiery Anjelica (Jacqueline Obradors) than the frankly boring Robin. *Six Days Seven Nights* is not a bad film, it's just not a very good one either.

Just about all the other reviews seemed to focus more on Heche's real-life role as Ellen Degeneris' girlfriend than her on-screen role as Harrison Ford's. It came up in a couple of media interviews with Ford, as well, but Ford refused to be drawn. 'I myself have very little interest in other people's personal lives,' he quite rightly said. 'Frankly, I don't give a damn.'

GROWN-UP DRAMA

Random Hearts was the third time Harrison Ford had worked under the eye of veteran director Sydney Pollack. Neither of the first two outings together had been spectacularly successful. *Presumed Innocent* (which Pollack produced) had performed respectably at the box office, but *Sabrina* was a bit of a disaster, both financially and critically. So why was Ford coming back for a third bite of that particular cherry?

Maybe it was because he hadn't done a romantic drama since 1978's *Hanover Street*. Maybe because he saw possibilities in the story of an internal affairs cop's affair with a US Congresswoman. Or maybe he thought it'd be third time lucky with Mr Pollack.

According to Ford, he'd been interested in the story since he first heard about it during the filming of *Sabrina*. 'Sydney told me the story and I responded to it very strongly, I told him, "I love the idea of this. Keep me in mind if you ever get a script that works."' So, what was it about the story that hooked him? 'I loved the different dramatic set-up. This is not a very plot-heavy movie, but the starting point – two characters lose their spouses on a commercial airline crash and then find out they were having an affair – that's a very powerful emotional beginning for me. The more that I heard about how the character behaved, the more interested I was. It's unusual material to make a love story from. And the way in which the characters behave is quite unusual as well. I was intrigued by that.'

The filmmakers added some action elements to the film that weren't in the original source novel. But Ford saw this more as expanding his character rather than pandering to an action hungry audience. 'I don't think that was put in to goose it up or to create an action atmosphere because it doesn't do that. What it's meant to do is to illuminate the character as he goes through this crisis in his life. We see its effects on him in his professional life as a policeman. In that way, I thought it was a very valuable parallel.'

Ford had good things to say about his co-star, glamorous Brit Kristen Scott-Thomas. 'She's an adult with a husband and kids who has an investment in the real world. When acting, she brings texture and definition to a character.'

Thomas likes Harrison too. 'He can fly planes, crack a whip, ride horses, seduce girls – he can do it. He knows what works, what buttons to push. One day, we were doing a scene, and I couldn't get it right – was being really pathetic. I was kicking up a fuss, and Harrison was eating peanuts. And he cracked one open and he pushed it toward me, these two nuts. That's what he was really pleased about, the fact that these two nuts just sat in their shells. It was like, you know, "Look, the world doesn't come to an end. There are peanuts – peanuts – that are designed perfectly."'

Far tougher for Ford than making philosophical points with peanuts was the task of living up to Sydney Pollack's expectations. 'He's a perfectionist. He's as hard on himself as he is on us. The detail of these character relationships is the plot of the movie. So you had the obligation to make it dramatically interesting to watch and participate in – and you couldn't rely on what you'd already given. The nature of drama is that you must keep the story going. And if the story is the nature of the characters and their relationship, then you have to weave something new into every scene.'

Though Ford has no ambitions for political office himself, the political subtext of the *Random Hearts* story captured Ford's interest. 'What interests me is the philosophy of government, the nature of government and its effect on the body politic, or vice versa. How we get to be the country we are, why we have the kind of representation we have, who we elect and how we elect them?'

Random Hearts opened on October 8, 1999 in the US and November 19 in the UK and took in around $70 million worldwide against a budget of $60 million so it was by no means a blockbuster success.

The critical reception was lukewarm. Roger Ebert of *The Chicago Sun-Times* wrote, 'You like the fact that the movie doesn't make one of these people good and the other bad, but makes both of them shell-shocked survivors with unexplored potential. You wish you could figure out what Harrison Ford is thinking, but then Ford has made a career out of hiding his thoughts.'

The San Francisco Chronicle offered, 'Kudos to Ford and to Dave Grusin's nice, understated jazz score. They do good work, but it's done in service to a hopelessly bland piece of machinery – a movie that's desperate to please but bereft of ideas.'

The San Francisco Examiner liked what Ford did, if not the film. 'Dutch is the hard-nose, smart-ass rogue cop with a chewy center Ford could play in his sleep, but he gives Dutch the haggard sense of purpose and bouts of anger and grief that a movie with absolutely no psychological depth needs. Although, the best moment in the film is the sight of Ford, in a Cary Grant fit, muscling his way into a closing elevator just to be near Thomas.'

I liked *Random Hearts* a whole better than *Six Days Seven Nights*. It seems to have been made with an adult audience in mind, which is pretty rare for a Hollywood film these days, and it was refreshing to see Ford play a romantic lead opposite an actress who looked closer to his age than the gamines he'd been paired with in his last couple of romantic outings. I could see what would have attracted Ford to the role. The film centres around the emotions of two relatively normal people who each have to deal with the double whammy of losing their spouses in an air crash then finding out they were having an affair as well. And emotions are something that few modern filmmakers seem comfortable confronting.

END OF AN ERA

As the 1990s drew to a close, Ford could look back, at age 58, at a career with some spectacular highs and a genuinely broad variety of roles to his credit. His standard fee for a movie role had risen to somewhere around the $20 million mark. He'd been happily married to Melissa Mathison, herself a successful screenwriter, for sixteen years. He spent as much time as he could on his ranch in Jackson Hole, Wyoming. It didn't really look like Harrison Ford had much more to achieve.

But at the end of 1999, the American Film Institute chose to honour Ford with a Lifetime Achievement Award. This placed his name alongside such movie luminaries as Dustin Hoffman, Clint Eastwood, James Cagney, Bette Davis, Alfred Hitchcock, James Stewart, Fred Astaire, Gregory Peck and Jack Nicholson. Several of Ford's colleagues turned out to say a few words about the actor at the black-tie dinner thrown in Ford's honour. George Lucas, who had cast Ford in his first significant role in *American Graffiti* said that the part, 'accomplished a great deal in Harrison's career – it took him right back to being a carpenter.'

Carrie Fisher raised a laugh when she began her remarks by saying, 'Hi, my name is Carrie and I'm an alcoholic. Sorry, wrong meeting. Actually, maybe not.'

Other speakers included Steven Spielberg, Sharon Stone, Anne Heche, Mike Nichols, Anne Archer, Daryl Hannah, David Schwimmer and most interestingly Brad Pitt, casting more doubts on the tabloids' claims that the two hadn't got on during the filming of *The Devil's Own*.

And, of course, the other subject that was brought up continually during the 1990s was whether Ford would ever reprise his role as Indiana Jones. Finally, he gave an interview in early 2000 for a New Zealand magazine that seemed to indicate he was ready to put on the leather jacket again.

'Yes, I think it's time for me to dust off my bullwhip and go in search of another fabulous quarry,' he said.

So what was it that changed his mind? 'Lots of things. There's popular demand for starters; then Steven and George have been on at me for years about a third sequel, and there's also the fact that any new Indiana movie will have to take in account that he's getting on a bit.

'And that appeals to me in a way,' he said. 'It could be fun. Why shouldn't Indiana be my age? If I'm fit enough, then so is he. What's wrong with an action hero being in his golden years? It just depends on what his obstacles are.

'There are racing drivers in their 70s – like Paul Newman, for instance. There are guys in their 70s I wouldn't want to come up against in a dark alley, like Clint Eastwood.

'It's not so much a question of age as vitality. While I'm not anxious to be the world's oldest action hero, I don't think it matters so much. It just depends on the quality of the story, the nature of the character.

'Sean Connery continues to be a viable leading man in action films – and he's even older than I am.'

'I never think about age. I liked being young, even though I had no success. But being 40 held no tears because I felt some of my best work lay ahead. At 50, I had no plans to fall apart, and coming up to 60, I have no intention of going to a retirement home. I expect to be around for a long time yet.'

There had been persistent rumours that the fourth Indiana Jones film would use the rejected script written by Christopher Columbus when Spielberg and Lucas were preparing for *Indiana Jones and the Last Crusade*. The story involves the Chinese Legend of The Monkey King and is set in Africa. Curious readers may want to Google the phrase 'columbus script Indiana Jones IV' to find websites that offer a download of Columbus' original script. But the real version of *Indiana Jones IV* was still several scripts and even more years away ...

CHAPTER 13

HARRISON FORD: MORE MOVIES, MORE GENRES

From spooky-spooky to cookie-cookie

'I'm like a fireman, y'know? When I go out on a call, I want a big fire, I don't want to put out a fire in a dumpster.' Harrison Ford

A t the beginning of the new millennium, Harrison Ford was approaching his 60s and looking forward to new challenges. For his first project, Ford became involved in the movie version of *Traffic*, with Steven Soderbergh, based on the UK tv mini-series. He was to play the part of a government drug czar whose daughter becomes a drug addict. The press reported that the part had originally been offered to Michael Douglas and when Ford came on board he asked for and got changes made to the script to enhance the quality of his part. In the end, Ford backed out of the project, but the changes to the role he'd instigated proved so sweeping and positive that Douglas reconsidered and accepted the part. Except that Ford refutes the story.

'Well, that story would be wrong,' said Ford. 'I made certain suggestions about the screenplay that would make it more attractive to me, and the producers were willing to indulge some of those suggestions. And I think they were pleased with the changes. The reason I decided not to do it is that the character had problems relating to his daughter that cast a pall on the character. And I didn't want to play another grim character so soon after *Random Hearts*.'

NOT SO SCARY MOVIE

Once free of his *Traffic* obligations, Ford wasted no time in signing up for his first project of the 2000s and supernatural thriller to be directed by Robert Zemeckis, who had directed *Forrest Gump* (1994) and was an old pal of Steven Spielberg, who'd produced most of his early films.

Zemeckis had formed a production company, Imagemovers, with Steve Starkey and Jack Rapke in 1998 and began to cast around for projects.

'During our first meetings, Bob said he was specifically looking for a film in the suspense genre,' said Starkey. 'When Dreamworks gave us Clark Gregg's script for *What Lies Beneath*, Bob immediately wanted to move forward.'

'Bob had a very strong vision for the film from the start,' concurs Rapke. 'He saw it as a pure suspense movie – the kind of thing that Hitchcock would have done in his day, but using the modern technology of today to help tell the story.'

'I think suspense and cinema are made for each other,' said Zemeckis. 'I mean there are certainly suspenseful books and stage plays, but I don't think anything can manipulate time and place and storytelling techniques the way a movie can. I've always wanted to try my hand at directing something really terrifying and mysterious.'

When it came to casting the film, there was little doubt about who would be the right actors for the roles. 'We looked at those roles and decided, in an ideal world, who our dream casting would be. Harrison Ford was Bob's first and only choice for Norman and we all thought Michelle Ffeiffer would be perfect for Clare. So, you know, the gods were with us and we got the two leads we were hoping for.'

Zemeckis was beyond happy with his choices. 'Harrison brings a kind of Rock of Gibraltar strength to the screen. To me, he's the definition of absolute stardom. And Michelle is truly gifted. She's completely believable as this vulnerable woman and at the same time conveys great inner strength. Along with her acting ability, she brings incredible beauty and a powerful screen presence to the role. You can't take your eyes off her.'

Both stars were enthusiastic about their experiences working with Zemeckis but, curiously, for completely different reasons. Pfeiffer said, 'I've always loved scary movies since I was a kid, but as an actress the genre was new territory for me, which is exactly what I was looking for. I'm also a huge fan of Zemeckis and have always wanted to work with him. He has this sort of childlike enthusiasm about moviemaking that is very infectious, so even though filming was incredibly hard work, he made it fun.'

Ford's reasons were more thoughtful, and more directly related to the craft of film-making, suggesting that Ford is just as knowledgeable as his director about the process. 'Bob is a spectacular craftsman,' stated Ford, 'and a very skilled storyteller. He is so good that he is able to take a film beyond its genre distinctions, as I think he did with this film. Also, the way he shot it made a real impression on me. He used complicated camera moves, allowing for really long takes, which gave his actors a chance to develop a scene in a more organic way.'

One aspect of the filming Pfeiffer didn't especially enjoy what the amount of time she was required to spend underwater. 'It was pretty uncomfortable. I don't like the water. I'm actually a bit phobic of the water. It's a claustrophobia kind of thing. And I had to take some scuba diving lessons to get over my fear of being under. I had to breathe with a tank to get into position and stay there until they would roll, and they would take that away from me, and then I'd have to do my action ... and yeah, it was kind of scary. And I was in the bathtub for a long time, too, which was really unpleasant.'

Ford's slight reservation about the picture was that audience might not accept him in what was close to being a horror film. 'The risk here is that people will say: "Hey! This is not what we want from you; we know where we can find the people that do this sort of thing and you should do something else." But hopefully, that won't be the case, because it's always been my ambition to play different kinds of characters in different kinds of films. This is perhaps my broadest departure so far ... but I love complication, I love an edge to the characters I play.'

Shooting began in the late summer of 1999 in Addison, Vermont. Scriptwriter Clark Gregg had suggested a New England setting for the story. 'While I never specifically named it, I had always envisaged the Spencers in a place like Burlington, Vermont, which is an academic community where I spent many summers with my theatre company. The region felt like a natural fit for someone like Norman to have grown up in and to be pursuing his life's work, so I was thrilled when Steve Starkey told me they had found a location near Burlington that seemed perfect.'

What Lies Beneath opened on July 21, 2000 in the US and on October, 20 2000 in the UK, and eventually took in $291 million worldwide making it a pretty big success. Critics were quick to point out the Hitchcock influences, but given that this is probably what Zemeckis intended and that the general cinema audiences wouldn't even have seen a Hitchcock movie, this was really no criticism at all.

Roger Ebert of the *Chicago Sun-Times* wrote, 'Pfeiffer is very good in the movie; she is convincing and sympathetic and avoids the most common problem for actors in horror films – she doesn't overreact. Her character remains self-contained and resourceful, and the sessions with the psychiatrist (Joe Morton) are masterpieces of people behaving reasonably in the face of Forces Beyond Their Comprehension. Ford is the most reliable of actors, capable of many things, here required to be Harrison Ford.'

The New York Times said, 'Mr Ford shambles through this picture like the real terror, the Creature Without a Pulse. He has the superficial details down to a science, using his voice like a cozy cotton blanket to drop over Ms Pfeiffer's shoulders.'

The San Francisco Chronicle said, 'When Pfeiffer enters the bathroom of their comfortable lakeside house in Vermont, it's fair to ask if the ghost she sees there is that of Alfred Hitchcock.' Then goes on to lambast Ford. 'Ford's performance is out of sync with the audience's expectations. A flash of the signature lopsided grin here seems phony. The Ford anger here is not righteous but a cover for marital infidelity. His display of comfortable confidence cannot last as his wife goes further around the bend.'

Most scathing of all was *The San Francisco Examiner* who said, 'Zemeckis, like Pfeiffer and Ford, knows the genre is somewhat beneath him. Some of the fun, at least in the last third, lies in watching dignified, middle-aged stars, Ford in particular, regress into struggling hacks who just want to make a stupid scary-movie homage. Ultimately, the film is as ridiculous, imbalanced and parodic as *Scary Movie*. It's a formal exercise in how to build the ideal thriller, then peel it away,' and concluded that the film was, 'a subpar Hitchcock retread that gets restless and unhinged enough in its finale to lose its mind and become the slasher flick it was leering at from the start.'

I think a lot of that criticism is unfair. Unlike many of these critics, I was brought up on Hitchcock and to be honest, this is neither the kind of film Hitchcock would ever have made, nor does it resemble any of Sir Alfred's films that I have ever seen. That said, the movie's biggest liability is that it is dull and this is not the fault of Zemeckis or either of the film's stars. The problem lies in a script that can't seem to make up its mind what it wants to be – psychological thriller or out-and-out scary ghost story. By sitting coyly on the fence it turns out to be neither, so you come away feeling cheated. Pfeiffer and Ford – and the audience, for that matter – deserve so much better.

An aside: during the publicity tours for *What Lies Beneath*, a story surfaced about M. Night Shyamalan working on a draft of the *Indiana Jones IV* screenplay. Ford was asked whether he'd spoken to Shyamalan about this and replied, 'A little bit.' So was Shyamalan writing the script? 'Can't really tell you that at the moment.' But Ford had spoken to him? 'Yep.' It's hard to glean much from that but Ford later confirmed that there had been some formal discussion with Shyamalan. 'You may know that M. Night Shyamalan is anxious to write the script, and I hope that a deal can be made, and I can make it in the next couple of years.'

Around the same time Ford announced he wouldn't be returning to the role of Jack Ryan in the next film in the series, *Sum of All Fears*, saying that he 'declined to continue with the Jack Ryan character as I didn't like the script they were offering me. I didn't think it would work for me.' Shortly after, Ben Afleck signed on for the role.

WE ALL LIVE IN A RUSSIAN SUBMARINE

When Harrison Ford was asked years earlier why he'd turned down the Jack Ryan role in the first Clancy movie *The Hunt for Red October*, he said that he found the character of Jack Ryan dull and would rather have played the part of the Russian sub commander that finally went to his Indiana Jones screen father Sean Connery. So presumably, when the chance came up to play a Russian sub commander in *K-19: The Widowmaker*, Ford jumped at the chance, a risky departure from the kind of roles he's most associated with. For one think, the character wasn't a traditional hero, in the accepted movie sense, and in some ways, Alexei Vostrikov wasn't even likeable.

'We wanted to keep him largely unsympathetic,' said Ford, 'knowing that would represent an emotional obstacle for the audience. We deliberately wanted to hold them at bay. We didn't bring the usual movie star, leading-man expectations, since that can prop up the character and give the license to take a lot of things for granted. This character doesn't allow for that. And that's what I found fascinating.'

The screenplay was based on a true incident during the 1960s. Ford, with his customary attention to detail, made the trip to Russia to meet some of the sailors who had been on board the K-19. 'On two occasions I had a chance, once in Moscow and once in St. Petersburg, to meet with members of the crew, all in their 70s now,' said Ford. 'Because a submarine is so compartmentalized and because the information about what was going on was not necessarily shared by those in command, they all had much different stories about what happened. They didn't all agree and it was a little confusing to sort it out. Some guys thought the pipes came from the torpedoes, some thought the pipes came from the missiles and really, it was hard to figure out what really happened.'

But the filmmakers didn't want what appeared to be conflicting facts to become a straitjacket for the storytelling. 'What we were looking for was a dramatic telling of the story of their sacrifice and devotion to duty. We were not so compelled to figure out which story was right but which story best helped tell the bigger story of the responsibilities of military command, the devotion to a political system, the devotion to your mates, your comrades and that was the story we wanted to tell. We were quite willing to take dramatic licence to give that story a more compelling, cinematic expression.'

'What I care about is that I have the opportunity to continue to work and that I have choices of good material that I can have some effect over the conditions under which I work and the quality of the material that I choose to work.' The control Ford's referring to is his additional duties on this picture as Executive Producer, which gave him a little more influence over the proceedings than he'd enjoyed previously.

And the accent? 'We had a very capable dialogue coach who helped enormously. I thought it was an important element in the storytelling. It reminded people consistently that this was a Russian story about Russians, so I thought it was useful dramatic device.'

However, though these Russians represented a regime that was hostile to the United States, Ford felt that was tangential to the human story. 'One of the things that was interesting to me was not to deal directly with a situation where we demonize our enemies but to understand. It's like Pogo, one of my favorite political philosophers, says, 'I've seen the face of my enemy and he is us.' Men behave like men regardless of the political system; the same tensions and the same issues are there under different kinds of government. What was interesting were the different theories of military leadership and the question of where moral responsibilities lie when you are charged with military leadership.'

But despite Ford's meeting with survivors of the original K-19 disaster, some members of that crew sent an open letter to the Venice Film Festival where the movie was showing, which said in part, 'We are surprised and saddened that the Venice Film Festival chose to give *K-19: The Widowmaker* its European premiere. It is unthinkably painful to us that this film will be considered a reference upon which the new generation of film goers, including our own children, will form ideas about us and our comrades.'

Ford countered that view by pointing out that it never was intended that *K-19: The Widowmaker* should be a documentary. 'I was peripherally aware of some of the problems when I became involved. Some crew members had seen an earlier version of the script which had some elements of commentary on Russian sailors that they found disquieting, which I did as well.

'Those elements were eliminated, not because the crew wanted them changed, but because of the rewrites that I asked for. What was unique about our attempt, as I saw it, was that we were trying to do an American film from a Russian point of view without editorializing or applying a jingoistic American attitude, which I don't believe had ever been done before. I think we eventually achieved that.'

A few journalists noticed that Ford was looking heavier in the movie as asked if he had been padded up for the role. 'Padding?' he said. 'You're so kind. No, that was all me. I just felt that people didn't work out so much at that time and I just stopped working out. I also found a different way of moving from watching a lot of film footage of Russians from the early sixties: lumpier, slow, less graceful. Part of the rigour of my character is caught in his spine and that attitude causes him to move a certain way.'

K-19 opened in the US on July 19, 2002, just six days after Ford's sixtieth birthday, and in the UK on October 25, taking a modest $13 million during its opening weekend. The movie was not a huge hit with the critics either and unsurprisingly, they fixated on

Harrison Ford's accent, his first in any of his films.

The Times said that a big factor in their disappointment with *K-19* was, 'Harrison Ford's accent. Ford plays a gruff Soviet submarine captain with an accent to match. It's clearly another bold move for him after playing the villainous husband in *What Lies Beneath*. Playing the captain is Ford's transition into Gene Hackman territory. He plays the curmudgeonly mentor and leaves all the running around to his energetic young sidekicks.'

The San Francisco Chronicle wrote, 'Ford and Neeson work well together. Their characters go on a journey, and by the time they get to the other side, they're different. We believe in their changes, even if we don't always believe in Ford's accent. At one point, he sounds as if he's trying to sound Irish. Still, no one could do stoic quite like Ford. In *K-19* he's so stoic that when he tries to smile, his eyes go screwy and his face goes lopsided. Like Humphrey Bogart.'

The Village Voice said, 'Ford, Hollywood commander in chief and heavyweight box office champ of the Reagan years, as navy captain Alexei Vostrikov, fiercely patriotic defender of the Motherland, registers foremost as a giant alienation effect. The actor himself adds to the general confusion by speaking his lines from behind a faintly embarrassed glower and in a discreetly Slavic-flavored English.'

Media carping aside, *K-19* was Ford's best film in a while. While the subject matter may not have been a crowd-pleaser, and the action – such as it was – not on a par with *Airforce One*, the film remains a heartfelt plea on behalf of foot-troops at the sharp end who are seen as expendable, at best, by their political leaders. *K-19* may not have been an American story ... but it might as well have been. And it was Kathryn Bigelow's best film since *Point Break*. As for Ford's accent, I couldn't see a problem with it. But it's an easy point to score for lazy reviewers.

During the media interviews for *K-19*, Ford was asked how he felt about turning 60. Ford was as ever stoic. 'It's just another birthday for me.'

GOLDEN GLOBES SUCCESS

Though the reviews for *K-19* hadn't been great, Ford must have taken some small consolation in being selected for a Career Achievement Award at the Golden Globes earlier in 2002. A report in the trade newspaper *Variety* suggested that it was this kind of success that's led to Ford having better than average influence over the direction of his own projects.

'As I've become more experienced, people have taken my notions a little bit more seriously,' he said. 'My traditional source of material, studio development, was drying up, and the better scripts and directors were not working through the studios as much as they were.' This led to Ford initiating and developing projects for himself more and more. He formed a relationship with a team of five agents at UTA and began nurturing a project with *Amores Perros* director Alejandro Inarritu about noted humanitarian aid worker Fred Cuny, who disappeared in Chechnya in 1995, which at the time of writing has still to materialize.

And it was at that same Golden Globes ceremony that Ford met his girlfriend Callista Flockhart when she reportedly splashed Ford – or his award, reports vary – with wine. Ford had separated from his wife Melissa Mathison, dated Minnie Driver for a while and then the Ford/Flockhart partnership led to a more public Ford and a media feeding frenzy in the tabloids, with all kinds of stories about Ford and Flockhart's life together, much of it speculation or just plain fiction.

'They write such rubbish, there is no longer any journalistic responsibility or test of truth,' said Ford at the time. 'Now it is the standard of our time. People [who write about celebrities] don't give a rat's ass about what they say about other people.'

When pressed about why he thought journos and the public were so interested in the lifestyles of the rich and famous, Ford took a stab at explaining ... with a touch of world-weariness 'I think I finally understand celebrity as a matter of people's interest in others that have – perhaps – what they imagine to be more of an effect over their lives,' he said. 'People feel a lack of effect in their own lives and feel they are at the whim and mercy of other people. They wrongly suspect people who are successful and are celebrities are inured to that, and of course they are not.' But just because he he'd grasped an understanding out the cult of celebrity didn't mean he had to like it. 'It is my private life, and I have a desire to keep it private. I don't want to play in that yard,' he said.

Callista Kay Flockhart was born on November 11, 1964 in Freeport Illinois. Her mother Kay was a schoolteacher and her father Ronald worked as an executive at Kraft Foods. Callista studied acting at Rutgers University in New Jersey and became involved in regional theatre work after graduation. Her Broadway debut came in 1994 when she played in *The Glass Menagerie* with Julie Harris. In 1996 she appeared in Chekov's *The Three Sisters* opposite Billy Crudup.

Flockhart was enjoying being a successful stage actress in New York, but a friend gave her a script for a new tv show and talked her into auditioning. The show, *Allie McBeal*, became an overnight phenomenon and Flockhart became an overnight superstar. Flockhart's life and lifestyle was dissected in the tabloids and in the celebrity gossip magazines. There was much media speculation around the possibility that Flockhart might have had an eating disorder, though she always denied it. But this may well have been because there simply wasn't very much to write about the actress. In 2001, still single – though she had previously been linked romantically with Ben Stiller, to whom she was engaged, Sam Mendes and Robert Downey Jr – she adopted a baby boy. 'It's the best thing I have ever done in my life and it really changes who you are,' she says. 'It's a miracle. Anybody who has children talks like this so I'm not unique and I am not special, but I am in love with my child in a way that I have truly never been in love before.'

A year after adopting Liam, she met Harrison Ford at the Golden Globes. 'I'm in love,' Harrison told reporters in 2003. 'We have a serious relationship. Calista's a really good mother and I enjoy participating in Liam's life.'

HOLLYWOOD SUICIDE

After the grim subject matter of *K-19*, it was no big surprise that Harrison Ford sought something lighter as his next project. This may have been why he turned down the lead in *Syriana*, which had been written with Ford specifically in mind. 'I saw a bit of (director) Steve Gaghan's movie *Syriana*,' Ford later remarked, 'and I wish I'd played the part that was offered to me – George's part. I didn't feel strongly enough about the truth of the material and I think I made a mistake. The film underwent some changes, and I think a lot of it is very truthful: the things that I thought weren't, were obviated after I left the table.'

While Ford may have felt that way after *Syriana* had been released, there's no getting away from the evidence that the actor preferred each successive movie to be a contrast of subject material to the last. And in that respect Gaghan's dark political thriller would have been too similar in tone to *K-19* for Ford's apparent career strategy.

So, sticking with his habitual body swerves when it comes to choosing his projects, Ford settled on an out-and-out comedy with new kid on the block Josh Hartnett. 'I hadn't done a comedy in awhile,' said Ford. 'The last was *Six Days Seven Nights* unless you count *K-19* which a lot of people do. So I was looking for a comedy and this idea came along.' The pair play Los Angeles cops who attempt to investigate a murder in the LA rap community while pursuing their off-duty ambitions to become a real estate broker and an actor.

A comedy, but not a buddy movie. 'These two characters are not buddies,' Ford said. 'They're guys who work together, who don't understand each other at all. I thought, that pretty much was reflected in our relationship, and I didn't try to disturb it.'

Hartnett confirms that Ford seemed to enjoy keeping him on edge during shooting. 'Over the course of the film we had our ups and downs,' says Hartnett. 'Harrison has this dry sense of humor, and he's very sarcastic. He's an intimidating guy.'

Following a somewhat awkward first meeting between the two at a Los Angeles deli, which left the awestruck Hartnett, 24, nearly speechless, production on the film began in late autumn 2002 on the streets in and around Hollywood. 'Harrison tested me to the limit, so I hated him for a while,' recalls Hartnett.

'He gave me a lot of [expletive] about the choices that I made. 'That's not a cop haircut.' Things like that. Other than Brad Pitt in *The Devil's Own*, I think I'm really only the second young guy he's worked with in his career, so when I kind of came into his territory, that's when he started to throw his elbows out. He might be the nicest guy in the entire world to everybody else.'

The way Ford sees it, whatever tension existed only helped make the *Hollywood Homicide* characters more believable. 'I didn't actively initiate any trouble,' he says, 'but neither did I dress his wounds. I just leave it lay like Jesus flung it. These two guys are not buddies. I did nothing to disturb that. Or Josh's discomfort. Or his questioning of whether or not I thought he was adequate.'

As always, Ford insisted on doing all his own 'physical acting', scorning the use of stunt doubles. This gave co-star Isaiah Washington some pause of concern. 'He forced me to do a lot of my own stunts because he did them,' Washington said in February 2003 at a benefit concert he attended at Cal State University, Fullerton. 'We were in the scenes together. I didn't have a choice. I told Harrison ... "I really don't think we should be doing this. This is dangerous. We could die." He said to me, "I'll see you on the other side." He's not someone you take lightly. He really enjoys doing the work,' Washington added.

Hollywood Homicide opened on June 13, 2003 in the US, taking $11 million on its opening weekend, and on August 29 in the UK.

The Guardian wrote, 'Harrison is implausibly paired with the fresh-faced youngster KC Calden, played by handsome young Josh Hartnett, who has a wide-ranging ability to be bad in comedy, drama and action.'

The New York Times seemed to like Ford's performance a lot better saying, 'He slips into the role as if it were a pair of well-worn loafers, the left inherited from Peter Falk, the right from Clint Eastwood, and then proceeds, with wry nonchalance, to tap-dance, shuffle and pirouette through his loosest, wittiest performance in years. It has been a long time since his gift for comedy – evident in the first *Star Wars* and Indiana Jones pictures, and also in Mike Nichols's *Working Girl* – has peeked out from behind that clenched, morose action-hero face. Mr Ford can be as gruff, decisive or brave as a given dramatic situation demands, but he is also sarcastic, foolish and, in his laconic, leathery way, downright silly.'

The San Franisco Chronicle said, 'As an actor, Ford has always understood himself well, and he uses himself here generously and without vanity. His Detective Gavilan represents savaged 21st century manhood at its bleakest, and it's a treat to see his sense of absurdist humor and comic grace in the role. He's abandoned but not wacky. Like Humphrey Bogart, Ford looks stern in repose but silly and almost demented when he smiles. Unlike Bogart, Ford is able to use this tendency, and modulate it, for maximum comic effect.'

Granted, *Hollywood Homicide* isn't the best thing Ford has ever done, but I thought it passed the time in an entertaining way. The unlikely teaming of Ford and Hartnett works quite well, and Ford seems to be enjoying mocking his own action star persona with some genuinely funny comedy turns which lift it – only slightly – above the usual Hollywood cop fair we've had to sit though over the last few years. It's not *Rush Hour* or even *Lethal Weapon 3* but it works well enough on its own undemanding terms.

Ford's 2003 consolation for the lukewarm reviews for *Hollywood Homicide* was getting his own star on the Hollywood Walk of Fame in May. 'There was a silent screen star in the Twenties whose name was Harrison Ford,' said Harrison Ford, 'and when I first came to Hollywood thirty five years ago, there was a star out in front of Franks with my name on it, but I never even thought about getting a star because I figured that most people figured for the last twenty years or so that that was my star. So, I wasn't all that worried about it. So, I was kind of surprised that they would do this, and happily, it's on the occasion of the opening of my latest film. So, that helps promote the film and I'm grateful for that opportunity. I'm near the Kodak Theater if you want to walk on me.'

The original Harrison Ford's star is still there, outside Musso and Frank's.

A QUICK ASIDE

Just before embarking on his next Hollywood project, Ford managed to find time to appear in a small-budget drama/documentary about snowboarding, *Water to Wine* (2004). Ford only agreed to appear in the film as 'Jethro the Bus Driver' as his son Malcolm played one of the snowboarders in the movie.

LO-TECH THRILLER

Ford's next project *Firewall* was a hi-tech thriller that put him back in the familiar territory of a family man battling the bad guys to protect his wife and kids. Cast opposite Ford as the endangered spouse was Virginia Madsen, who returned to the public's attention in the Oscar-nominated *Sideways*.

It was Ford himself who contacted Madsen to see if she was interested in being in *Firewall*. 'As a member of the team I was nominated to call her and encourage her to commit. I left a message on her answering machine. It was a very typical professional call. We were anxious to have her join us. We had sent the script and we hadn't heard. She was at a moment when she getting likely as many offers as she's ever had in her life.'

Madsen thought at first some one was playing a joke on her. 'I thought that someone was pulling my leg because I got the Oscar nomination and I had wanted to do the Harrison Ford movie, and I thought it was going to another actress. So first I was like, 'That's not funny!' and I was real blasé 'Hi, it's Virginia Madsen, Harrison.' Then it began to dawn on me that it's him. You can't imitate him, and as soon as he said, 'Well, I think that you would make a very good wife for me.' I was like, 'So do I!''

Despite having been around major stars for over twenty years, Madsen was still a little awed by Ford. 'And he looks like he does on-screen. A lot of actors don't – they're smaller. Or they're not bathed or something. Or they don't communicate well. But Harrison walks in … and he looks like that guy. So I just spent a lot of time just looking at him, going, "Well, there he is. Love to watch him go."'

Madsen took on the role of on-set mother hen to the child actors. 'I was always scolding people for swearing. It's a very adult environment on any movie set. You've got one or two kids in the midst of all these big guys and there's off-colour humour … and I'm like "Shh … stop that! Language!" And I was always scolding them, just because I felt like these two kids were not like show business kids. They weren't precocious yet and they've worked a lot, but they've got really good parents. And I responded to the fact that they weren't jaded. They were still innocent. I guess I didn't want showbiz to invade them. And Harrison was very protective, too.'

When asked about his protectiveness, Ford deadpanned, 'What the fuck is she talking about?' then broke up laughing. He then continued, 'No, I have children, and I respect that, and I respect their innocence. But these are not innocent children; these are highly trained professional actors in little bodies. Both of them are remarkably gifted young actors, and it's just a joy to watch them.'

When asked about the tough-looking fight sequences in *Firewall*, Harrison Ford was his usual deprecatory self. 'It's acting. It's smoke and mirrors. It's choreography. It's understanding the physics of a fight scene. It's breaking it down into manageable pieces and placing the camera in the right place to reflect the energy of a fight scene. It's articulating it with a beginning, middle and an end and it's a short story, that fight scene, in a way. And you have to make sure that there is story in it. Otherwise it becomes a mush of the action.'

His co-star Paul Bettany took a different view. 'He's a tough son of a bitch. I threw that bastard through a window seven times and not only did he get up and get thrown again, he rebuilt the window in between. I hit that bloke. I really wound up on him one time because he wanted to feel the punch, and I was pulling it and he had a pad on. He wanted to be able to react to it and so he asked for a bit more and a bit more and a bit more, and finally I let loose on him and he said, 'That's it.' It's quite humiliating. I've given Harrison Ford my best shot and he got right back up.'

Firewall opened on February 10, 2006 in the US, taking in $13.5 million on its opening weekend and a total of $48.7 million in domestic rentals, and on March 31 in the UK.

Variety was cool towards the film, saying, 'Despite its preoccupation with technology, *Firewall* really wants to be about heart – about an average guy rising to the challenge in order to protect his family. While Ford can achieve that posture in his sleep, he's left to do so in a vehicle that the average filmgoer will be more eager to hack out of than into.'

The Guardian liked the film better and wrote, 'Harrison Ford shows that at 63, he still has the chops to play leading male – more or less – and for my money he carries it off in this enjoyable and decently crafted Hitchcockian thriller, with *Wimbledon* director Richard Loncraine behind the camera.' Another critic who's evidently never seen a Hitchcock movie ...

The Los Angeles Times thought the film was a 'reasonable facsimile of a successful thriller' and added, 'As for the always empathetic Ford, he starts the film looking vaguely weary and ends up increasingly exasperated, irritated and distraught. This is largely due to the multiple perils Joe Forte's script places him in, but it's hard not to wonder if the film itself didn't start to get on his nerves.'

The *San Francisco Chronicle* liked the film well enough, calling it 'a reasonably solid B movie' but thought, 'it's enough of a leap of faith to believe that Ford, at 63, could keep up with a juicy younger wife (Virginia Madsen) much less with the young, sleek, borderline-psycho criminal mastermind, played by Paul Bettany.'

Firewall wasn't one of Ford's best, by a long way. You have to wonder what Ford saw in a story that had been done better before. The granddaddy of the family-held-hostage-by-criminals movies is *The Desperate Hours*, William Wyler's 1955 shocker in which three escaped gangsters, played with grim ruthlessness by Humphrey Bogart, Dewey Martin and Robert Middleton, invade the home of mild-mannered shop manager Frederic March and terrorise his clean-cut suburban family. What made the film controversial at the time was the idea of criminal lowlifes holding sway in a decent neighbourhood. What garnered the film critical acclaim was the fact that it concentrated on the drama of the interplay between the regular folk and the killers holding them at gunpoint. *Firewall* was unable to score in either of these departments. The idea of gangsters targeting an ordinary family is just too familiar from the news bulletins these days and *Firewall* effectively dodges any opportunities for real drama but taking the action movie route, so it gets bogged down in how Ford is going to beat the bad guys instead of exploring the characters. By the end of the film I didn't feel I had learned anything about Jack Stanfield, his wife Beth or any of the thugs led by Bill Cox. To his credit, Ford isn't coy in offering opinions about either of his last two projects. 'Once in a while, you take shots on things,' says Ford ruefully, 'and it doesn't work out. You might well accuse *Hollywood Homicide* of a certain lack of ambition. But I don't think *Firewall* suffers from a lack of ambition. It just suffers from failure to get itself together and be as interesting as it might have been.'

END OF A DYNASTY

There was a devastating turn of events for Harrison Ford during the filming of *Firewall*, when his manager of 30 years, Patricia McQueeny died in hospital on September 4, 2005 after a brief illness. She was 77.

McQueeney was born Patricia Noonan in Bridgeport Connecticut in 1927, married actor Robert McQueeny in 1944 and moved to New York, where their three children were born. After 12 years, the marriage failed and McQueeney began work as a model, under the name of Patricia Scott, and then moved into television. Towards the end of the 1950s, she worked on the *Today* program as co-host to Dave Garroway. In 1964, she relocated to Los Angeles, working in tv commercials. She joined Fred Roos and Gary Marshall at Compass Management where she got her first taste of talent management. After leaving Compass, McQueeney set up on her own and began to look after a small but select band of Hollywood actors that included Cindy Williams, Candy Clark, Mackenzie Phillips, Charlie Martin

Smith, Teri Garr and Frederic Forrest.

Her first big success was when many of the actors on her books landed roles in George Lucas' smash-hit *American Graffiti*, but as Harrison Ford's career picked up speed, McQueeney eventually concentrated exclusively on Ford's career.

BEYOND THE FIREWALL?

For a time, Ford's next scheduled project after *Firewall* was to be a picture with the working title of *Godspeed*, to be produced by *Titanic* director James Cameron's Lightstorm production company. The movie was to be a thriller set in deep space, scripted by Ryne Douglas Pearson and produced by Cameron, Rae Sanchini and Jon Landau. However, both this and the Beacon Communications/Warner Bros production *The Wrong Element* that Ford had also committed to star in, seemed to vanish from the production schedules and have apparently stalled. Ford confirmed this when interviewed in Australia during the early part of 2006. '*Godspeed* is gone, that was a space project with James Cameron.'

Next up was to be a period thriller about the hunt for John Wilkes Booth, the assassin of Abraham Lincoln. 'That would seem to be next,' allowed Ford. In it, Ford was to play Lt Colonel Everton Conger, who was in command of the troops that tracked down Booth. On April 26, 1865, Conger had Booth trapped in a barn and ordered the structure fired to drive Booth out. Sgt Boston Corbett shot Booth in the neck and killed him and Conger took possession of Booth's personal effects which, legend has it, included a diary that was never seen again. Conger's reward for the successful end to his mission was $15,000. *Manhunt* was scheduled for release in the summer of 2007. But for whatever reason, the movie was shelved and Ford withdrew from the production, reportedly because of scheduling conflicts with the fourth Indiana Jones film. However, some reports have it that *Manhunt* is merely postponed, rather than cancelled.

The next project Ford was associated with was *Battle for Fallujah*. Produced by Michael Shamberg, whose projects have included *Word Trade Centre* and *Garden State*, the movie is based on a controversial book by Bing West about the US Marine mission to free the captured American Blackwater contractors, who were later executed, their bodies burned and hung from a bridge before television cameras. Understandably, there has been some furore – particularly among fans – about Ford's plans to play General Jim Mattis who led the mission. At the time of writing, this was still listed at imdb.com as being 'in production', with a release date of 2009, though Harrison Ford's name was no longer attached to the project.

Then there was *Crossing Over* and, of course, *Indiana Jones and the Kingdom of the Crystal Skull* ...

CHAPTER 14

HARRISON FORD: BACK TO BASICS

From there to here and back again

'I hadn't worn the Indiana Jones costume for 18 years,
but early in the production process the costume was sent
to my house so I could try it on … and it fit like a glove.'
Harrison Ford

It was always inevitable, despite all the denials over the years, that there would be a fourth Indy film. We all knew it. It was just a matter of when. Then finally, almost out of the blue, it was announced. *Indiana Jones and the Kingdom of the Crystal Skull* was finished and would be released 22 May 2008.

The genesis of the script had been a long, drawn-out process with many stumbles along the way. Just before Lucas, Spielberg and Ford committed to make *Indiana Jones and the Last Crusade*, Chris Columbus, writer of *Gremlins* and later director of the Harry Potter franchise, had been engaged to create a screenplay for *Indiana Jones III*. The storyline he came up with involved the Monkey King of Chinese legends and was reportedly an enjoyable, humorous romp. But in the end, the team decided that they didn't want to spend four months filming in the African jungles and the Columbus script was shelved. A different story for the third Indy film was written by Jeffrey Boam based on the Quest for the Grail idea that Lucas had pushed so strongly for.

Franchise director Steven Spielberg had ended the third Indy film with a visual closure for the stories, tying up the first three films into a self-contained trilogy. 'I shot Indiana Jones riding a horse into the sunset because I thought that brought the curtain down on the story,' said Spielberg. Yet as early as 1992 Lucas had been working on ideas for another Indy adventure, though no agreement between the Lucas, Spielberg and Ford had been reached.

It was Ford himself who finally pushed for another instalment. 'Harrison presented me with the Best Picture Oscar for *Schindler's List* in 1994, and when we went backstage, he said he was ready to make another Indiana Jones movie.'

'It had to be right,' said Spielberg. 'I wanted to recapture the magic that we were able to achieve in three movies in the '80s. I wasn't trying to improve on Indiana Jones; I was just trying to reanimate the character. My goal was to make this movie a blood relative of the first three.'

SO MANY SCRIPTS

At the same time, another script, with the working title *Indiana Jones and the Saucer Men from Mars* was under development by Jeb Stuart, writer of *Die Hard* and *Another 48 Hrs*. This story had Indy on a quest for an alien cylinder covered in strange symbols and featured army ants, a fight on a rocket sled and Indiana surviving a nuclear explosion in a fridge. The climactic set-piece is a battle between the US military and flying saucers. But it was Ford who wasn't keen on the flying saucer angle and, reportedly, Spielberg resisted this idea too.

So, a draft of a tale involving a quest for a crystal skull was produced by Boam in 1995.

Then M. Night Shyamalan was hired to write another draft, but ran into trouble because Lucas' attention seemed to be focussed on the *Star Wars* prequels and quit the project. There were reports that Stephen Gaghan, who went on to write *Traffic* and *Syriana*, and Tom Stoppard (who'd contributed some dialogue to *Last Crusade*) were invited to write drafts, but these efforts came to nothing.

Work on *Indy IV* progressed little after that and it seemed as if the three main players had lost interest in bringing the world-weary adventurer back to life.

In the meantime, the earlier Columbus script turned up on the internet and many speculated at the time that it would be the basis for the fourth movie.

Then in 2002, Frank Darabont, who'd adapted *The Shawshank Redemption* and scripted episodes of *The Young Indiana Jones Chronicles* tv series, was hired to write a screenplay. Working closely with Steven Spielberg, his story was set in the 1950s and brought back the characters of Marion Ravenwood and Willie Scott. Spielberg was satisfied with the result and took it to Lucas for approval, but George didn't like it and rejected it.

'Steven was very, very happy with the script and said it was the best draft of anything since *Raiders of the Lost Ark*,' Darabont told the chud.com website in 2006. 'That's really high praise and gave me a real sense of accomplishment, especially when you love the material you're working on as much as I love the Indiana Jones films. And then you have George Lucas read it and say, 'Yeah, I don't think so, I don't like it.' And then he resets it to zero when Spielberg is ready to shoot it that coming year, [which] is a real kick to the nuts. You can only waste so much time and so many years of your life on experiences like that, you can only get so emotionally invested and have the rug pulled out from under you before you say enough of that.'

Two years later, Jeff Nathanson who'd written the *Rush Hour* sequels and *Catch Me If You Can*, came on board to do a version of the script. After a year's work, the scripting chores were then taken up by David Koepp, writer of *Jurassic Park*, *Mission: Impossible* and *Spider-Man*. A further two years of work took Koepp up to the end of 2006, when Lucas announced that the script was ready and that filming would commence during 2007. Lucasfilm seemed to be keeping its options open and several titles were registered with the Motion Pictures Association of America, including 'Indiana Jones and the Destroyer of Worlds', '… and the Fourth Corner of the Earth', '… and the City of Gods' (the title of Frank Darabont's script), '… and the Lost City of Gold', and even, tantalisingly, '… the Quest for the Covenant'.

Though it might seem like it was just Lucas and Spielberg shepherding the *Indy IV* script to completion, there was another player to be satisfied. 'George works on the germination of the idea,' Ford explained to cinematical.com at the 2008 Cannes Film Festival. 'He and Steven work with a writer they have agreed on, there are adjustments to be made – by the way, these guys, they're a little busy, they do other things, other than Indiana Jones movies – so it's not a full-time job to get one of these scripts together. But when it's ready, and we all agree, when they do their process, it comes to me, and I have my little say about it, and the recipe is adjusted. It's a meal for three, so maybe a touch more of this or a little too much salt … we work it all out amongst us until we're all confident that we have something of the quality that we've done in the past.'

Of course there was the question of 'the past' meaning it was 20 years having passed since Indy was last on screen. So the script would inevitably have to deal with Indy – and Ford – being two decades older. 'Age has its virtues and it has its disadvantages, and I think we embrace the reality of the passage of twenty years of time. We're not coy about it, you know, constantly commenting on it, but the guy is twenty years older.'

Not that Ford is going to let a little thing like being 64 slow him down. To prepare for filming, he undertook a strict low-carb, high-protein diet of fish and vegetables and trained three hours a day under the watchful eye of personal trainer Jamie Milnes, who's worked with Ford since *Hollywood Homicide*. The regimen was tailored to Ford's existing level of fitness and the fact that lack of time was a big constraint. 'I have set work for Harrison to do each session and when it's done he leaves, whether it's 20, 30 or 50 minutes,' said Milnes. 'We put the emphasis on movements that integrate the whole body in multiple planes of motion with high athletic demand. This gives us the most bang for the buck, especially when he is pressed for time. This type of training does, however, require a high level of fitness.'

As some measure of the level of fitness Ford has maintained over the years, Ford cited trying on the Indy outfit in almost two decades. 'I hadn't worn the Indiana Jones costume for 18 years,' he told *E! Behind the Scenes*, 'but early in the production process the costume was sent to my house so I could try it on so we could see where we'd have to change its size. And I put it on and … it fit like a glove. I felt really comfortable and ready to go.'

THE OTHER PLAYERS

'I'd never actually met Harrison before the first day of shooting,' said Cate Blanchett, cast as the villain Dr Irena Spalko. 'My first encounter with him as an audience member was as this character, when I saw the Raiders films. It seemed perfectly right that the first time I should meet him, he'd be in the Indy costume.'

Kingdom of the Crystal Skull also saw the return of Marion Ravenwood, played by Ford's co-star from *Raiders of the Lost Ark*, Karen Allen. 'I was delighted that Karen could rejoin us,' said Ford at Cannes. 'She's the original relationship for Indiana Jones. We know Indiana Jones through the character that Karen played in the original film, and we learn more about him.'

Karen Allen seemed to slip easily back into character. 'Well, they have a history even before the film begins,' said Allen. 'We know that they've known each other, which comes forward right away, when she socks him in the jaw, we know that there's some history that never gets filled in, but they go back a long way. But it felt very seamless. When I walked on the set to do the camera test in Los Angeles, and Harrison knocked on my door, and I opened the door, and suddenly, we're standing there, talking to each other as though weeks had gone by. It just felt very easy to me.'

Another pivotal character in the film is Indy's new teenage sidekick played, with more than a tip of the peaked cap to Brando's moody and magnificent turn in *The Wild One* (1950), by Shia laBeouf. Certainly Karen Allen valued his contribution. 'Shia's just a delight, as far as I'm concerned. He's very, very funny and – I don't know how much I can describe particular scenes in the film – but there's some moments where Shia has some quite challenging tasks he had to perform in the film, and there's just some very, very, very funny, wonderful moments with Shia where he was just above and beyond the call of duty. He's an incredibly talented young actor, I find him very eloquent as an actor. With his face, he says a lot ... he's remarkable. I'm really very impressed with him, and I had an awfully good time with him.'

Shia LaBeouf signed on for the film in April 2007, without even reading the script, so excited was he about being asked to do an Indy film. To prepare for his role, LeBeouf repeatedly watched the previous three Indiana Jones films and undertook a training regimen to gain fifteen pounds of muscle. (Interestingly, it was LaBeouf who first spoke the film's official title publicly, at the 2007 MTV Music Awards – which surely must have been sanctioned by Lucasfilm.)

The fourth member of the Jones 'family' for this adventure was respected British actor John Hurt. As the perpetually bewildered Professor Harold Oxley, he didn't have a great deal to do apart from mutter cryptic phrases from Milton and T. S. Eliot that would provide the clues needed to get Indy's party to the City of Gold. But unlike LaBeouff, Hurt wanted to read the script before he signed on. He had previously heard about actors who signed on to a Steven Spielberg film before reading the script, since 'Spielberg – you know, *God* – was doing it!' but Hurt felt, 'I need to have a little bit of previous knowledge even if God is doing it.' So the filmmakers sent a courier with the script from Los Angeles over to London, left the script with Hurt at three in the afternoon, reclaimed it at eight that evening and flew it back the following day.

THE SHOOTING STARTS

Unlike the previous Indiana Jones films, which travelled the world in pursuit of the most exotic locations, Spielberg tried to confine most of the shooting to the United States, saying he did not want to be away from his family for an extended period. Principle photography began on June 18, 2007 at Deming, New Mexico. Then, an extensive chase scene set at Indiana Jones's fictional Marshall College was filmed between June 28 and July 7 at Yale University in New Haven, Connecticut (where Spielberg's son Theo was studying).

The first unit then moved on to Hilo, Hawaii which stood in for the Peruvian jungles until August. *Indiana Jones and the Kingdom of the Crystal Skull* was the biggest film shot in Hawaii since *Waterworld*, and has contributed an estimated $22 to $45 million to the local economy. Because of an approaching hurricane, Spielberg was unable to shoot a fight at a waterfall, so he sent the second unit to Brazil's and Argentina's Iguaçu Falls. This footage was digitally added into the main action, which was shot at the Universal backlot.

About half the film was scheduled to shoot on five sound stages at Los Angeles: Downey, Sony, Warner Bros, Paramount and Universal. Then filming moved to Chandler Field in Fresno, California, standing in for Mexico City International Airport, on October 11, 2007. After shooting some aerial shots of Chandler Airport and a DC-3 on the morning of October 12, 2007, filming wrapped. Although he originally found no need for re-shoots after viewing his first cut of the film, Spielberg decided to add an establishing shot, which was filmed on February 29, 2008 at Pasadena, California.

In the last 20 years, there have been many changes in the way films are made. Certainly the technology has changed beyond recognition. But, though both Lucas and Spielberg had been shooting their movies in digital format for some considerable time, Spielberg made the decision to shoot *Crystal Skull* on conventional 35mm movie cameras to re-capture the feel of the first three Indy movies. Cinematographer Douglas Slocombe had retired from film-making so Spielberg's regular cinematographer Janusz Kaminski studied Slocombe's techniques by watching the first three movies repeatedly until he could emulate Slocombe's shooting style.

The stunts, too, have changed. 'They have figured out new things in safety so myself and the stuntman can do more,' said Ford. 'For instance, when you see a car and a bus converging and we are in the middle on a motorcycle we are on a thin wire with a special harness ...' Although the filmmakers wanted to avoid relying as heavily on CGI as, say, the Star Wars prequels, digital processing was used to remove the safety wires from shot during post-production. In the end, there were around 450 effects shots in the movie.

However, not everything went as smoothly as it could have done. In one sequence, Ford was driving a military truck through a breakaway wall that was rigged to explode as the truck made contact. 'It was supposed to look like the car was causing the wall to fly through the air and that I was driving through it, but it came just a millisecond before I went through ... And I looked down and right next to me on the seat there's this big-assed box of explosives that had survived. If it had gone off, it would have caused a stitchable,' by which Ford means a wound that would have required surgical stitching, something he's no stranger to. 'I didn't get hurt on this one at all. I've got war wounds but they are all athletic or stupid, not because of a heroic willingness to endure pain or take risks.'

Of course, the people involved in the Indy films have been on the team for over 20 years, too. This led to some marked differences, as well as similarities, for Karen Allen between working on *Raiders* and on *Crystal Skull*. 'When we made *Raiders of the Lost Ark*, Steven was working with a lot of people for the first time, and my impression coming onto this set in the very beginning was, they have an amazing kind of team. Janusz Kaminski and all the people that Steven works with, it just felt so seamless, just like a well-oiled team of people, so there was something in that that felt really great to me, you know. They almost don't even have to speak; they make hand signs to each other across the room and people are moving and doing things, and that felt kind of different, because I remember Doug Slocombe, who was doing the first one ... everybody was kinda trying to learn everybody's language. One thing that was so extraordinary to me coming onto a film like this for the first time, in London at Elstree [Studios] when we were shooting *Raiders*, was just the extraordinary craft of the building of the sets, which just blew my mind. I'd never seen anything like that before, and I have to say that the craft of the sets in this film also blew my mind, almost on a daily basis. You'd walk into these sets that were being built, and I felt just like a little kid a lot of times. It was just like, "Wow! How'd they do this, and aren't we lucky to be working on these sets?"'

After such a long wait, with many of the teenagers who had thrilled to the first three Indiana Jones adventures taking their own teenagers to see *Kingdom of the Crystal Skull*, it was inevitable that the fourth film would be a resounding financial success. Yet the critical reception was oddly muted.

The Guardian's Peter Bradshaw wasn't hugely impressed. Seeing the film at Cannes, he commented, 'despite the genuine excitement, and one blinding flash of the old genius, this new Indy film looks like it's going through the motions.' Sadly, the flash of genius Bradshaw is referring to is the daft scene with the atomic bomb and the fridge, so that's a thumbs-down, then.

Rolling Stone made no bones about its feelings. '*Crystal Skull* is hit-and-miss like the clunky 1984 sequel, *Indiana Jones and the Temple of Doom*. And instead of the elegiac tone that lifted 1989's presumptive valedictory, *Indiana Jones and the Last Crusade*, director Steven Spielberg and producer George Lucas have gotten sillier.'

Said Ken Turan of the *LA Times*, 'it was inevitable that this film was going to fall within a very narrow range in terms of quality. It was either going to be a worse or better-than-average Indiana Jones film.'

Roger Ebert of the *Chicago Sun-Times* allowed that, 'if you liked the other Indiana Jones movies, you will like this one, and if you did not, there is no talking to you.'

I liked *Indiana Jones and the Kingdom of the Crystal Skull* a lot. If I had to rank it, I'd put it joint second, equal with *Last Crusade* behind *Raiders*. Ford is magnificent. He *owns* the role of Indy. It's not just Ford playing himself, because he doesn't do that. And it's not Ford acting the part of Indy. It goes into a territory beyond that, where he takes on the persona of Indy and completely suspends our disbelief. It is an extraordinary performance and it's a shame he'll probably not be properly recognised for that. The set-pieces are every bit as thrilling as you might fairly expect from an Indiana Jones adventure and Blanchett's turn as the evil Dr Spalko is note-perfect, though her accent veers towards pantomime at times. And then there are some odd lapses in logic.

The first howler I spotted was when Indy is trying to find the artefact for the Russians in the warehouse during the opening scenes of the film. Indy demands cartridges from his captors, rakes out the gunpowder – don't bullets have cordite rather than gunpowder? – and flings it in the air so the magnetism emitted by the artefact can sweep the cloud of powder in the appropriate direction. But ask any ten-year old boy if gunpowder is magnetic. Go on ... see? Of course it isn't. Then there's the small matter of surviving an atomic blast by hiding in a fridge ... suspension of disbelief is one thing, but that was downright silly. Don't try this at home, children.

But despite my two minor reservations, I thought *Crystal Skull* made splendid fist of bringing back Indie for a new generation of movie-goers, many of whom genuinely wouldn't have seen any of the earlier Indie films.

WHAT NEXT?

Since *Indiana Jones and the Kingdom of the Crystal Skull* we've also seen Harrison Ford in *Crossing Over*, actually filmed before the Indy movie, where he is just one of a larger ensemble cast rather than the outright focus of the story and in 2009 he was set to appear in the worthy-sounding drama *Crowley*, about a couple's desperate search to find a cure for their children's rare genetic disorder. That project underwent a title change and was to emerge as *Extraordinary Measures*. But, almost expectedly, George Lucas has hinted in interviews that he is open to the idea of a fifth Indiana Jones film ...

CHAPTER 15

HARRISON FORD: LIFE AFTER INDY

From Action to Acting

'Am I grumpy? I might be. But I think maybe sometimes it's misinterpreted. I've always been an independent son of a bitch. So, if I'm grumpy, then call me grumpy. I'm all right with that.' Harrison Ford

If I'd been Harrison Ford just coming off the gruelling shoot for *Indiana Jones and the Kingdom of the Crystal Skull*, I'd have been looking to take a year off, or at least choose a project that wouldn't involve quite as much running, jumping and falling down. And at first glance, it looks like his next-released project fit that bill exactly. Yet the announcement that Ford was signed to head the cast of *Crossing Over* came in April 2007, over a year before principal photography on *Indiana Jones 4* began. Perhaps even more surprisingly, the filming of *Crossing Over* also happened in 2007, so although it was released after Indy, *Crossing Over* was actually filmed first. The delay in release was due to some wrangling between director Wayne Kramer and Executive Producer Harvey Weinstein over how the final cut of the movie should look.

The project originated with Kramer as early as 2002. 'I wanted to show how the system works from the law enforcement side and from the side of the immigrants,' said Kramer. 'It's not black and white, or us versus them. It's not people trying to invade our border and do us harm. These are people just like you and me, looking for a better life. Some are educated, some aren't. Some have come for refugee status, some for economic gain. Some want to live in a country with freedom of speech, and some just want to get into the entertainment industry!'

Kramer himself arrived in the US from South Africa in 1986 and in 2000 took the oath of US citizenship. 'It was a very emotional experience for me. The very day I became eligible for naturalization, I had my forms in the mail. First you have to go for an interview and after you pass that, they set an oath-taking ceremony date for you a couple months later. You wait for that day, and it is a crossing over. And it's transcendent because you now feel like you have all the rights of the society.'

Crossing Over sets out to cover the issue of immigration to the US using the same kind of format as *Traffic* or perhaps *Crash*. Though many reviewers criticised the movie precisely for taking that approach, including Roger Ebert of the *Chicago Sun-Times*, *Rolling Stone*'s Peter Travers and David Edwards of the UK's *Daily Mirror*, it's a template that works well given the complex and many-facetted subject matter the filmmakers are trying to present to an audience in a two-hour time slot.

So although there is a large and ethnically diverse cast, each group with their own story to tell, it's Harrison Ford's character that holds the narrative together. Kramer tells his story from the point of view of a veteran ICE office Max Brogan, a man who's worked for the system for decades and is himself from immigrant stock. 'I needed someone who could make the audience, male and female, feel this was a decent guy caught up in a tough job,' said Kramer. 'Harrison Ford is obviously an American icon with the gravitas of a tough leading man like William Holden or Robert Mitchum.'

Ford saw his character as less of an elder statesman, bringing gravitas to the role, and more as a guy who hasn't been able to keep up with a changing world. 'Max is a bit burnt out,' said Harrison Ford in a post-filming interview, 'and has come to the point where he doesn't quite fit in anymore. He's a little less strict with the rules than some of the newer agents, and it puts him in conflict with people at work.'

The other attraction of the part was that Ford wouldn't be carrying the whole movie on his shoulders, making it a bit of an easier job than the daunting shoot for Indiana Jones which was already on Ford's radar at this point. 'I became interested in doing something where it was an ensemble cast, where I didn't feel responsible for the screenplay or the overall success of the project,' said Ford. 'I just showed up and I did my work, which I enjoyed quite a bit.'

Cliff Curtis plays Brogan's ICE partner, agent Hamid Baraheri, a naturalised US citizen of Iranian parentage. 'Harrison definitely has an iconic presence, but he's a lot more fun in person than you'd ever guess. With a twinkle in his eye, he deconstructs his own star status.'

Hamid's sister Zahara, born in the US and completely assimilated into that society, is played by Melody Khazae, sporting a mildly gothy look, which is heartily disapproved of by the character's family. For Khazae, the film set had a bit of a party atmosphere, what with all the other actors of Iranian descent. 'It was like a real Persian party – everything extravagant, great food and music, just the way we do it,' said the actress. 'I felt like I was going to an aunt's house and getting the evil eye for looking like I did.'

British-born Alice Eve plays Claire Shepherd, an Australian actress trying to win US citizenship. Ray Liotta plays the sleazy Green Card adjudicator who sees in Claire the opportunity for some old-fashioned sexual exploitation. Though Alice didn't do many scenes with Ford, she was very aware of his presence on-set. 'Harrison Ford is so cool ... I guess you can do that if you've been a carpenter. He just walks around, he's easy, you don't feel like he's a star, you don't feel like he's demanding anything. And he's still hot.'

Ironically, the reality of casting so many actors of non-US origin caused a very real set of immigration headaches for the filmmakers. 'We had to contend with getting foreign actors over to LA and ensure that they had the right visas to enter the country and work on our film. Anyone who applies for a visa is suddenly thrown into a bureaucratic nightmare in America,' Kramer explains.

The subject matter of *Crossing Over* was always going to be contentious. As soon as you represent any one cultural group on the Hollywood screen, there a queue of critics lining up to decry the portrayal for whatever reason fits their agenda best. An entire sub-plot about an honour killing within the Iranian community in the film was chopped about and the dialogue was rewritten to turn the incident into a 'teaching a lesson' scenario that gets 'out of hand'. Nowhere on the soundtrack now is the phrase 'honour killing' uttered. The reasons given for this pre-emptive censorship on the part of the producers vary, but it meant that every frame with actor Sean Penn was excised from the film. Some say Penn wanted to be removed from the film after Iranian-American groups complained about the portrayal of such an incident in the film. Penn himself said his decision to withdraw his work from the project was a creative one and Executive Producer Harvey Weinstein said that it was Penn's agent that demanded his client's scenes be cut. There's evidence of further tampering. Director Kramer delivered a finished print of 140 minutes. At Weinstein's direction, the studio then cut that down to 113 minutes, which is a lot of screentime by anyone's stopwatch.

Kramer was, understandably, incensed by this and was moved to post on the HighDefDirect.com forum, 'The theatrical cut of the film is NOT my film. Harvey Weinstein (in collusion with other parties) cut out about twenty plus minutes of my film and restructured everything. There's an entire Sean Penn framing device missing, including a great Alice Braga performance. It plays like a *Twilight Zone* episode on the US/Mexico border and connects to a major storyline within the film. The Penn storyline, in fact, was the very material that my 1995 short film was based on. The sex scenes in *Crossing Over* were also eviscerated (as well as the sexual dialogue toned way down) and the resolution to the Jim Sturgess/Alice Eve storyline was cut out. I can't really get into the politics of why the Sean Penn scenes were removed – a lot has already been written about it on the internet, mostly accurate (it's completely absurd!), but the film I directed was far grittier and more textured that what was released – or should I say, barely released. If you lived outside of New York or LA, you didn't even know the film came out – and even if you lived in those cities, I'm not sure you knew about it either. I seem to have a shitty track record of getting decent distribution for my films. Lionsgate did fine with *The Cooler*, but it never expanded beyond a few hundred theaters. *Crossing Over*'s highest theater count was 42, I think. It was a really bad experience in post-production on that film and even now, Harvey Weinstein is cockblocking a Director's Cut on DVD. He screwed up the theatrical release and he still won't concede that he damaged the film and the perception of the film and won't agree to release the real film I made. I was really proud of the film I directed and I think there are great performances (even in the theatrical cut), but when you cut out all connective tissue and major plot points and take the edge off a gritty indie film, you're going to be left with a mediocre piece of work and it sucks because as a director it's almost impossible to remove your name. I only hope one day that we'll see a genuine Director's Cut on *Crossing Over*, because I think we made a really good film. It just wasn't released that way. I don't know whether there will be a Blu Ray release of the theatrical cut. I'm not on very good terms with the company and I won't be participating in any of their extras (so don't expect a director's commentary) until they agree to release a Director's Cut. But the truth is, I just don't think they give a shit over there. Please feel free to contact Weinstein Company and request a Director's Cut of *Crossing Over* – it will be worth it if you've enjoyed my previous films (even if you haven't).'

The film opened in just nine theatres in the United States on 1 March 2009 to decidedly lukewarm business taking just $77 thousand in its first weekend against an estimated budget of $25 million. By the end of the month, as Kramer says, its distribution peaked at 42 theatres – by contrast *Indiana Jones and the Kingdom of the Crystal Skull* opened on 4260 screens in the US alone. So it's fairly apparent that Harvey Weinstein's release strategy wasn't designed to maximise ticket sales. Though that was far from the movie's only problem. As it turns out, the theatrical release of *Crossing Over*, such as it was, was not all that well received by the critics either.

Roger Ebert of the *Chicago Sun-Times* was damning with his faint praise when he said, 'Harrison Ford supplies the strong central strand in the story, but sometimes it grows so implausibly melodramatic, we're distracted. Ashley Judd's character provides insights in the way our legal system handles immigration, and the Australian [sic] actress (Alice Eve) shows what she is willing to do for the venal official (Liotta), who happens to be Judd's husband.'

Rolling Stone was being kinder when their critic, Peter Travers, said, 'Ford brings a quiet intensity to Max Brogan, the immigration cop whose years on the job haven't hardened him to the plight of the illegals he busts in sweatshops and ass-kicks back to Mexico. His partner, Hamid Baraheri (a terrific Cliff Curtis), has a meltdown during a store robbery that results in a monologue about citizenship that would stop a lesser movie cold.'

Mike LaSalle of the *San Francisco Chronicle* also singled Ford out for praise when he wrote, '[Ford's] role is more that of a witness than a participant, but he lends integrity and truth to his role as a compassionate INS officer. Indeed there's more genuine conviction in Ford's face, more complexity, honesty and ability to incite compassion, than everything else in *Crossing Over* combined.'

Though not everyone agreed. 'Ford … chugs through *Crossing Over* looking displeased with the dialogue,' complained Michael Phillips of the *Chicago Tribune*.

And it looks like Scott Foundas writing in the *Village Voice* was able to recognise glimmers of Kramer's original intention when he said, '*Crossing Over* begins earnestly enough as an old-fashioned exercise in Stanley Kramerish consciousness-raising, with Ford wearing existential angst on his sleeve as a callous colleague reprimands him: "Jesus Christ, Brogan! Everything is a Goddamn humanitarian crisis with you!"'

However, overall critical reception of *Crossing Over* wasn't enthusiastic, which doubtless contributed to the movie's lacklustre performance at the US box-office.

I would very curious indeed to see Kramer's cut of the film, if only be allowed to make my own mind up, rather than having faceless studio executives do it for me. As it stands, I thought *Crossing Over* did a sterling job of telling a spectrum of stories around the subject of immigration to the United States. Comparisons with movies like *Crash* are, to say the least, tenuous. *Crossing Over* has neither the budget – nor, I suspect, the intention – to take on big budget blockbusters like *Traffic* on their own turf. Kramer's film is much more of an indie-style effort and, appears to be a heartfelt try at telling a human story around subject matter that the director knows from first-hand experience. Whether Kramer truly had the gravitas to pull it off will remain a mystery until we can get to see his original edit.

EXTRAORDINARY CRITICISM

If Harrison Ford thought he was leaving controversy behind with his next released project, *Extraordinary Measures*, he was wrong. In 2004, Ford had read an article in *The Wall Street Journal* about John Crowley, a father who was battling bureaucracy to find a cure, or at least a treatment, for his two young children, both of whom suffered from a rare wasting disease called Pompe Syndrome. With no hope in sight, Crowley set about forming a company, raising money and engaging specialists in the field to develop a treatment that would give hope to thousands of parents just like himself.

'I was in business with my production partners, Michael Shamberg, his partner, Stacey Sher, and Carla Shamberg, Michael's wife,' explains Ford, 'and we were looking for material to develop for movies that I could be in and we came across this material in *The Wall Street Journal*, read the follow-up book by Geeta Anand and thought that there was a germ of a good idea for a movie in there, something different to what I normally am involved in, and a chance to build an interesting part for myself in that story. We started to try and find a screenwriter that could capture what we were looking for and we hit upon Robert (Robert Nelson Jacobs) and he did two or possibly three drafts before we started. Well, I think there was a wonderful collaborative atmosphere involving Michael and all of the other production partners who have developed a couple of stories in the past that were stories of real humanity and people doing positive things – *Erin Brockovich*, *World Trade Center* being two of them. And so we went through the process, we found a script, we were satisfied with the script, we found Tom, and the rest is show business history.'

The part that Ford had developed for himself was Dr Robert Stonehill. Though based on a true story, Ford's character is really an amalgam of several scientists who were prominent in the quest for a treatment for Pompe.

There was always the danger that the project might be seen as an overblown, 'disease-of-the-week' daytime tv-movie, something Ford was wary of from the start. 'I think we're all against creating a polemic, a bully pulpit to proclaim our point of view about these things,' said Ford emphatically. 'I think we wanted to present the reality of the situation and let the audience decide for themselves. I think that's why we didn't take an easy swipe at the pharmaceutical industry. I think we portrayed it the way it really is. And, we wanted to concentrate on the kids and on the relationships, the human relationships, and not get into that level of detail on the rest of it.'

As Ford was credited as the Executive Producer – which is the title usually accorded to the person who came up with the idea for the project or in some way kick-started it – Ford was in a good position to get the film to come together the way he wanted it to. 'Oh, yeah, I'm Executive Producer here, so I was involved from the very beginning. It's a collaborative enterprise; I don't remember who came up with what, but I got to pick the music, and the pick-up truck ... I got to describe a character that I wanted to play. I was investing six years of my time in the development of this, and I felt that there was no sense in playing the conventional idea of what a scientist is. It wouldn't have been dramatically interesting for the audience. And it wouldn't have been interesting for me, as a character.'

He seemed pleased with the contribution Brendan Fraser made to the film. 'What Brendan brought, from the very first time we read through material together and when we talked about it, was an authenticity. He didn't attempt an imitation of John Crowley. He just reached into his own experience and his own emotions and understood, and because he understood and because he felt, he's had a lot of experience. He may downplay it but he's had a lot of opportunities and experience to work with good people in the past and he's learned how to do it really well. So, I had a great time working with him. It was fun.'

During its opening weekend, 24 January 2009, *Extraordinary Measures* gathered a fairly respectable $6 million on 2500 American screens. The following fortnight pulled in another $5 million. With an estimated budget of $31 million, the movie wasn't setting the film business alight, but was on track to make back some profit for its investors.

Needless to say, the critics jumped on the film's perceived 'worthiness' as it biggest liability. They weren't terribly forgiving of Ford's contribution to the movie, either.

Roger Ebert at the *Chicago Sun-Times* wrote that Ford's character, 'seems inspired more by Harrison Ford's image and range. He plays the doctor using only a few spare parts off the shelf. (1) He likes to crank up rock music while he works. (2) He doesn't return messages. (3) He's so feckless he accidentally hangs up on Crowley by pulling the phone off his desk. (4) He likes to drink beer from longneck bottles in a honky-tonk bar and flirt with the waitress. (5) "I'm a scientist, not a doctor," he says. He's not interested in Pompe patients, only the chemistry of the disease.'

Rene Rodriguez of the *Miami Herald*, on the other hand, quite liked Ford's performance. 'There is some fun to be had in watching Ford as a crabby professor – what Indiana Jones might have become if he had hung up his whip at 60. But Dr Stonehill, like everyone else in *Extraordinary Measures*, is a superficial sketch – a compendium of likes (fishing, classic rock) and dislikes (people, his ex-wife's cats) that never really digs into the intriguing man's life.'

Amy Biancolli of the *San Francisco Chronicle*, somewhat cynically I think, accused both Ford and Fraser of 'actorliness' in attempting to inject some drama. 'The movie pits Ford and Fraser in fantastic bouts of righteous screaming – growling, spitting, vein-popping,' she wrote. 'The histrionics are all quite actorly and convincing. Medical research might be dramatic as hell for those who do it, but hunched nerds in lab coats don't offer much excitement for average moviegoers. Better to toss in a few raw slabs of scenery-chewing to keep them awake.'

And interestingly, the British critics were a bit more forgiving in their comments. 'Harrison Ford is convincing as the difficult research scientist essential to the project,' wrote *The Observer*'s Philip French, 'and there are a few harsh observations about the roles of venture capitalists and their number-crunchers in the highly competitive bio-tech field.'

And *Reuters* allowed that, 'The best thing about the movie is Ford's effortless star performance as the curmudgeonly Stonehill. Although the conception of the eccentric genius doesn't break any new ground, Ford underplays masterfully.'

I think that last one got it about right. As he's gotten older, Ford's acting has gotten more subtle and understated. He's able to convey emotions and unspoken thoughts with just the slightest shift of expression. I don't know what film Ms Biancolli saw, but I don't think it was the same one I did.

RED SKY IN THE MORNING

After two fairly grim releases in a row, Harrison Ford would normally be looking for a comedy around this time. What he signed on for, in *Morning Glory*, was indeed exactly that, but also with something of value to say about how media-driven the world has become. It was that undercurrent that gave Ford something he could get behind. The first thing he saw in the script was, 'The quality of the writing, the wit, the intelligence of it all … and the opportunity to play something different to what I usually play. And a good film. I thought it was a really ambitious script.'

Having said that, Ford was also drawn to the project because on the other people involved. 'What also attracted to me to the role was I liked the people involved in the movie. JJ Abrams (the producer) told me he was developing a part for me and when I read it I thought, "Well done, JJ. It's a good opportunity for me". I also liked the work of (director) Roger Michell. Rachel McAdams and Diane Keaton are actors I also admire so there was no reason not to do the movie.' When pinned down, Ford revealed there was another reason to play the part of Mike Pomeroy. 'He's an ass. But, I could also see that the events of the film had an impact on him and he had an impact on Rachel's character, Becky. The emotional context that comes out of Mike and Becky's relationship is a bonus.'

But in most of the interviews Ford gave promoting *Morning Glory*, he was always able to find a space to squeeze in his own view of the news-cycle culture in the media.

'I regret – a bit – that we've become such a fragmented society,' said Ford to one reporter. 'We don't as a national community have a source of news that we all recognise as free of opinion. The news business has devolved to the point where we can each go to a news outlet that will repeat back to us the prejudices we come with. So that everybody has their own source of news. It's like religion or philosophy. It's not news. News used to be free of opinion and it used to be the pride of a newsman that he didn't bring his own opinion, but gave you the opportunity to think about what was happening, they reported the facts.' It might not be the forum to mention it, but I agree entirely with Harrison Ford on this point. Even the UK's respected BBC News seems to have become infected with the taint of tabloidism.

Ford's portrayal of grumpy news anchor Mike Pomeroy, currently slumming it on a morning television news show, gave him the opportunity to once more do something different from the action hero personae he's become known for. 'Am I grumpy?' asked Ford of *The Daily Telegraph*, then acknowledged, 'I might be. But I think maybe sometimes it's misinterpreted. I've always been an independent son of a bitch. So, if I'm grumpy, then call me grumpy. I'm all right with that.'

Morning Glory is about how new-girl news producer Becky Fuller (Rachel McAdams) is suddenly saddled with an aging news-anchor, Mike Pomeroy, who really doesn't want to be doing her ligh-hearted breakfast show on a New York television station. Ford's character is balanced off by the casting of Diane Keaton as his co-host. No stranger to comedy, Keaton has a track record of working with some of the best in the business, most notably Woody Allen. Ford has never worked with Keaton before this, which Ford puts down to the different circles they move in. 'We do different kinds of films. I describe her as being part of the intellectual branch of the service and I'm in the commando branch. You know, the jumping and falling down department.' When asked whether he had any preconceptions entering into a project with Keaton, he replied, 'I didn't really. I have always thought she was a wonderful actress and it was really fun to work with her. She really knew what she wanted to get out of her character in each scene and she was tenacious about getting it. I thought she was great to work with. She was inventive, spontaneous and always kept it fresh.'

Also in the supporting cast are Patrick Wilson as fellow producer Adam Bennett, the other side of Becky Fuller's under-written romance, and the always reliable Jeff Goldblum as Becky's boss at the IBS channel, who could also have been given more to do.

Morning Glory opened on 14 November 2010 in the US and on 21 January 2011 in the UK. American box-office business was encouraging with the film taking over $9 million during its opening weekend. To date the movie's taken $31 million in US ticket sales, which isn't too bad a performance given the film's estimated $41 million budget.

The critics were split over what kind of job Ford did in *Morning Glory*. 'I do wish, though, that Ford had found a more interesting attack on his bull-headed character,' grumbled Michael Phillips in the *Chicago Tribune*. 'His performance is built entirely on discomfort – the character's own, as well as the unease it generates in others. Ford lays it on so thickly, he keeps grinding the scenes to a halt.'

The Miami Herald's Rene Rodriguez wasn't much more complimentary, writing, 'This was a perfect opportunity for him to loosen up and have some much needed fun, but the actor seems to have grown listless and more reticent to emote with age. Like Pomeroy, he simply can't be bothered. There's no Han Solo left in him; there's just grumpy old man.'

Uncharacteristically, Roger Ebert, writing for *The Chicago Sun-Times*, said, 'Ford is not a demonstrative actor. Sometimes he can barely rouse himself to growl. Here he's kind of inspired. When he's anchoring with Keaton, his double takes are flawless. When they get into a duel of who says "bye" last, they do it with impeccable timing. Ford doesn't venture beyond his usual acting range, but within it he creates a character with a reluctantly human inside.'

And *USA Today*'s Scott Bowles, thought that Ford was 'dandy as a beleaguered newsman watching his profession circle the drain. He's an actor who has lost range over the years, but his sneer and grimace work here. He manages three smiles and one laugh through the entirety of the film. But, given his new boss, the irritation is reasonable.'

For my money, *Morning Glory* was a pretty good comedy with some genuinely funny moments. Ford delivered an excellent performance as the dinosaur news journalist who appears to have outlived his usefulness, bringing just the right note of disillusionment to the character of Mike Pomeroy. And Rachel McAdams' turn as the eternally perky news producer held the whole stew together.

SIX-GUNS AND BEMS

For his follow-up to *Morning Glory*, Harrison Ford settled, reluctantly at first, on a movie adaptation of a relatively obscure comic book called *Cowboys & Aliens*.

The genesis of the comic was probably even more complicated than the start-up of most movies. Back in the 1990s there was a small comic company called Malibu. They were responsible for some modestly successful but interesting properties, *Men in Black* being one. Because Malibu looked like they were doing quite well, they were offered a buy-out by industry giant Marvel Comics. Marvel took over publishing a number of existing Malibu comics, all of which failed in around a year under their new owners. However, Malibu president Scott Mitchell Rosenberg still had a couple of unpublished properties up his sleeve and in 1997 Universal Pictures and Dreamworks partnered to buy the *Cowboys & Aliens* property pitched by Rosenberg. Director Steve Oedekerk was hired to write and direct as his follow-up to *The Nutty Professor II: The Klumps*. We can only speculate about what kind of movie Oedekerk was planning at that stage, because the deal stalled the following year when Oedekerk jumped ship to make *The Incredible Mr Limpet* with Jim Carrey. That project also has yet to materialise.

The rights to *Cowboys & Aliens* passed to Columbia in 2004, though no visible progress was made. In 2006 Rosenberg released a graphic novel of the project with art by Luciano Lima. In 2007, Universal and Dreamworks were once again in control of the movie rights and approached Robert Downey Jr for the role of former Union Army soldier Zeke Jackson. It was Downey who mentioned the project to Jon Favreau during the filming of *Iron Man 2* and Favreau stepped up as director of the film in 2009. Then Downey left the project early in 2010 to make *Sherlock Holmes: A Game of Shadows* and a month later Daniel Craig was cast for the Downey role, by this time renamed as Jake Lonergan. And in April 2010, Harrison Ford was signed. The producers were looking to move away from the comedy version that Oedekerk had been planning to bring the movie into the action genre – they had the right stars to do that.

Screenwriters Mark Fergus and Hawk Ostby who had written the screenplay for *Iron Man* were brought in to change the tone of the original Steve Oedekerk script. 'We were brought onto *Cowboys & Aliens* just as the *Iron Man* shoot was wrapping up,' said Ostby, 'and were offered a chance to create an entire story universe on a blank slate. There was an existing graphic novel, which we very much admire, but we chose instead to be inspired by the novel's indelible cover art: a cowboy on horseback, racing away from a looming spaceship overhead.'

'It occurred to us as we started writing our first draft, "Why hasn't anyone done this before? These two genres belong together,"' adds Mark Fergus. 'We imagined the epic grandeur of John Ford's *The Searchers*, infused with the magic of Spielberg's *Close Encounters of the Third Kind*.'

Even then, Steven Spielberg wasn't entirely satisfied with the script and assigned Alex Kurtzman and Roberto Orci (co-creators, with JJ Abrams, of *Fringe*) to give the screenplay another polish. Kurtzman and Orci already had the screenplays of *Transformers*, *Mission Impossible III* and the *Star Trek* reboot on their resume, so were in familiar territory with *Cowboys & Aliens*. Kurtzman and Orci's colleague Damon Lindelhof, who had worked as line producer on *Lost* and as co-producer on *Star Trek*, helped with the re-writes until they had a final shooting script Spielberg was happy with.

'What I respect about Alex (Kurtzman) and Bob (Orci),' said Spielberg, 'is that they wanted to keep this concept authentic. They've made it all real from the standpoint of the characters. Even if the aliens never came down in this film, there's still a tremendous story of conflicted characters in a range war. It's one that starts to bubble up to the surface in the very first act of *Cowboys & Aliens*. If it was just cowboys, it would be a pretty darn good cowboy story. If it was just aliens, it would be a pretty good alien story unto itself, but then when you combine the two, it's wonderful.'

This was the script that the producers sent to Harrison Ford to get him interested in playing the role of Woodrow Dolarhyde, embittered Civil War veteran and land baron.

Said director Favreau of Ford, 'For my generation, he's like John Wayne. When people

The Harrison Ford Story

sit in their seats, they're bringing everything that has come before to their experience of watching a movie. You can't separate the actor from his work. He has a roguish quality. He's always charming but with unpredictability; you never knew what he was going to do. There is a danger to him that we thought fit this role.'

Early reports stated that Ford wasn't initially convinced that the idea would work. 'He became interested after I showed him the concept art and explained that our approach was serious in tone; we weren't going to play this as a joke. Our goal was to juxtapose these two classic forms to create something new and exciting.'

Yet in an entertaining interview with Favreau after the film was completed, Ford was a bit more forthcoming about his early reaction to reading the script. 'Well, I read thirty pages … and then I threw the script across the room. Then I called my agent and I said, "I don't get it. There's nothing in this for me. Why are you asking me to do this?" And he said, "Have a little faith. This is the way of the world now. You're an older person, maybe you don't understand how things work. Read the rest of the script." So I read the rest of the script. And I said, "I don't get it, there's nothing in this for me." So then I said, "Why I don't go and see this guy (Jon Favreau) …" By this point I was thinking that this is something I clearly haven't done before. And one of the things I should be doing at this stage [in my career] is the thing I haven't done before. As much as I've been part of what they call sci-fi movies, I always approached them as kind of fairy tales. I didn't even think about the sci-fi stuff. And [Jon] convinced me that there was a human story in here that was at least as important as the other elements and it was that opportunity – and the opportunity to work with someone who appeared to be intelligent and collaborative and insightful about the telling of the story.'

Principle photography began 30th June 2010 in New Mexico and took three months. The location filming held its share of hazards for the cast. 'There was no air and a lot of reflected heat off the white cliffs,' said Ford. 'They searched around for snakes before we shot. That was reassuring. I came sort of "horse ready". I auditioned a couple of horses, three or four, before I ever came out. I found one horse that is so good, I'm trying to buy him right now. Yeah, so I'm really happy with my horse and he's relatively happy with me.'

The first bit of filming was done in the dark and Ford recalls an incident where he was doing better with his horse than the stuntmen who were on camera to fill out the posse. 'The first scene we did, riding, was at night … And there's gopher holes. Then Jon [Favreau] introduced another element that's really anathema to horses and that's fire. They decide to light the torches with a propane torch, with this sharp hissing sound. So I said, "I gotta be first. I'm leading this pack." The first time I did it I rode up to my mark, then I look and there's an empty horse next to me, because the stunt guy had come off his horse way back.'

Another story that was widely reported was that Ford's hat became the focus of the production team for longer than it merited. Ford had wanted to play the role bareheaded, avoiding the obvious comparisons to Indiana Jones a cowboy hat would invite. But filming under the New Mexico sun would have been impossible without some kind of head-covering. Ford takes up the story: 'I opened the newspaper to read an interview with all seven producers about the part they played in picking my hat [for the film]. None of the discussions happened in front of me. I was very particular about the hat. They had a lot to say, but it was Mary Zophres [costume designer] and I that picked the hat. Then submitted the hat for approval. The last thing I wanted was for it to look like Indiana Jones. I mean when I first read the script, the guy had a whip. That was a pretty obvious, too. "No. No whip. And a different hat". You don't need seven producers to tell you that. But costume is character. It makes my job easier. If you can see it, I don't have to talk about it. I don't have to create a behaviour that tells you what you can already see. Mary had just come off *True Grit* and had great experience with the western and the wisdom to know this was not the same kind of movie.'

The making of *Cowboys & Aliens* seemed to be an especially enjoyable experience for the oft-times grumpy Ford. Ford has never made any secret of the fact he dislikes any kind of intrusion by the media into his private life and has a pretty low-threshold of boredom when it comes to the obligatory and inevitable round of media appearances and interviews that follow each movie role. Playing on that facet of Ford's character allowed the director the opportunity for an engaging practical joke at 2011 San Diego ComicCon where Favreau led the actor onto the stage in handcuffs for an unannounced appearance to help promote the movie to the 6000-strong crowd.

'It's been really gratifying, I have to say,' Ford said. 'A lot of that is because of Jon, who has surprised me with his spirit and his insight, and I only say that I was surprised because I knew him better as an actor than as a filmmaker. He's a very clever actor but as a director he's shown that he can solve the problems that come up every day and not become mechanical.'

Part of that was probably because Favreau took the time to invest in the human story and not rely – Roland Emmerich-like – on the special effects to carry the film. '[With *Cowboys & Aliens*] you're dealing in human scale' said Ford. 'The whole mistake that can be made with the power of the computer and CGI is to take things out of human scale. And because you can make a force of 2000 cow-sized ants instead of one very dangerous ant, you end up with something the human mind looks at and says, "Oh, that's fascinating, but I have no experience of that, I don't relate to that emotionally." And that never happened in *Cowboys & Aliens*.'

Then there was the fact that, during the filming in New Mexico, Ford had taken a day off to marry his partner of eight years, actress Calista Flockhart, in a private ceremony in Santa Fe on 15th June 2010 at the mansion of New Mexico Governor Bill Richardson, under the legal supervision of Chief Justice Charles Daniels.

Cowboys & Aliens had its premiere at the San Diego Comic Art Convention on 23rd July 2011 and was released in American theatres on 29th July. By 4th September, the movie had managed to pull in $133.5 million at the US box office against a rather high estimated budget of $163 million. The UK release was on 17th August.

The critics were grudgingly complimentary. Movie trade bible *Variety* seemed surprised to have liked the film and commented of Ford, 'Thirty years ago, Ford could have easily tackled the lead role in such an adventure; here, he goes against type, bringing an intriguing emotional dimension to a character who would traditionally ride under a black hat.'

Mike LaSalle of the *San Francisco Chronicle* was also pleased with Ford's contribution, remarking, 'the movie's most inexhaustible source of delight is Harrison Ford as a cranky old entrepreneur in an Indiana Jones hat. It's a given in every Ford movie that he's ticked off about something. The trick is to give him a reason to be so surly. Space aliens taking his son? Alien death rays burning up his cattle? OK, these are good reasons. Ford doesn't exactly play for laughs, and in fact the movie provides him with several dramatic moments that he seems to relish. But Ford knows who he is onscreen and what he has come to mean over the decades. He knows exactly where the laughs are, and he nails every one of them.'

USA Today's Claudia Puig dismissed Ford's efforts with a terse, 'his grouchy performance is one-note.'

And Kenneth Turan of the *Los Angeles Time* commented, 'Though the permanently apoplectic Dolarhyde is supposed to be a holy terror, the actor unintentionally plays him on the edge of caricature.'

The *New York Daily News*' Joe Neumaier probably came closest to my own view on the film when he wrote, 'Ford is kicky and loose as an old saddle bag, though the story gives him little to do.'

I think Ford did what he could with an underwritten role. His portrayal of Dolarhyde is clever and quite subtle in that you don't even notice his character softening quietly as the movie unspools so that, by the end, he's quite the changed man. Ford carries this off with deft professionalism. However, he's acting in a project that is beneath the talents of most involved in it. *Cowboys & Aliens* is a triumph of concept over content. It's a terrific idea to match 19th Century frontier gunmen against hi-tech extraterrestrials, but somehow there just doesn't seem to be enough Wild West in the film. How much more exciting it would have been with an alien attack on an 1873 railway locomotive, or at least a stagecoach. And I think the involvement of the Apache tribe was probably a sub-plot too far. Still, an entertaining, if undemanding, action movie pitched perfectly for the summer blockbuster marketplace.

At the time of writing, it's not known what Ford's next movie project will be. If Ford's career planning in the past is anything to go by, we can probably expect something that's not science fiction, comedy or worthy drama, as he's covered those genres in his last four projects. But I think what most of us want to see is a new Indiana Jones adventure ...

CHAPTER 16

HARRISON FORD: THINKING ACTOR

Carpenter, Actor, Common Man, Sage

'What's so attractive about Harrison Ford is that you wouldn't recognise him on the street. You wouldn't know him in a crowd, you might not even know him at a small cocktail party of a dozen people. He really is a chameleon. When he's acting, he becomes the character he's playing, and afterwards, he reverts to being Harrison Ford, wood-cutter and furniture maker. His magic is that he's a very accessible, common guy.' Steven Spielberg, director of the *Indiana Jones* movies.

Harrison Ford has been around the movie acting business for forty years. From his first film, *Dead Heat on a Merry-Go-Round* (1967), to his most recent, *Cowboys & Aliens* (2011), his attitudes to fame, wealth and success have remained surprisingly consistent. He is proof, if proof were ever needed, that becoming a big-time movie star needn't change one's life for the worse. He has displayed an admirable ability to keep the craziness of Hollywood, and film-making in general, firmly in perspective.

He isn't over-awed with his own on-screen image and can always be counted on for a breath of common sense in an all-too-loony business.

'My mission when I started in the business,' he smiles, 'was simply not to have to do anything else for a living. And now, my only mission is to do good work. For me, that depends on the idea, the script. I can't foresee what will come up in the future, so I can't have focused ambition. I have a lot of carpentry projects. I know that much. I design all the things I make at home. I used to be much more involved with carpentry. I just don't have the time any more to put hand to hammer.'

Ford is too level-headed a person to let media name-tags like 'Star' bother him too much. 'I don't consider myself to be a star,' he told *Starburst* magazine shortly after the release of *Star Wars*. 'I'm much too aware of the functionality of that word. I don't happen to think I'm good enough. I'm a perfectionist and I always think I could have done things better. That's one reason why I never see rushes of any film I am making. I never know how the character is going to work out. I never really know, not even when I eventually see the final movie. Because I can't stand to see myself. I know how much better it might have been if I'd had the intelligence at the time – that's the worst part about filming, absolutely the worst part. Now, I just want to keep on working. You grow older and your career changes. All the better. I just hope things are still as scary as they are now for my next seven years. Well, not scary – but needing to keep on your toes. I'd like to be surprised at the parts offered me. I'd like roles that I'd never imagined for myself. If you start churning out bull, it lives on long after you've flushed yourself. It's still up there, 40ft high and 60ft wide screaming, "Bull! Bull! This guy was a fraud."'

Ford's acquaintances and associates have also described Ford as a perfectionist. 'Someone I know bought a truck from Harrison,' said a friend of Ford, 'and it was in the neatest, most spotless, most perfect condition, immaculate to the tiniest detail. He doesn't do anything lightly, he's very intense.' Ford acknowledges this with a wry smile, 'I'm probably impossible for me to live with. I get along much better with other people than I do with myself. I do not consider myself fun at a party. I'm judgemental in the extreme about my work, I'm demanding of other people in terms of their energy and their willingness to explore thoughts and exchange real ideas. I wear myself out.'

Wary as Ford may have been about the term 'star', there's no arguing that *Star Wars* made him a media personality. With just about every person in the civilised world having seen the film, he had to cope with the fact that he was recognised in public as being Han Solo.

'Under certain circumstances, if I'm where people expect to see that sort of person – or whatever they think that sort of person is like – then I'm generally more recognisable than if I'm someplace ordinary people congregate, which is the place I'm more likely to be. But a lot of people recognise me, and some of them say something about it, and some of them don't. But I'm aware when I'm pegged. Basically, I don't like it, because it takes me out of my favourite position, which is the unseen observer. It puts me in a position of being observed, which has no profitability whatsoever. I generally have no problem with the people who approach me. But often they don't know who the hell I am, or they don't care. Sometimes they think my name is Han Solo, and sometimes they don't know what my name is. Some know quite well what my name is and all about the movies I've been in. And when I'm asked to sign an autograph, I'll sign it – if I'm not having sex at the time or doing something important. I don't have any trouble dealing with people. People are generally very kind. It may change.'

As well as being spotted on the streets by *Star Wars* fans, Ford noticed that suddenly he had fan mail. But rather than allowing himself to be buried in a deluge of letters asking for anything from an autograph to a piece of clothing, Ford passed the chore on. 'I get my mail dealt with by the studios, but there are times when you look out the window and see a pair of eyes peering back at you through the bushes.'

In fact, Ford is far more interested in being an actor than a star. 'At this point in my career,' he said at the time of *Raiders'* release, 'I'd like to do more contrasting roles.

My attitude is a reflection of my early TV experiences, and a lack of a formal theatrical discipline. I just don't have the patience to do methodical, safe, repetitious formula acting. I like film acting because every experience is new – new sets, new actors, new directors. The stage is a confining medium where everything is too calculated.

'I also prefer film because I have such a poor memory. What I do – my method if you will – is to convince myself to believe in the reality of a situation. The Let's Pretend School of Acting.

'Actually, my approach calls upon my survival skills the same way boy scouts leave kids alone in the woods with two matches and a pocket knife. You get a scenario of action, some words, and you are expected to travel between two points in a believable manner. What goes on in my mind is so personal and above explanation that it's torturous to reveal.

'Of course, I have technical tricks and fundamental skills, but they were largely self-taught, because I was such a bad learner. I profit from experience. I think acting classes teach you how to act in acting classes. I've made an awful fool of myself on film a number of times as a result, but that's how I learn.'

Ford expanded on this by adding, 'It's a process of constant assessment. If you added a pinch of stuff earlier on, you've got to assess the fact that even though you don't taste it yet, you know it's in there and it's going to come through in the final stew. It's just very complicated, an unending enterprise, some of which goes on in your head, some in your gut. But that's the job. That's what the job of acting is.

'I do know my limitations, though. If I ever found myself thinking, "I could do *Streetcar* better than Brando," I'd wash my mind out with soap. I am simply happy to be working. Film acting is an honest, professional activity and an experience that I enjoy. I only ever wanted to make a decent living out of it.

'I must admit that I've been extremely lucky. That's an oft-repeated homily, but true. My success is more accident than accomplishment.'

Yet Ford is careful to distinguish between believing in the characters he is portraying and losing himself in them. 'I don't live out my fantasies,' he said in 1981, 'I choose from amongst what is offered to me at any given time. I look for parts that contrast with the last thing I've done. I don't wish to do the same thing twice, and I try to put as much distance between past characters as possible. The reason I choose something depends on a lot of things. Whether I like the people involved and think I can get along properly with them. Whether I think it's good and worthwhile to do. A lot of different elements enter into it ... whether I want to work at that time.'

The creating of a character is one of the things that will draw Ford to one project or another. 'I have very particular feelings about the characters I play, but my way of articulating them is through the medium of film, not in 25 words or less. I couldn't do that for myself. I grow a character, rather than delineate him from the word 'go'. I'm more interested in making a character up out of the story parts. I prefer to work that way than to impose a character as a whole piece onto the film to start with, although it's sometimes necessary to do that. And I try to put as much of myself into the characters as possible – not my recognisable self – but my mind is always there. I don't know how you could not put elements of yourself into a part – or why it would be profitable to keep those elements out. It's the unique thing about a person – any person – which makes him or her interesting.'

Ford likes to think of acting as a kind of logical progressive process – more a craft than an art – and is fond of comparing it to carpentry. 'Both are crafts,' he told *The Times*. 'I taught myself acting the same way I taught myself carpentry. You submit yourself to the logic of the craft. My approach to both jobs is almost entirely technical. What I learnt from carpentry, above all, was the work ethic. I used to be very lazy, but now I find I can't enjoy myself when I'm not working. It's allied to my problem of not being able to distract myself when I'm waiting around on a film set. Those big films, like *Star Wars* and *Raiders,* are technically very complex, so that the actors have to wait a long time between takes. I sit and stare at the walls or I walk around and bump into the front and the back of my trailer. Either I'm thinking about the next scene or I'm in a state of mental suspension. I can't read or concentrate on anything else. It's the worst thing about being an actor, for me.'

As well as waiting around for the floor crews to prepare the physical effects on movie, you'd think Ford would be pretty tired of reacting to blank blue screens, where the filmmakers will later drop in the special effects scenes of space ships battling one another or hideous creatures closing in for the kill. Not Ford.

'I wish I could take everyone with me on a film so they could get a clear idea of what the process of film-making is like, really, in practical terms. Special effects include miniatures, which are done in the post-production phase; matte shots, in which part of what you see on the screen is live-action, includes actors, with some background matted in; mechanical effects, such as craft going up on wires. All of these things have *nothing* to do with the acting process. The supposed difficulty of acting with special effects does not exist. It's not difficult to imagine that if this room was a set, I'm seeing the approach of a dozen star cruisers coming towards us, or to imagine, if this was a set, there were an ocean and tennis courts out there, any more than there would be a dozen star ships. So what is the difference? It's exactly the same.'

None of which is to say that there are *no* problems attached to working within the constraints of special effects. 'If we were matting in starships outside this window, I'd be obliged not to move past the frame on this side or that side of the window. But I'm getting money for that. That's no problem. Special effects are no more difficult than having to work with another person. If you and I were in a scene, and you were lit from back there, I'd be obliged not to move from here. It might be necessary for me to be here for the framing. If I moved to there, they'd have to cut [Ford indicates 'here' to 'there' with the slightest inclination of the head]. That's the kind of constraint you're under. I quite enjoy dealing with all the technical problems. If I were obliged not to move from here to there, I'd be able to find a source of inspiration. When it came time for my close-up, I'd be rivetted here for some reason. Either I would stare at you in a way that would prohibit my moving or something else. But it's always weaving the bits together to make something as real as possible.'

One very real problem attached to films which contain a dazzling array of special effects is that they are received with varying degrees of suspicion by both critics and the Hollywood establishment. The film industry has, without marked success, tried to imitate the Lucas style of movie making by creating special effects extravaganzas at the cost of the stories and the characters. The critics seem to have laid the blame for this explosion unfairly and squarely at the door of George Lucas, dubbing his films 'comic book movies', an accusation which Ford doesn't take kindly to.

'In Europe, I think films tend to be more like literature. The concerns are literary. In America, we have evolved a film that is, perhaps, different. And I feel there is as much opportunity for expression and action in a scene without dialogue as in a scene with. So I don't see that similarity with comic books. Because it's not literature doesn't mean it's a comic book for me. And I think that's the extension that's being made. If it's not full of serious, metaphysical concerns, then it must be a comic book.

'I'm aware that there are very complicated ideas in some comic books, but this kind of comment does not seem to apply, but a number of times I've heard this said ... that the characters are less real than they might be in other circumstances.

'I work hard to avoid making a character too simple. I think in *Raiders of the Lost Ark,* the screenwriters, the people who created the concept of the character, did me a great service as an actor by providing me with a strong opening scene in which you *think* you know everything about the character, and then you get a hard cut to the same person under circumstances you would never have anticipated. Now this produces anything but a two-dimensional character, *I* think. But I suppose I should leave that judgement to other people.

'I see my films as *films.* I see the characters as expressive, as full as the film has time. I don't see a limitation on the experience that "a film being like a comic book" suggests to me. If a film *is* like a comic book, then to me, it's not enough like a film.

'And the other criticism – while we're at it! – is how do you feel being upstaged by special effects, being in a film where the characters are totally unimportant compared to the special effects. And I usually say to that comment: Who's at fault here? We're talking about awfully good directors here. I don't think they do that. If they do – where is the audience during this period of time? They've no emotional touchstone on the screen. They're just sitting there watching trucks collide with no people in them. That's not interesting. *Nobody* would be interested in that situation.

'But I think this also proceeds from a cultural difference between what film has *come* to mean in Europe and in America. . .

'I for one feel that intellectual concerns are probably better dealt with in books. There's more depth of potential for intellectual definition in a book than, maybe, in a film. Although there's more chance for empathy, more chance for emotional contact in a film than in a book.

'I also think there is a kind of idea in Europe, and among European critics, that entertainment is less than salutary. Entertainment is something we should look down our noses at.

'This, I think, is very wrong. We, in America, have gone through a cycle of films that were full of social commentary and social relevance. What happened in America is that all the socially relevant film did was co-opt the problem. They spoke about a problem and then they presented a solution that was really a movie solution. Not a real solution for the real world. It was imposed by the mechanism, by the necessity to be, to a certain degree, commercially successful.'

THE HALLMARKS OF SUCCESS

As with any other person in the movie business who has rocketed, in this case quite literally, to success, Harrison Ford has to contend with people who want to hitch their wagon to the tail of his comet. One of the ways in which this trend is most apparent is in the number of unsolicited scripts that cascade through the post with his name on the wrapper.

'By and large, every time I'm in a successful film, I receive a whole bunch of material, imitations from people looking to get the same job done, and I don't read those. Then there's another level of stuff that comes in and I simply do not agree with the intentions of what those people are after. That's the second biggest body of rejections. And then if I can find something with an idea I can live with and if the character is not the same as I've played last time, then I will begin to consider who's involved and when it's going to happen. About twenty a week come into the office. They send them to my business manager as well as my agent. My car mechanic gets a stack, too! The only point of departure is the last thing I've done. I have been associated with a lot of successful entertainment. I don't necessarily want to be taken seriously, but I would like to do some serious roles. Unfortunately one must be thought of as serious before one is offered serious roles.'

But for Ford, the most important thing when considering a new acting role is not to have his judgement swayed by the financial rewards attached to the job. 'Never do it for the money,' he says. 'That's the biggest lesson. The potential for embarrassment and humiliation is much too great to do it for the money. But now I can decide not to do it for the money. As an aesthetic principle. It's what made the difference between being able to work and not being able to work. When I was doing television, I wasn't making a living as an actor. I was working ten times a year. But I wasn't making a decent living and I had no prospects. I wasn't learning anything about what I was doing. I wasn't appearing in anything that had enough quality in it to enable me to live up to my potential, or go beyond it. So I quit being an actor, not because I didn't want to be an actor, but because I didn't want to make money doing that bull over and over again. I thought I would wear out my face and wear out my welcome and I would never get another chance at the kind of stuff I wanted to do. So for eight years I did carpentry and appeared in three or four movies, all good ones. So I was then beginning to be associated with good work.'

When quizzed over whether it is difficult to cope with the pressures financial and career success has brought, Ford answers a little dismissively. 'I was never level-headed before, so it hasn't been an enormous change in my life. There's an enormous change in the freedom. Money for me is just an enormous amount of freedom, and I enjoy it. I was poor for a long, long time and now I don't have any problem with making money.

'And how could success bother me? I struggled for so long, and I always saw other actors, younger than me, making it big. I wondered if it would ever be my turn. But life is like that, sometimes. I believe if you wait long enough, you'll get your reward. Or just deserts, as the case may be. I've done work I'm proud of, like in Coppola's films *The Conversation* and *Apocalypse Now*. Those are very highly regarded, and when I'm famous enough, maybe people will look back and say, "gee, I didn't know he was a good actor, too." I've done comedy, romance, you name it. But it's the teens, the kids, who have given me this success. They're the ones who not only saw me as Han and Indy, but they kept going back, making those films the biggest hits of all time.

'It is today that counts, not what was yesterday or will be tomorrow. Fifteen years ago when I was starting, I could not have handled this degree of success. I am a late bloomer. I resisted maturity because I had to learn my job and that takes a long time. In a way, I still resist maturity. I like to play – fortunately my work is my pleasure.'

Nevertheless, all this success did have a negative side effect on Ford's life. It coincided with the breakdown of his marriage of fifteen years to his college sweetheart, Mary, the mother of his two sons. 'We simply grew apart and, although she has custody of our two sons, we've remained as amicable as possible in the circumstances. They don't live too far away from me and I see the boys regularly, which is great. They're pretty well adjusted and seem to be taking my success in their stride.

'I probably wasn't easy to be married to. I respond to a sort of barometric pressure and this is a stressful occupation. In the dark spaces of my personality I show it. I can be moody. I am independent, but not solitary. I like people in ones and twos, not parties. I'm a very ordinary person whose fear is being stuck in a typical Hollywood party for an eternity. If I die and don't go to Heaven, you just might find me in purgatory in a disco.'

When pressed, Ford admits there are some good aspects to his celebrity. 'You can get the table you want in a restaurant,' allows Ford. 'Not the best table right inside the front door or where everybody can see you, but the quieter table off to the side. It gets you doctors' appointments. But what is the worth of that? Nothing. The real coin of the realm is freedom. What is a great pleasure is the freedom to make choices, do the projects that you want to do with directors you want to work with, to have some control over the stories and the way a film is released and sold. And the freedom to explore, take chances and maybe talk people into doing something they don't think is such a good shot, because you really want to do it.'

HARRISON FORD ON POLITICS

Harrison Ford has never been shy about offering his opinions on acting and about Hollywood and the film business, but he's a bit more reluctant to share his views on politics than many of his movie star contemporaries. Whenever a journo has tried to draw Ford into a political discussion, the actor has neatly sidestepped the issue and steered the conversation on towards calmer waters. Even the easy target of then-sitting president George W. Bush failed to draw Ford's fire. 'I grew up in the mid-west,' said Ford in an interview in early 2006. 'You don't ask what a person's religion is, you don't ask what their politics are, you don't ask how much money they make and I pretty much still have that attitude about it.

'It's none of anybody's business and I don't advantage anyone by telling them what my personal politics are. The arguments are much too subtle to be entered in that way, to my mind.

'There are things that I think are happening in the world that are egregious mistakes but I'm only operating out of my own box and I don't have any expertise. I'm a voter ... I have one vote, that's all I should have.'

Though none of that stopped Ford having a say about the involvement of the United States in Iraq. 'I think something needs to be done to help alleviate the conditions which have created a disenfranchised and angry faction in the Middle East,' Ford told an Australian journalist in 2003. 'I don't think military intervention is the correct solution,' he said. 'I regret what we as a country have done so far.'

And Ford was initially evasive about his most publicly political act – his refusal to fight in the Vietnam war. 'I was a conscientious objector in the Vietnam war, but I didn't have an option, that was just the way I felt.' he said. Then in a later interview, he elaborated. My conscientious objection wasn't based on a history of religious affiliation, which made it difficult at the time. I went back to my philosophy training from college. I remembered Paul Tillich's phrase, "If you have trouble with the word God, take whatever is central or most meaningful to your life and call that God". I always had trouble with the notion of God in a stand-up form. So I developed a thesis and took the Biblical injunction to love thy neighbour as thyself as the central and most meaningful thing in my life. I combined it all and typed for days and sent it off and never heard a word. Never got called in.'

HARRISON FORD=BOX OFFICE?

Harrison Ford's success has been at that level for the last 35 years where the mere mention of his name in connection with a movie – any movie – is almost enough to guarantee a profit. Such a thought has always alarmed Ford. 'I don't expect every film I make to be a box-office success, period. This is something that never even occurs to me. As often as it's happened, how could you anticipate that it would happen again? My luck is enormous.

'But my skills at seeing into the future are really not as great as my luck. Also I'm not looking for commercial viability. I'm lucky enough to have had enough success that I feel I can deal with a certain number of films that are not going to be big, commercial successes.

'Every film you make has to have the potential to make its money back and make a fair enough profit, so that people won't feel they've wasted their time.

'So, yes, I want that. But I also like to make films for a smaller segment of the audience. You just don't take the demographics then make up a script that reflects the concerns of the broadest number of people. You work in another way – from the other direction.'

With all this acting success it seems a little surprising that Harrison Ford didn't go the way of other successful stars and set up his own production company, to develop pet projects for himself, nor did he go the directing route. In the years following the successes of the Star Wars and Indiana Jones franchises, Ford had an especially strong view on that kind of career path.

'So far I haven't been able to figure out a way of becoming involved in a process like that. One of the major problems in developing a property for yourself, or having something developed for you, is that it tends to be made *for you*. And who you are is what you want to change.

'I would prefer to come to something that has a strength of its own, a life of its own, and then add something to that. If I feel somebody makes something for me, they're going to use what they think are my strengths. Maybe they'll try to stretch me a little bit. But they'll always have me in mind. I want them to have a character in mind. Then I want to come in at the last minute.

'I don't even want to hear that somebody has written something with me in mind.'

That view has mellowed a little in the last decade or so, with Ford actively involved in the development of *Extraordinary Measures* and being credited as Executive Producer.

And directing? That route has worked out pretty well for actors like Kevin Costner, Mel Gibson and Clint Eastwood ... 'I simply have no ambitions in that area. That job involves too much planning and preparation. I'm more of an on-the-spot, spontaneous individual. Frankly I have no long-term goals. I'm just getting used to the idea of not having to worry about money any more. Actors who want to turn director are a pain. It's just enough to research a part, period, and go out there and do it. My advice to other actors? Rely on experience and intuition, and get a good night's sleep. Who wants to be a director?'

AND NOW, THE END IS NEAR …

What would have made a perfect ending for this book would have been for Harrison Ford to announce his retirement after *Indiana Jones and the Kingdom of the Crystal Skull*. Sacrilege? Perhaps, but think about it. No one can claim that the last ten years' worth of Ford films have been great. The last really good movie he was in before *Indy 4* was *Airforce One*, and his choices of vehicle since haven't been the best. That may be for various reasons. Perhaps there just aren't the quality scripts out there. But whatever the cause, a decade's worth of so-so films would suggest that now's the time to head back to Jackson Hole and pull up the drawbridge.

Lord knows, he doesn't need the money …

And there's the age thing. At this point in their careers, most other star actors (I know Ford hates that word, but it describes him perfectly) are taking smaller character roles. Christopher Walken and Harvey Keitel are two actors who seem to have gone this route. I'm sure Ford feels just as fit now as he did at 40, but it's a perhaps unpleasant truth that today's audiences are looking for younger male leads and that's not a trend I invented.

Certainly Ford isn't entertaining any thoughts of taking the same route as his *Last Crusade* co-star Sean Connery. 'Kick back and work for Scotland's freedom?' says Ford jokes, making a sly reference to Connery's pet cause of home rule for Hibernia. 'I don't think I'll make that same choice. But, sure. I think I might decide to do other things, but I think it's a ways down the line. I'm still having as much fun and taking as much pleasure, and I'm as intellectually stimulated by the process, as I ever was.'

There are, of course, other counter-arguments. The strongest is Ford's work ethic. Few would argue that Ford isn't one of the hardest working actors in American cinema. His entire upbringing – and he's spoken of this on the record many times – is that you *work* for a living until you can't work any more. 'I'm not a person who can occupy my time with recreation,' he told *Readers Digest*. 'I need a challenge. I need the intellectual stimulation. I'm a member of a community on each film, working in concert to try to bring an idea to life. It's a great job.' It's unlikely that Ford will change this life-view any time soon. It's a fact that he simply loves making movies. And that's a hard thing to walk away from. Finally, despite Ford's protestations to the contrary, I think he likes being a star. There's hardly an actor in the business that wouldn't carry on acting for free as long as it meant they could hear the applause of the audience. While that might not be literally true in Ford's case, it's almost certainly a metaphorical fact.

And yes, if Ford retired, it would mean I wouldn't have to update this book in another ten years' time … but at least we could finally have the definitive Ford biography.

The final word on *that* subject must go to Harrison Ford himself. When asked if he could have any writer in history write his biography, who would he choose, his reply was characteristically terse.

'I don't want anybody writing my biography.'

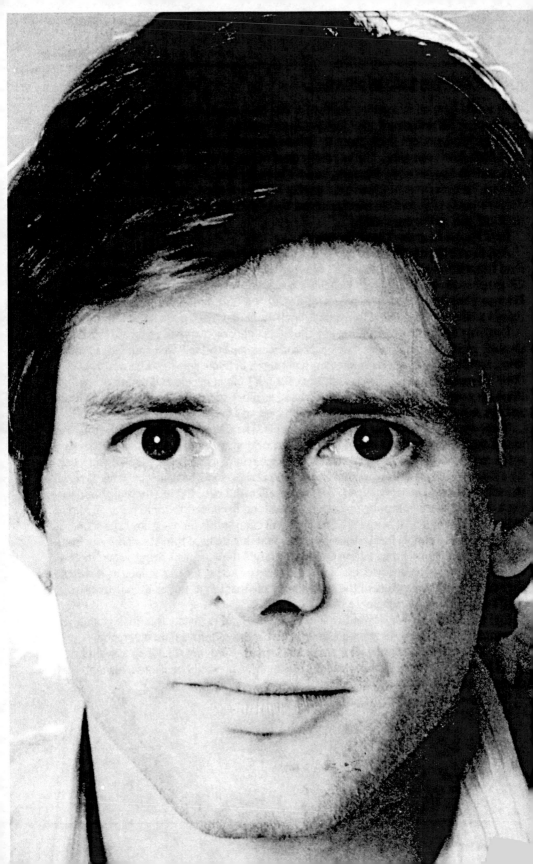

HARRISON FORD: FILMOGRAPHY

Dead Heat on a Merry-Go-Round (1966)

Starring James Coburn (as Eli Kotch), Camilla Sparv (Inger Knudson), Aldo Ray (Eddie Hart), Nina Wayne (Frieda Schmid), Robert Webber (Milo Stewart), Rose Marie (Margaret Kirby), Todd Armstrong (Alfred Morgan), Marian Moses (Dr Marion Hague), Michael Strong (Paul Feng), Severn Darden (Miles Fisher), James Westerfield (Jack Balter), Philip E. Pine (George Logan), Simon Scott (William Anderson), Ben Astar (General Mailenkoff), Lawrence Mann (Officer Howard), Michael St.Angel (Captain William Yates), Alex Rodine (Translator), Albert Nalbandian (Willie Manus), Tyler McVey (Lyman Mann), Roy Glenn (Sergeant Elmer K. Coxe), Harrison Ford (Bellboy).

Directed by Bernard Girard, Screenplay by Bernard Girard, Cinematography by Lionel Linden, Edited by William Lyon, Art direction by Walter M. Simonds, Music by Stu Phillips, Produced by Carter DeHaven. Production Company DeHaven-Girard for Columbia. Time 107 mins.

On Reg 1 DVD through Sony Pictures
On Reg 2 DVD through Sony Pictures Home Entertainment

Luv (1967)

Starring Jack Lemmon (as Harry Berlin), Peter Falk (Milt Manville), Elaine May (Ellen), Nina Wayne (Linda), Eddie Mayehoff (Attorney Goodhart), Paul Martman (Doyle), Severn Darden (Vandergrist), and Harrison Ford.

Directed by Clive Donner, Screenplay by Elliott Baker, based on the play by Murray Schisgal, Cinematography by Ernest Laszlo, Edited by Harold F. Kress, Production Design by Albert Brenner, Set Decoration by Frank Tuttle, Costume Design by Donfeld, Makeup by Ben Lane, Special Effects by Geza Gaspar, Produced by Martin Manulis. Production Company Jalem. Time 96 mins.

The Long Ride Home (1967, aka: A Time for Killing, US)

Starring Glenn Ford (as Major Walcott), George Hamilton (Captain Bentley), Inger Stevens (Emily Biddle), Paul Petersen (Blue Lake), Max Baer (Sgt Luther Liskell), Todd Armstrong (Lt

Prudessing), Timothy Carey (Billy Cat), Kenneth Toby (Sgt Cleehan), Richard X.Slattery (Corp Paddy Darling), Duke Hobbie (Lt Frist), Dean Stanton (Sgt Dan Way), James Davidson (Little Mo), Harrison J. Ford (Lt Shaffer), Charlie Briggs (Sgt Kettlinger), Kay E. Kuter (Owelson), Dick Miller (Zollic officer), Craig Curtis (Bagnef), Emile Miller (Col Harries), Marshall Reed (Stedner), Jay Ripley (Lovingwood), Dean Goodhill (Bruce).

Directed by Phil Carlson, Screenplay by Halsted Welles, based on the novel Southern Blade by Nelson and Shirley Wolford, Cinematography by Kenneth Peach, Edited by Roy Livingston, Art Direction by Daniel Heller, Music by Mundell Lowe, Produced by Harry Joe Brown. Production Company Columbia/Sage Western Pictures. Time 88 mins.

On Reg 2 DVD through Blaqout as French Import

Journey to Shiloh (1967)

Starring James Caan (as Buck Burnett), Michael Sarrazin (Miller Nalls), Brenda Scott (Gabrielle Du Prey), Don Stroud (Todo McLean), Paul Petersen (J.C.Sutton), Michael Burns (Eubie Bell), 'Michael Vincent (Little Bit Buck), Harrison Ford (Willie Bill Beardon), John Doucette (Gen Braxton Bragg).

Directed by William Hale, Screenplay by Gene Coon, based on the novel *Fields of Honour* by Will Henry, Cinematography by Enzo A.Martinelli, Edited by Edward W. Williams, Art Direction by Alexander Golitzen & George Patrick, Makeup by Bud Westmore, Stunts by Bob Herron, Produced by Howard Christie. Production Company Universal Pictures. Time 101 mins.

On Reg 2 DVD through Noble Entertainment

The Intruders (TV, 1967, released 1970)

Starring Don Murray (as Sam Garrison), Anne Francis (Leora Garrison), Edmond O'Brien (Col William Bodeen), John Saxon (Billy Pye), Gene Evans (Cole Younger), Edward Andrews (Elton Dykstra), Shelly Novack (Theron Pardo), Harry Dean Stanton (Whit Dykstra), Stuart Margolin (Jesse James), Zalman King (Bob Younger), Phillip Alford (Harold Gilman), Harrison Ford

(Carl), John Hoyt (Appleton), Marlene Tracy (Kate Guerrera), Ken Swofford (Pomerantz), Robert Donner (Roy Kirsh), Edward Faulkner (Bill Riley), James Gammon (Chaunce Dykstra), Gavin MacLeod (Warden), Len Wayland (George Ganzer).

Directed by, William A. Graham, Screenplay by William Douglas Lansford, from a story by Dean Riesner, Cinematography by Ray Flin, Film Editing by Howard Terrill, Original Music by Dave Grusin, Art Direction by Lloyd S. Papez, Set Decoration by John McCarthy Jr. & James Redd, Makeup by Bud Westmore, Produced by Bert Granet, Executive Producer James Duff McAdams. Production Company Universal TV. Time 100 mins.

Getting Straight (1970)

Starring Elliott Gould (as Harry Bailey), Candice Bergen (Jan), Robert F. Lyons (Nick), Jeff Corey (Dr Wilhunt), Max Julien (Ellis), Cecil Kellaway (Dr Kasper), John Lormer (Vandenburg), Leonard Stone (Lysander), William Bramley (Wade Linden), Jeannie Berlin (Judy Kramer), John Rubenstein (Herbert), Richard Anders (Dr Greengrass), Brenda Sykes (Luan), Jenny Sullivan (Sheila), Gregory Sierra (Garcia), Billie Bird (Landlady), Harrison Ford (Jake), Elizabeth Lane (Alice Linden), Hilarie Thompson (Cynthia), Irene Tedrow (Mrs Stebbins), Joanna Serpe (Room-mate), Scott Perry (Airline Representative).

Directed by Richard Rush, Screenplay by Robert Kaufman, based on the novel by Ken Kolb, Cinematography by Lazlo Kovacs, Edited by Maury Winetrobe, Original Music by Ronald Stein, Art Direction by Sydney Z. Litwack, Produced by Richard Rush. Production Company The Organisation. Time 125 mins.
On Reg 1 DVD through Sony Pictures

American Graffiti (1973)

Starring Richard Dreyfuss (as Curt), Ron Howard (Steve), Paul Le Mat (John), Charles Martin Smith (Terry the Toad), Cindy Williams (Laurie), Candy Clark (Debbie), Mackenzie Phillips (Carol), Wolfman Jack (Disc Jockey), Harrison Ford (Bob Falfa), Bo Hopkins (Joe), Manuel Padilla (Carlos), Beau Gentry (Ants), Kathleen Quinlan (Peg), Suzanne Somers (Blonde in T-Bird), Debralee Scott (Falfa's Girl).

Directed by George Lucas, Screenplay by George Lucas, Gloria Katz and Willard Huyck, Cinematography by Haskell Wexler, Ron Eveslage and Jan Dalquen, Edited by Verna Fields and Marcia Lucas, Sound and recording by Walter Murch, Casting by Fred Roos and Mike Fenton, Coproduced by Gary Kurtz, Produced by Francis Ford Coppola. Production Company Lucasfilm Ltd/Coppola Company. Time (original release) 110 mins, (re-release) 112 mins.
On Reg 1 DVD through MCA Home Video
On Reg 2 DVD through Universal: 8205598

The Conversation (1974)

Starring Gene Hackman (as Harry Caul), John Cazale (Stan), Allen Garfield (Bernie Moran), Frederic Forrest (Mark), Cindy Williams (Ann), Michael Higgins (Paul), Elizabeth MacRae (Meredith), Terri Garr (Amy), Harrison Ford (Martin Stell), Mark Wheeler (Receptionist), Robert Shields (Mime), Phoebe Alexander (Lurleen), Robert Duvall (The Director).

Directed by Francis Ford Coppola, Screenplay by Francis Ford Coppola, Cinematography by Bill Butler, Edited by Walter Murch and Richard Chew, Music by David Shire, Produced by Francis Ford Coppola and Fred Roos. Production Company The Coppola Company/Paramount Pictures. Time 113 mins.
On video through CIC Video: VHL/BEL 2051: 110 mms.
On Reg 1 DVD through Paramount: 113 mins.
On Reg 2 DVD through Miramax: BED881219

Judgment: The Court Martial of Lieutenant William Calley (TV, 1975)

Starring Tony Musante (as Lt. William Calley), with Richard Basehart (George Lattimer), Olive Clark, Harrison Ford (Frank Crowder), Linda Haynes (Calley's girl), Bo Hopkins, (prosecuting attorney), William Lucking (The Captain), Steve Mitchell (head juror), Bruce Kimball (juror), Frank McRae (Mr Langham), Jan Merlin (Capt Briggs), Stanley Kramer (Host).

Produced & Directed by Stanley Kramer, Art Teleplay by Henry Denker, Edited by Gary Anderson and Jim McElroy, Art Direction by Edward Stephenson, Costume Design by Tom Dawson, Casting by Jane Feinberg and Mike Fenton, Associate Producer Michael Manheim. Time 101 mins.

On Reg 1 DVD through Platinum Disc.

(James Michener's) Dynasty (TV, 1976)

Starring Sarah Miles (as Jennifer Blackwood), Stacey Keach (Matt Blackwood), Harris Yulin (John Blackwood), Harrison Ford (Mark Blackwood), Tony Schwartz (Harry Blackwood), Amy Irving (Amanda Blackwood), Charles Weldon (Sam Adams), Stephanie Faulkner (Lucinda), Karmin Murcello (Elvira), John Carter (Benjamin McCullum), Sari Price (Margaret McCullum), Gerrit Graham (Carver Blackwood), Dennis Larson (Mark, age 12), Gary Lee Cooper (Mark, age 6).

Directed by Lee Philips, Teleplay by Sydney Carroll, based on the novel by James Michener, Cinematography by William Cronjager, Film Editing by George Jay Nicholson, Art Direction by Perry Ferguson, Original Music by Gil Melle, Produced by Buck Houghton, Executive Producer David Frost. Production Company David Paradine TV Productions/Marjay Productions for NBC's *Saturday Night at the Movies*, Time 99 mins.

On DVD from Platinum Disc

The Possessed (TV, 1977)

Starring James Farentino (as Kevin Leahy), Joan Hackett (Louise Gelson), Claudette Nevins (Ellen Sumner), Eugene Roche (Sgt Taplinger), Harrison Ford (Paul Winjam), Ann Dusenberry (Weezie Sumner), Diana Scarwid (Lane), Dinah Manoff (Celia), Carol Jones (Alex), P. J. Soles (Marty), Ethelinn Block (Barry), Susan Walden (Student), with Lawrence Bame, James R. Parkes, Catherine Cunneff.

Directed by Jerry Thorpe, Teleplay by John Sacret Young, Executive Story Consultant William Blinn, Cinematography by Chuck Arnold, Film Editing by Michael A. Hoey, Art Direction by Frederick P. Hope, Original Music by Leonard Rosenman, Special Effects by Joseph A. Unsinn, Manager of Talent Casting for NBC TV Network Joe Scully, Produced by Philip Mandelker, Executive Producer Jerry Thorpe. Production Company NBC Television. Time 76 mins.

On Reg 1 DVD through Warner Archives

Star Wars (1977)

Starring Mark Hamill (as Luke Skywalker),
Harrison Ford (Han Solo), Carrie Fisher (Princess Leia Organa), Peter Cushing (Grand Moff Tarkin), Sir Alec Guinness (Ben "Obi-wan" Kenobi), Anthony Daniels (C-3PO), Kenny Baker (R2-D2), Peter Mayhew (Chewbacca), David Prowse (Lord Darth Vader), Phil Brown (Uncle Owen Lars), Shelagh Fraser (Aunt Beru Lars), Jack Purvis (Chief Jawa), Biggs (Dennis Lawson).

Written and directed by George Lucas, Cinematography by Gilbert Taylor, Edited by Paul Hirch, Marcia Lucas and Richard Chew, Production design by John Barry, Music by John Williams, Special effects supervisor John Dykstra, Sound effects by Ben Burtt, Production Supervisor Robert Watts, Produced by Gary Kurtz. Production Company Lucasfilm Ltd. Time: 121 mins.

On Video through CBS/Fox Video: 1052: 116 mins.

On Reg 1 DVD (as part of the Star Wars Trilogy Box Set) through Twentieth Century-Fox

On Reg 2 DVD (as part of the Star Wars Trilogy Box Set) through Twentieth Century-Fox: 27233DVD

Heroes (1977)

Starring Henry Winkler (as Jack Dunne), Sally Field (Carol), Harrison Ford (Kenny Boyd), Val Avery (Bus Driver), Olivia Cole (Jan Adcox), Hector Elias (Dr Elias), Dennis Burkley (Gus), Tony Burton (Chef), Michael Cavanaugh (Peanuts), Helen Craig (Bus Depot Manager), John P. Finnegan (Mr Munro), Betty McGuire (Mrs Munro), John O'Leary (Ticket Clerk), Tom Rosqui (Second Patrolman), Fred Struthman (Nathan), Caskey Swain (Frank), Earle Towne (Leo Sturges), Verna Bloom (Waitress), Kenneth Augustine (Charles), Rick Blanchard (Andy), Louis Carillo (Stokes), Robert Kretschman (Robert), Lee Cohn (Patient), Dick Ziker (Artie).

Directed by Jeremy Paul Kagan, Screenplay by James Carabatsos, Cinematography by Frank Stanley, Edited by Patrick Kennedy, Music by Jack Nitzsche, Production Design by Charles Rosen, Produced by David Foster and Lawrence Turman. Production Company Turman-Foster Company. Time 107 mins (cut from 113 mins).

On video from MCA-Universal

On Reg 1 DVD through Universal Studios: 112 mins.

On Reg 2 DVD through Freemantle

Force 10 from Navarone (1978)

Robert Shaw (as Maj Keith Mallory), Harrison Ford (Lieutenant Colonel Mike Barnsby), Barbara Bach (Maritza Petrovich), Edward Fox (SSgt Dusty Miller), Franco Nero (Capt Nikolai Leskovar), Carl Weathers (Sgt Weaver), Richard Kiel (Capt Drazak), Alan Badel (Maj Petrovitch), Michael Byrne (Maj Schroeder), Philip Latham (Cmdr Jensen), Angus MacInnes (1st Lt Doug Reynolds), Michael Sheard (Sgt Bauer), Petar Buntic (Marko), Leslie Schofield (Interrogation Officer 1), Anthony Langdon (Interrogation Officer 2), Richard Hampton (Interrogation Officer 3), Paul Humpoletz (Sgt Bismark), Dicken Ashworth (Nolan), Christopher Malcolm (Rogers), Nick Ellsworth (Salvone), Jonathan Blake (Oberstein), Roger Owen (MP Walter Blake), Frances Mughan (Farrell), Mike Sirett (Force Ten Team), Graeme Crowther (Force Ten Team), Jim Dowdall (Force Ten Team), Michael Osborne (Lt Cmdr Vincent Ryan), Patrick Allen (Narrator)

Directed by Guy Hamilton, Screenplay by Robin Chapman and Carl Foreman, based on the novel by novel by Alistair MacLean, Original Music by Ron Goodwin, Cinematography by Christopher Challis, Film Editing by Raymond Poulton, Casting by Irene Lamb, Production Design by Geoffrey Drake, Art Direction by Fred Carter, Special Effects by René Albouze, Stunts by Eddie Stacey, Associate Producer David W. Orton, Co-produced by John R. Sloan and Anthony B. Unger, Produced by Oliver A. Unger. Production Company American International Pictures (AIP). Time 118 mins.

On Reg 1 DVD from MGM: 93 mins.
On Reg 2 DVD from UCA Catalogue: 121 mins.

Apocalypse Now (1979)

Starring Marron Brando (as Colonel Kurtz), Robert Duvall (Lt Col Kilgore), Martin Sheen (Capt Willard), Frederic Forrest (Chef), Albert Hall (Chief), Sam Bottoms (Lance), Larry Fishburne (Clean), Dennis Hopper (Photo Journalist), G. D. Spradin (General), Harrison Ford (Col Lucas), Jerry Zesmer (Civilian), Scott Glenn (Coby). Produced and directed by Francis Coppola, Screenplay by John Milius and Francis Coppola, Narration written by Michael Herr, Cinematography by Vittorio Storaro, Supervising editor Richard Marks, Edited by Walter Murch, Gerald B. Greenberg and Lisa Fruchtman, Music by Carmine Coppola and Francis Coppola, Production design by Dean Tavoularis, Sound montage and design by Walter Murch, Executive assistants Melissa Mathison and Jack Fritz, Associate producer Mona Skager, Co-produced by Fred Roos, Gray Frederickson and Tom Sternberg. Production Company Omni Zoetrope Ltd. Time 148 mins.

On video through CIC Video: VHE 2030
On Reg 1 DVD through Paramount Home Video
On Reg 2 DVD through Paramount Home Video P9157DVD

Hanover Street (1979)

Starring Harrison Ford (as David Halloran), LesleyAnne Down (Margaret Sellinger), Christopher Plummer (Paul Sellinger), Alec McCowen (Major Trumbo), Richard Maur (2nd Lt Jerry Cimino), Michael Sacks (2nd Lt Martin Hyer), Patsy Kensit (Sarah Sellinger), Max Wall (Harry Pike), Shane Rimmer (Col Ronald Bart), Keith Buckley (Lt Wells), Sherrie Hewson (Phyllis), Cindy O'Callaghan (Paula), Di Trevis (Elizabeth) Suzanne Bertish (French Girl), Keith Alexander (Soldier in Barn), Jay Benedict (Corp Daniel Giler), John Ratzenberger (Sgt John Lucas), Eric Stine (Farrell), Hugh Frazer (Capt Harold Lester), William Hootkins (Beef).

Directed by Peter Hyams, Screenplay by Peter Hyams, Cinematography by David Watkin, Edited by James Mitchell, Music by John Barry, Associate producers Michael Rachmil and Harry Benn, Produced by Paul N. Lazarus III, Executive producer Gordon G.T.Scott, Production Company Hanover Street Productions. Time 108 mins.

On video through Columbia Video: CVT/CBT 10097: 105 mins.
On Reg 1 DVD through Sony Pictures
On Reg 2 DVD through Sony Pictures CDR10097

The 'Frisco Kid (1979)

Starring Gene Wilder (as Avram Belinski), Harrison Ford (Tommy Lillard), Rammon Bieri (Mr Jones), Val Bisloglio (Chief Gray Cloud), George Ralph DiCenzo (Darryl Riggs), Leo Fuchs (Chief Rabbi), Penny Peyser (Rosalie), William Smith (Matt Diggs), Jack Somack (Samuel Bender), Beege Barkett (Sarah Mindl), Shay Duffin (O'Leary), Walter Janowitz (Old Amish

Man), Joe Kapp (Monterano), Clyde Kusatsu (Mr Ping), Cliff Pellow (Mr Daniels), Allan Rich (Mr Bialik), Henry Rowland (lst Amish Farmer), Vincent Schiavelli (Brother Bruno), John Steadman (Booking Agent), Ian Wolfe (Father Joseph), Steffen Zacharias (Herschel Rosensheine), Eda Reiss Medin (Mrs Bender), Tommy Lillard (Sheriff).
Directed by Robert Aldrich, Screenplay by Michael Elias and Frank Shaw, Cinematography by Robert B.Hauser, Edited by Maury Winetrobe, Irving Rosenblum and Jack Horger, Music by Frank De Vol, Associate producer Melvin Dellar, Produced by Mace Neufeld, Executive producer Howard W. Koch Jr, Production Company Warner Bros, Time: 119 mins.
On video through Warner Home Video: WEVIWEX 61095: 118 mins.
On Reg 1 DVD through Warner Home Video
On Reg 2 DVD as European Import

More American Graffiti (1979)
Starring Candy Clark (as Debbie Dunham), Bo Hopkins (Little Joe), Ron Howard (Steve Bolander), Paul Le Mat (John Milner), Mackenzie Phillips (Carol/Rainbow), Charles Martin Smith (Terry 'The Toad' Fields), Cindy Williams (Laurie Bolander), Anna Bjorn (Eva), Richard Bradford (Major Creech), John Brent (Ralph), Scott Glenn (Newt), James Houghton (Sinclair), John Lansing (Lance), Manuel Padilla Jr (Carlos), Ken Place (Beckwith), Mary Kay Place (Teensa), Tom Ruben (Eric), Doug Sahm (Bobbie), Will Seltzer (Andy Henderson), Monica Tenner (Moonflower), Ralph Wilcox (Felix), Carol Ann Williams (Vikki), Wolfman Jack (Himself), Rosanna Arquette (Girl in Commune), Tom Baker (Cop #1), Eric Barnes (Sergeant Dutton), Becky Bedoy (Girl in Bus), Buzz Borelli (The Freak), Ben Bottoms (Perry), Patrick Burns (Musician #1), Tim Burrus (Slick Eddie), George Cantero (Guard), Chet Carter (Race Starter), Dion M. Chesse (Delivery Man), Gil Christner (Ed), Don Coughlin (Cop #2), Mark Courtney (Kevin Bolander), Michael Courtney (Teddy Bolander), Denny Delk (Police Sergeant), Frankie Di (Trophy Girl), Steve Evans (Race Announcer), Nancy Fish (Police Matron), Rocky Flintermann (The Neighbor), Michael Frost (Musician #2), Jon Gries (Ron), Paul G. Hensler (Lieutenant), Julie Anna Hicks (Child in Commune), Robert Hirschfeld (Delivery Man),

Erik Holland (Ole),Jay Jacobus (Congressman), Naomi Judd (Girl in Bus), Leslie Gay Leace (Girl in Bus), Delroy Lindo (Army Sergeant), Dwight Reber (Pilot), Sandra Rider (Girl in Commune), Kevin Rodney Sullivan (Lieutenant), Morgan Upton (Mr Hunt), John Vella (Big Guy), Dan Woodworth (Student Leader), Clay Wright (Pilot), Harrison Ford (Officer Bob Falfa, uncredited), with Country Joe & The Fish as themselves.
Written and Directed by Bill L. Norton, based on characters created by George Lucas, Gloria Katz & Willard Huyck, Original Music by Eugene Finley, Cinematography by Caleb Deschanel, Film Editing by Tina Hirsch & Duwayne Dunham, with Marcia Lucas (uncredited), Casting by Gino Havens & Terry Liebling, Art Direction by Ray Storey, Set Decoration by Doug von Koss, Costume Design by Aggie Guerard Rodgers, Makeup artist Don Le Page, Hair stylist Paul LeBlanc, Dialogue editor Ben Burtt, Special Effects by Don B. Courtney, Visual Effects by Peter Donen, Stunts David S. Cass Sr. & Greg Walker, Produced by Howard G. Kazanjian, Executive Producer George Lucas. Production Company Lucasfilm Ltd. Time 110 mins.
On Reg 1 DVD through Universal)
On Reg 2 DVD as Dutch Import
Also on Reg 1 DVD (as part of the American Graffiti box set) through MCA Home Video

The Empire Strikes Back (1980)
Starring Mark Hamill (as Luke Skywalker), Harrison Ford (Han Solo), Carrie Fisher (Princess Leia Organa), Billy Dee Williams (Lando Calrissian), Anthony Daniels (C-3PO), Kenny Baker (R2-D2), Peter Mayhew (Chewbacca), Frank Oz (Yoda), Sir Alec Guinness (Ben "Obi-wan" Kenobi), Jeremy Bulloch (Boba Fett), John Hollis (Lando's Aide), Jack Purvis (Chief Ugnaught), Des Webb (Snow Creature), Clive Revill (Voice of the Emperor), Kenneth Colley (Admiral Piet), Julian Glover (General Veers), Dennis Lawson (Wedge).
Directed by Irvin Kershner, Screenplay by Leigh Brackett and Lawrence Kasdan, from a story by George Lucas, Cinematography by Peter Suschitsky, Production design by Norman Reynolds, Music by John Williams, Edited by Paul Hirsch, Special effects supervised by Brian Johnson and Richard Edlund, Associate

producer Robert Watts, Produced by Gary Kurtz,
Executive producer George Lucas. Production
Company Lucasfilm Ltd. Time 124mins.
On video through CBS/Fox Video: 1425/40
On Reg 1 DVD (as part of the Star Wars Trilogy
Box Set) through Twentieth Century-Fox
On Reg 2 DVD (as part of the Star Wars Trilogy
Box Set) through Twentieth Century-Fox
27233DVD

Raiders of the Lost Ark (1981)

Starring Harrison Ford (as Prof Indiana Jones),
Karen Allen (Marion Ravenwood), Paul Freeman
(Belloq), Ronald Lacey (Toht), John Rhys-Davies
(Sallah), Denholm Elliot (Brody), Wolf Kahler
(Dietrich), Anthony Higgins (Gobler), Alfred
Molina (Satipo), Vic Tablian (Barranca), Don
Fellows (Col Musgrove), William Hootkins (Maj
Eaton).
Directed by Steven Spielberg, Screenplay by
Lawrence Kasdan, from a story by George
Lucas and Philip Kaufman, Cinematography
by Douglas Slocombe, Production designed by
Norman Reynolds, Music by John Williams,
Edited by Michael Kahn, Visual Effects
supervised by Richard Edlund, Associate
producer Robert Watts, Produced by Frank
Marshall, Executive producers George Lucas
and Howard Kazanjian. Production Company
Lucasfilm Ltd. Time 115 mins.
On video through CIC Video: VHR/BER 2076:
112 mins.
On Reg 1 DVD (as part of the Adventures of
Indiana Jones box set) through Paramount
Home Video
On Reg 2 DVD (as part of the Adventures of
Indiana Jones box set) through Paramount
Home Video PHE8400

Blade Runner (1982)

Starring Harrison Ford (as Rick Deckard),
Rutger Hauer (Roy Batty), Sean Young
(Rachael), Edward James Olmos (Gaff), M.
Emmet Walsh (Bryant), Daryl Hannah (Pris),
William Sanderson (Sebastian), Brion James
(Leon), Joe Turkel (Tyrell), Joanna Cassidy
(Zhora), James Hong (Chew), Morgan Paull
(Holden), Kimiro Hiroshige (Cambodian Lady),
Carolyn DeMirjian (Saleslady), Robert Ozkazaki
(Sushi Master), Hy Pyke (Taffy Lewis), Kevin
Thompson (Bear), John Edward Allen (Kaiser).

Directed by Ridley Scott, Screenplay by
Hampton Fancher and David Peoples, based on
the novel *Do Androids Dream of Electric Sheep*
by Philip K.Dick, Cinematography by Jordan
Cronenweth, Production designed by Lawrence
G.Paul, Music by Vangelis, Supervising editor
Terry Rawlings, Special effects supervised by
Douglas Trumbull, Richard Yuricich and David
Dryer, Visual futurist Syd Mead, Associate
producer Ivor Powell, Produced by Michael
Deeley, Executive producers Brian Kelly and
Hampton Fancher. Production Company The
Blade Runner Partnership. Time 114 mins.
On Video through Warner Home Video: WEV/
WEX 70008: 111 mins.
On Reg 1 DVD (Director's Cut) through Warner
Home Video
On Reg 2 DVD (Director's Cut) through Warner
Home Video D012905 – currently OOP
Remastered Director's cut on Reg 1 DVD
(Director's Cut) through Warner Home Video
Remastered Director's cut on Reg 2 DVD
(Director's Cut) through Warner Home Video
Final cut box set on Reg 1 DVD (Director's Cut)
through Warner Home Video
Final cut box set on Reg 2 DVD (Director's Cut)
through Warner Home Video

Return of the Jedi (1983)

Starring Mark Hamill (as Luke Skywalker),
Harrison Ford (Han Solo), Carrie Fisher
(Princess Leia Organa), Billy Dee Williams
(Lando Calrissian), Anthony Daniels (C-3PO),
Peter Mayhew (Chewbacca), Sebastian Shaw
(Anakin Skywalker/ Darth Vader), David Prowse
and Bob Anderson (Darth Vader), Ian McDiarmid
(The Emperor), Frank Oz (Yoda), James Earl
Jones (voice of Darth Vader), Sir Alec Guinness
(Ben "Obi-wan" Kenobi), Jeremy Bulloch (Boba
Fett).
Directed by Richard Marquand, Screenplay
by Lawrence Kasdan, based on a story by
George Lucas, Cinematography by Alan Hume,
Production designed by Norman Reynolds,
Music by John Williams, Edited by Sean Barton,
Marcia Lucas and Duwayne Dunham, Special
visual effects by Dennis Muren, Ken Ralston and
Richard Edlund, Makeup and creature design by
Phil Tippett and Stuart Freeborn, Sound design
by Ben Burtt, Co-produced by Robert Watts and
Jim Bloom, Produced by Howard Kazanjian,

Executive producer George Lucas. Production Company Lucasfilm Ltd. Time 123 mms.
On Reg 1 DVD (as part of the Star Wars Trilogy Box Set) through Twentieth Century-Fox
On Reg 2 DVD (as part of the Star Wars Trilogy Box Set) through Twentieth Century-Fox 27233DVD

Indiana Jones and the Temple of Doom (1984)

Starring Harrison Ford (Indiana Jones), Kate Capshaw (Willie Scott), Ke Huy Quan (Short Round), Amrish Puri (Mola Ram), Roshan Seth (Chauar Lal), Philip Stone (Captain Blumburu), Roy Chiao (Lao Che), David Yip (Wu Han), Ric Young (Kao Kan), Raj Singh (Liule Maharajah), D. R. Nanayakkarah (Shaman), Dharmadasa Kuruppu (Chieftain), Stany de Silva (Sajnu), Pat Roach (Chief Guard).
Directed by Steven Spielberg, Screenplay by Willard Huyck and Gloria Katz, based on a story by George Lucas, Cinematography by Douglas Slocombe, Supervising editor Michael Kahn, Production designed by Elliot Scott, Special effects supervisor Dennis Muren, Mechanical effects supervisor George Gibbs, Stunt arrangers Vic Armstrong and Glenn Randall, Music by John Williams, Associate producer Kathleen Kennedy, Produced by Robert Watts, Executive producers George Lucas and Frank Marshall. Production Company Lucasfilm Ltd. Time 117 mins (US 118 mins).
On Reg 1 DVD (as part of the Adventures of Indiana Jones box set) through Paramount Home Video
On Reg 2 DVD (as part of the Adventures of Indiana Jones box set) through Paramount Home Video PHE8400

Witness (1985)

Starring Harrison Ford (as Det Capt John Book), Kelly McGillis (Rachel Lapp), Josef Sommer (Chief Paul Schaeffer), Lukas Haas (Samuel Lapp), Jan Rubes (Eli Lapp), Alexander Godunov (Daniel Hochleitner), Danny Glover (Det Lt James McFee), Brent Jennings (Det Sgt Elden Carter), Patti LuPone (Elaine), Angus MacInnes (Det 'Fergie'), Frederick Rolf (Stoltzfus), Viggo Mortensen (Moses Hochleitner), John Garson (Bishop Tchantz), Beverly May (Mrs Yoder), Ed Crowley (Sheriff), Timothy Carhart (Zenovich),

Sylvia Kauders (Tourist Lady), Marian Swan (Marilyn Schaeffer), Maria Bradley (Casey Schaeffer), Rozwill Young (T-Bone, Suspect in Bar).
Directed by Peter Weir, Screenplay by Earl W. Wallace & William Kelley, based on a story by William Kelley, Pamela Wallace & Earl W. Wallace, Original Music by Maurice Jarre, Cinematography by John Seale, Film Editing by Thom Noble, Casting by Dianne Crittenden, Production Design by Stan Jolley, Set Decoration by John H. Anderson, Makeup by Marie Delrusso, Associate Producer Wendy Stites, Co-produced by David Bombyk, Produced by Edward S. Feldman. Production Company Paramount Pictures. Time 112 mins
On video through Paramount
On Reg 1 DVD through Paramount
On Reg 2 DVD through Paramount: EC103020

The Mosquito Coast (1986)

Harrison Ford (as Allie Fox), Helen Mirren (Mother Fox), River Phoenix (Charlie Fox), Conrad Roberts (Mr Haddy), Andre Gregory (Reverend Spellgood), Martha Plimpton (Emily Spellgood), Dick O'Neill (Mr Polski), Jadrien Steele (Jerry Fox), Michael Rogers (Francis Lungley), Hilary Gordon (April Fox), Rebecca Gordon (Clover Fox), Jason Alexander (Hardware Clerk), Alice Sneed (Mrs Polski), Tiger Haynes (Mr Semper), William Newman (Captain Smalls), Melanie Boland (Mrs Spellgood), Butterfly McQueen (Ma Kennywick), Michael Opoku (Bucky), Adolpho Salguero (Drainy), Rafael Cho (Leon), Sofia Coc (Alice), Margarita Coc (Veryl), Wilfred Peters (Dixon), Luis Palacio (Peaselee), Juan Antonio Llanes (Mercenary), Abel Woolrich (Mercenary), Jorge Zepeda (Mercenary).
Directed by Peter Weir, Screenplay by Paul Schrader, based on a novel by Paul Theroux, Original Music by Maurice Jarre, Cinematography by John Seale, Film Editing by Thom Noble, Casting by Dianne Crittenden, Production Design by John Stoddart, Art Direction by John Wingrove, Set Decoration by John H. Anderson, Costume Design by Gary Jones, Makeup by Judy Lovell, Associate Producer Neville C. Thompson, Produced by Jerome Hellman, Executive Producer Saul Zaentz. Production Company Jerome Hellman

Productions, The Saul Zaentz Company. Time 117 mins.
On Region 1 DVD through Warner Home Video

Frantic (1988)

Starring Harrison Ford (as Dr Richard Walker), Betty Buckley (Sondra Walker), Emmanuelle Seigner (Michelle), Djiby Soumare (Taxi Driver), Dominique Virton (Desk Clerk), Gérard Klein (Gaillard), Stéphane D'Audeville (Bellboy), Laurent Spielvogel (Hall Porter), Alain Doutey (Hall Porter), Jacques Ciron (Le Grand Hotel Manager), Roch Leibovici (Bellboy 2), Louise Vincent (Tourist), Patrice Melennec (Hotel Detective Le Grand Hotel), Ella Jaroszewicz (Restroom Attendant), Joëlle Lagneau (Florist), Jean-Pierre Delage (Florist), Marc Dudicourt (Cafe Owner), Artus de Penguern (Waiter), Dominique Pinon (Wino), Richard Dieux (Desk Cop), Yves Rénier (Inspector), Robert Ground (US Security Officer), Bruce Johnson (Marine Guard), Michael Morris (US Embassy Clerk), Claude Doineau (US Embassy Clerk), John Mahoney (US Embassy Official).
Directed by Roman Polanski, Screenplay by Roman Polanski & Gérard Brach, with Robert Towne and Jeff Gross (uncredited), Original Music by Ennio Morricone, Cinematography by Witold Sobocinski, Film Editing by Sam O'Steen, Production Design by Pierre Guffroy, Costume Design by Anthony Powell, Chief Makeup Artist Didier Lavergne, Produced by Tim Hampton & Thom Mount. Production Company: Mount/Warner Bros. Time 120 mins.
On Reg 1 DVD through Warner Home Video
On Reg 2 DVD through Warner Home Video

Working Girl (1988)

Starring Harrison Ford (as Jack Trainer), Sigourney Weaver (Katharine Parker), Melanie Griffith (Tess McGill), Alec Baldwin (Mick Dugan), Joan Cusack (Cyn), Philip Bosco (Oren Trask), Nora Dunn (Ginny), Oliver Platt (Lutz), James Lally (Turkel), Kevin Spacey (Bob Speck), Robert Easton (Armbrister), Olympia Dukakis (Personnel Director), Amy Aquino (Alice Baxter), Jeffrey Nordling (Tim Rourke), Elizabeth Whitcraft (Doreen DiMucci), Maggie Wagner (Tess's Birthday Party Friend), Lou DiMaggio (Tess's Birthday Party Friend), David Duchovny (Tess's Birthday Party Friend), Georgienne

Millen (Tess's Birthday Party Friend), Caroline Aaron (Petty Marsh Secretary), Jim Babchak (Jr Executive), Zach Grenier (Jim), Ralph Byers (Dewey Stone Reception Guest), Leslie Ayvazian (Dewey Stone Reception Guest), Steve Cody (Cab Driver), Paige Matthews (Dewey Stone Receptionist), Lee Dalton (John Romano), Barbara Garrick (Phyllis Trask), Madolin B. Archer (Barbara Trask), Etain O'Malley (Hostess at Wedding), Ricki Lake (Bridesmaid).
Directed by Mike Nichols, Screenplay by Kevin Wade, Original Music by Carly Simon, Cinematography by Michael Ballhaus, Film Editing by Sam O'Steen, Casting by Juliet Taylor, Production Design by Patrizia von Brandenstein, Art Direction by Doug Kraner, Set Decoration by George DeTitta Jr, Costume Design by Ann Roth, Makeup Artist Joseph A. Campayno, Produced by Douglas Wick, Executive Producers Robert Greenhut & Laurence Mark. Production Company 20th Century Fox. Time: 115 mins.
On Reg 1 DVD through 20th Century Fox

Indiana Jones and the Last Crusade (1989)

Starring Harrison Ford (as Indiana Jones), Sean Connery (Professor Henry Jones), Denholm Elliott (Dr Marcus Brody), Alison Doody (Dr Elsa Schneider), John Rhys-Davies (Sallah), Julian Glover (Walter Donovan), River Phoenix (Young Indy), Michael Byrne (Vogel), Kevork Malikyan (Kazim), Robert Eddison (Grail Knight), Richard Young (Fedora), Alexei Sayle (Sultan), Alex Hyde-White (Young Henry, scenes deleted), Paul Maxwell (Panama Hat), Isla Blair (Mrs Donovan, as Mrs Glover), Vernon Dobtcheff (Butler), J.J. Hardy (Herman), Bradley Gregg (Roscoe), Jeff O'Haco (Half Breed), Vince Deadrick Sr (Rough Rider), Marc Miles (Sheriff), Ted Grossman (Deputy Sheriff), Tim Hiser (Young Panama Hat), Larry Sanders (Scout Master).
Directed by Steven Spielberg, screenplay by Jeffrey Boam from a story by George Lucas & Menno Meyjes, Original Music by John Williams, Cinematography by Douglas Slocombe, Film Editing by Michael Kahn, with George Lucas(uncredited), Casting by Maggie Cartier, Mike Fenton, Valorie Massalas & Judy Taylor, Production Design by Elliot Scott, Art Direction by Stephen Scott, Set Decoration by Peter Howitt, Costume Design by Joanna Johnston

& Anthony Powell, Chief Makeup Artist (Prosthetics) Nick Dudman, Stunts coordinated by Vic Armstrong, Associate Producer Arthur F. Repola, Produced by Robert Watts, Executive producers George Lucas & Frank Marshall. Production Company Lucasfilm Ltd. Time 127 mins.
On Reg 1 DVD (as part of the Adventures of Indiana Jones box set) through Paramount Home Video
On Reg 2 DVD (as part of the Adventures of Indiana Jones box set) through Paramount Home Video PHE8400

Presumed Innocent (1990)
Starring Harrison Ford (as Rusty Sabich), Brian Dennehy (Raymond Horgan), Raul Julia (Sandy Stern), Bonnie Bedelia (Barbara Sabich), Paul Winfield (Judge Larren Lyttle), Greta Scacchi (Carolyn Polhemus), John Spencer (Det Lipranzer), Joe Grifasi (Tommy Molto), Tom Mardirosian (Nico Della Guardia), Anna Maria Horsford (Eugenia), Sab Shimono ('Painless' Kumagai), Bradley Whitford (Jamie Kemp), Christine Estabrook (Lydia 'Mac' MacDougall), Michael Tolan (Mr Polhemus), Madison Arnold (Sgt Lionel Kenneally), Ron Frazier (Stew Dubinsky), Jesse Bradford (Nat Sabich), Joseph Mazzello (Wendell McGaffney), Tucker Smallwood (Det Harold Greer), Leland Gantt (Leon Wells), Teodorina Bello (Ernestine), David Wohl (Morrie Dickerman), John Michael Bennett (Guerasch), Bo Rucker (Mike Duke), Peter Appel (Glendenning), John Ottavino (Chet), Robert Katims (Cody), Joseph Carberry (Mr McGaffney), John Seitz (Louis Balestrieri), Bill Winkler (Tom), John C. Vennema (Judge Mumphrey), Michael Genet (Court Clerk), Richard L. Newcomb (Undercover Cop), Ed Wheeler (Arresting Detective), Jim Miles Watson (Arresting Detective #2), DeAnn Mears (Loretta, Horgan's Secretary).
Directed by Alan J. Pakula, screenplay by Frank Pierson & Alan J. Pakula, based on the novel by Scott Turow, Original Music by John Williams, Cinematography by Gordon Willis, Film Editing by Evan A. Lottman, Casting by Alixe Gordin, Production Design by George Jenkins, Art Direction by Robert Guerra, Set Decoration by Carol Joffe, Costume Design by John Boxer, Makeup Artist Fern Buchner, Produced by

Sydney Pollack & Mark Rosenberg, Executive producer Susan Solt. Production Company Mirage/Warner Bros. Time 127 mins.
On Reg 1 DVD through Warner Home Video
On Reg 2 DVD through Warner Home Video D012034

Regarding Henry (1991)
Starring Harrison Ford (as Henry Turner), Annette Bening (Sarah Turner), Michael Haley (Court Clerk), Stanley Swerdlow (Mr Matthews (as Stanley H. Swerdlow)), Julie Follansbhee (Mrs Matthews), Rebecca Miller (Linda), Bruce Altman (Bruce, Henry's Partner), Elizabeth Wilson (Jessica, Henry's Secretary), Donald Moffat (Charlie Cameron), Mikki Allen (Rachel Turner), Aida Linares (Rosella), John MacKay (George), Mary Gilbert (Julia), Peter Appel (Eddie the Doorman), Harsh Nayyar (Liquor Store Owner), John Leguizamo (Liquor Store Gunman), Harold House (Policeman), Robin Bartlett (Phyllis), Cynthia Martells (ICU Nurse), James Rebhorn (Dr Sultan), Brian Smiar (Dr. Marx, Chief of Staff), May Quigley (Hillary), Bill Nunn (Bradley, Physical Therapist), Marjorie Monaghan (Julie), Emily Wachtel (Nurse Gloria), Kai Soremekun (Loretta), Suzanne O'Neill (Real Estate Broker), Glen Trotiner (Elevator Man), J.J. Abrams (Delivery Boy), Jack P. Mclaughlin (Taxi Driver), Louis Cantarini (Hot Dog Vendor), Kirby Mitchell (Rudy, Lawyer), William Severs (Lawyer), Mark Irish (Lawyer), Bernadette Penotti (Lawyer), Jim Gardner (Lawyer), Fred Fehrmann (Lawyer), Alva Chinn (Lawyer), Henry Stram (Waiter), Kia Graves (Jennifer), Benjamin Hendrickson (Daniel, Phyllis' Boyfriend), Susan Forristal (Brenda), Ralph Byers (Gerald), Joan Kindred (Party Guest), Hollis Granville (Butler), Anne Stone (Anne, Charlie's Secretary).
Directed by Mike Nichols, Screenplay by J.J. Abrams, Cinematography by Giuseppe Rotunno, Film Editing by Sam O'Steen, Original Music by Hans Zimmer, Casting by Ellen Lewis Juliet Taylor, Production Design by Tony Walton, Art Direction by Dan Davis, William A. Elliott, Set Decoration by Susan Bode & Cindy Carr, Costume Design by Ann Roth, Makeup by Joseph A. Campayno, Stunts by Vic Armstrong, Associate Producer Susan MacNair, Co-produced by J.J. Abrams, Produced by Mike Nichols & Scott Rudin Executive Producer Robert

Greenhut. Production Company Paramount
Pictures. Time 108 mins.
On Reg 1 DVD through Paramount Home
Entertainment
On Reg 2 DVD through Paramount Home
Entertainment

Patriot Games (1992)

Harrison Ford (as Jack Ryan), Anne Archer
(Dr Caroline "Cathy" Ryan), Patrick Bergin
(Kevin O'Donnell), Sean Bean (Sean Miller),
Thora Birch (Sally Ryan), James Fox (Lord
Holmes), Samuel L. Jackson (Lt Cmdr Robby
Jackson), Polly Walker (Annette), J.E. Freeman
(Marty Cantor), James Earl Jones (Adm James
Greer), Richard Harris (Paddy O'Neil), Alex
Norton (Dennis Cooley), Hugh Fraser (Geoffrey
Watkins), David Threlfall (Insp Highland), Alun
Armstrong (Owens), Berlinda Tolbert (Sissy
Jackson), Hugh Ross (Barrister Atkinson),
Gerald Sim (Lord Justice), Pip Torrens (First
Aide), Thomas Russell (Ashley), Jonathan Ryan
(Jimmy O'Reardon), Andrew Connolly (Charlie
Dugan), Karl Hayden (Paddy Boy), Claire
Oberman (Lady Holmes), Oliver Stone (Young
Holmes), Tom Watt (Electrician), P.H. Moriarty
(Court Guard), Rebecca Mayhook (Schoolgirl),
Lucia Noyce (Schoolgirl at Crossing).
Directed by Phillip Noyce, Screenplay by W.
Peter Iliff and Donald Stewart, based on the
novel by Tom Clancy, Cinematography by Donald
McAlpine & Stephen Smith, Film Editing by
William Hoy & Neil Travis, Original Music by
Clannad, James Horner, Casting by Amanda
Mackey Johnson & Cathy Sandrich, Production
Design by Joseph C. Nemec, Art Direction by
Joseph P. Lucky, Costume Design by Norma
Moriceau, Makeup by John R. Bayless & Michael
Key, Stunt Coordinator Martin Grace, Stunts
Terry Leonard, Stunt double (for Harrison Ford,
uncredited) Vic Armstrong, Produced by Mace
Neufeld & Robert Rehme, Executive producer
Charles H. Maguire. Production Company
Paramount Pictures. Time 117 mins
On Reg 1 DVD through Paramount Home
Entertainment
On Reg 2 DVD through Paramount Home
Entertainment PHE8356

The Fugitive (1993)

Starring Harrison Ford (as Dr Richard Kimble),
Tommy Lee Jones (Marshal Samuel Gerard),
Sela Ward (Helen Kimble), Julianne Moore (Dr
Anne Eastman), Joe Pantoliano (Deputy Marshal
Cosmo Renfro), Andreas Katsulas (Frederick
Sykes), Jeroen Krabbé (Dr Charles Nichols),
Daniel Roebuck (Deputy Marshal Robert Biggs),
L. Scott Caldwell (Deputy Marshal Poole),
Tom Wood (Deputy Marshal Noah Newman),
Ron Dean (Detective Kelly), Joseph F. Kosala
(Detective Rosetti), Miguel Nino (Chicago
Cop #1), John Drummond (Newscaster), Tony
Fosco (Chicago Cop #2), Joseph F. Fisher (Otto
Sloan), James Liautuad (Paul), David Darlow (Dr
Alexander 'Alec' Lentz).
Directed by Andrew Davis, Screenplay by Jeb
Stuart & David Twohy from a story by David
Twohy, based on characters created by Roy
Huggins, Cinematography by Michael Chapman,
Film Editing by Don Brochu, David Finfer,
Dean Goodhill, Dov Hoenig, Richard Nord &
Dennis Virkler, Original Music by James Newton
Howard, Casting by Amanda Mackey Johnson &
Cathy Sandrich, Production Design by J. Dennis
Washington, Art Direction by Maher Ahmad,
Set Decoration by Rick Gentz, Costume Design
by Aggie Guerard Rodgers, Makeup Supervisor
Peter Robb-King, Special Effects Coordinator
Roy Arbogast, Stunt Coordinator Terry
Leonard, Co-produced by Stephen Brown, Nana
Greenwald & Peter Macgregor-Scott, Produced
by Arnold Kopelson, Executive Producers Roy
Huggins & Keith Barish. Production Company
Warner Bros. Time 130 mins.
On Reg 1 DVD through Warner Home Video
On Reg 2 DVD through Warner Home Video
D021000

Clear and Present Danger (1994)

Starring Harrison Ford (as Jack Ryan), Willem
Dafoe (John Clark), Anne Archer (Cathy
Muller Ryan), Joaquim de Almeida (Col
Felix Cortez), Henry Czerny (Robert Ritter),
Harris Yulin (James Cutter), Donald Moffat
(President Bennett), Miguel Sandoval (Ernesto
Escobedo), Benjamin Bratt (Captain Ramirez),
Raymond Cruz (Domingo Chavez), Dean Jones
(Judge Moore), Thora Birch (Sally Ryan),
Ann Magnuson (Moira Wolfson), Hope Lange
(Senator Mayo), Tom Tammi (FBI Director
Emile Jacobs), Tim Grimm (FBI Agent Dan
Murray), Belita Moreno (Jean Fowler), James

Earl Jones (Adm James Greer), Jorge Luke (Sipo), Jaime Gomez (Sgt Julio Vega), Jared Chandler (Radioman), Greg Germann (Petey), Ellen Geer (Rose).

Directed by Phillip Noyce, Screenplay by Donald Stewart, Steven Zaillian & John Milius, based on the novel by Tom Clancy, Original Music by James Horner, Cinematography by Donald McAlpine, Film Editing by Neil Travis, Casting by Mindy Marin, Production Design by Terence Marsh, Art Direction by William Cruse, Set Decoration by Jay Hart & Mickey S. Michaels, Costume Design by Bernie Pollack, Stunt Coordinator Dick Ziker, Associate Producer Lis Kern, Co-produced by Ralph S. Singleton, Produced by Mace Neufeld & Robert Rehme. Production Company Paramount Pictures. Time 141 mins.

On Reg 1 DVD through Paramount Home Entertainment

On Reg 2 DVD through Paramount Home Entertainment PHE8357

Sabrina (1995)

Starring Harrison Ford (as Linus Larrabee), Julia Ormond (Sabrina Fairchild), Greg Kinnear (David Larrabee), Nancy Marchand (Maude Larrabee), John Wood (Tom Fairchild), Richard Crenna (Patrick Tyson), Angie Dickinson (Mrs Ingrid Tyson), Lauren Holly (Elizabeth Tyson, MD), Dana Ivey (Mack), Miriam Colon (Rosa), Elizabeth Franz (Joanna), Fanny Ardant (Irène), Valérie Lemercier (Martine), Patrick Bruel (Louis), Becky Ann Baker (Linda), Paul Giamatti (Scott).

Directed by Sydney Pollack, Screenplay by Barbara Benedek & David Rayfiel, based on an earlier screenplay by Billy Wilder, Samuel A. Taylor & Ernest Lehman, based on the play by Samuel A. Taylor, Cinematography by Giuseppe Rotunno, Film Editing by Fredric Steinkamp, Original Music by John Williams, Casting by David Rubin, Production Design by Brian Morris, Art Direction by John Kasarda & Jeremy Conway, Set Decoration by George DeTitta Jr & Amy Marshall, Costume Design by Gary Jones & Ann Roth, Harrison Ford's costumes Bernie Pollack, Produced by Sydney Pollack & Scott Rudin, Executive Producers Lindsay Doran & Ronald L. Schwary. Production Company Paramount Pictures. Time 127 mins.

On Reg 1 DVD through Paramount Home Entertainment

On Reg 1 DVD through Paramount Home Entertainment PHE8176

The Devil's Own (1997)

Starring Harrison Ford (as Tom O'Meara), Brad Pitt (Rory Devaney/Francis Austin McGuire), Margaret Colin (Sheila O'Meara), Rubén Blades (Edwin Diaz), Treat Williams (Billy Burke), George Hearn (Peter Fitzsimmons), Mitch Ryan (Chief Jim Kelly (as Mitchell Ryan), Natascha McElhone (Megan Doherty), Paul Ronan (Sean Phelan), Simon Jones (Harry Sloan), Julia Stiles (Bridget O'Meara), Ashley Carin (Morgan O'Meara), Kelly Singer (Annie O'Meara), David O'Hara (Martin MacDuf), David Wilmot (Dessie), Anthony Brophy (Gerard), Shane Dunne (Young Frankie), Martin Dunne (Frankie's father), Gabrielle Reidy (Frankie's mother), Samantha Conroy (Frankie's sister), Baxter Harris (Customs agent).

Directed by Alan J. Pakula, Screenplay by David Aaron Cohen, Vincent Patrick & Kevin Jarre, based on a story by Kevin Jarre, Cinematography by Gordon Willis, Film Editing by Tom Rolf & Dennis Virkler, Original Music by James Horner, Casting by Alixe Gordin, Production Design by Jane Musky, Art Direction by Robert Guerra, Set Decoration by Leslie Bloom, Costume Design by Joan Bergin & Bernie Pollack, Makeup & Hair Stylist (for Brad Pitt) Jean Ann Black, Chief Makeup Artist Rosie Blackmore, Special Effects Supervisors Edward Wiessenhaan & Harrie Wiessenhaan, Stunt Double (Harrison Ford) John Alden, Stunt Double (Reuben Blades) Daniel W. Barringer, Stunt Coordinator Doug Coleman, Associate Producers Shari Hamrick Karen L. Thorson, Produced by Robert F. Colesberry & Lawrence Gordon, Executive Producers Lloyd Levin Donald Laventhall. Production Company Columbia Picture Corporation. Time 111 mins.

On Reg 1 DVD through Sony Pictures

On Reg 2 DVD through Columbia Pictures CDR94773

Air Force One (1997)

Starring Harrison Ford (as President James Marshall), Gary Oldman (Ivan Korshunov), Glenn Close (Vice President Kathryn Bennett),

Wendy Crewson (Grace Marshall), Liesel Matthews (Alice Marshall), Paul Guilfoyle (Chief of Staff Lloyd 'Shep' Shepherd), Xander Berkeley (Secret Service Agent Gibbs), William H. Macy (Major Caldwell), Dean Stockwell (Defense Secretary Walter Dean), Tom Everett (National Security Advisor Jack Doherty), Jürgen Prochnow (General Ivan Radek), Donna Bullock (Deputy Press Secretary Melanie Mitchel), Michael Ray Miller (Colonel Axelrod), Carl Weintraub (Lt. Colonel Ingraham), Elester Latham (AFO Navigator), Elya Baskin (Andrei Kolchak), Levani Outchaneichvili (Sergei Lenski), David Vadim (Igor Nevsky), Andrew Divoff (Boris Bazylev), Ilia Volokh (Vladimir Krasin), Chris Howell (Major Perkins), Spencer Garrett (Thomas Lee, White House Aide), Bill Smitrovich (General Northwood), Philip Baker Hall (US Attorney General Andrew Ward), Albert Owens ('Football' Colonel), Willard E. Pugh (White House Communications Officer), Michael Monks (Assistant Press Secretary), (Russian President Petrov), Messiri Freeman (Future Postmaster General), Thomas Crawford (Mike, Steward), Fenton Lawless (Joey, Steward), Dan Shor (Notre Dame Aide), David Gianopoulos (Agent Johnson), Glenn Morshower (Agent Walters).

Directed by Wolfgang Petersen, Screenplay by Andrew W. Marlowe, Cinematography by Michael Ballhaus, Film Editing by Richard Francis-Bruce, Original Music by Jerry Goldsmith, Additional Music Joel McNeely, Casting by Janet Hirshenson & Jane Jenkins, Production Design by William Sandell, Art Direction by Carl Aldana & Carl J. Stensel, Set Decoration by Ernie Bishop, Costume Design by Erica Edell Phillips, Key Makeup Artist Kevin Haney, Stunt Coordinator Doug Coleman, Stunt Double (Harrison Ford, uncredited) John Alden, Special Effects coordinator Terry D. Frazee, Visual Effects supervisor Richard Edlund, Associate Producers Peter Kohn & Mary Montiforte, Produced by Wolfgang Petersen, Armyan Bernstein, Gail Katz & Jonathan Shestack, Executive Producers Marc Abraham, Thomas A. Bliss & David V. Lester. Production Company Beacon Communications LLC/Columbia Pictures Corporation/Radiant Productions. Time 124 mins.
On Reg 1 DVD through Sony Pictures

On Reg 2 DVD through Touchstone BED888315

Six Days Seven Nights (1998)

Starring Harrison Ford (as Quinn Harris), Anne Heche (Robin Monroe), David Schwimmer (Frank Martin), Jacqueline Obradors (Angelica), Temuera Morrison (Jager), Allison Janney (Marjorie, Robin's Boss), Douglas Weston (Philippe Sinclair, Resort Manager), Cliff Curtis (Kip), Danny Trejo (Pierce), Ben Bode (Tom Marlowe, Helicopter Pilot), Derek Basco (Ricky, Helicopter Crewman), Amy Sedaris (Robin's Secretary), Long Nguyen (Pirate), Jake Feagai (Pirate), John Koyama (Pirate), Jen Sung Outerbridge (Pirate), Michael Chapman (Mechanic), E. Kalani Flores (Tahitian Priest at Funeral), Ping Wu (Infirmary Orderly), Greg Gorman (Photographer), Hoyt Richards (Model), Odile Corso (Model).

Directed by Ivan Reitman, Screenplay by Michael Browning, Original Music by Randy Edelman, Cinematography by Michael Chapman, Film Editing by Wendy Greene Bricmont & Sheldon Kahn, Casting by Michael Chinich & Bonnie Timmermann, Production Design by J. Michael Riva, Art Direction by Richard F. Mays, Set Decoration by Lauri Gaffin, Costume Design by Gloria Gresham, Hair Stylist (for Ford) Michael Kriston, Makeup Artist (for Ford) Michael Laudati, Visual Effects Supervisor David Goldberg, Stunt Coordinator Doug Coleman, Stunt Double (for Harrison Ford, uncredited) John Alden, Associate Producers Terry Norton & Michael Palmieri, Co-produced by Sheldon Kahn & Gordon A. Webb, Produced by Roger Birnbaum, Wallis Nicita & Ivan Reitman, Executive Producers Julie Bergman Sender, Daniel Goldberg & Joe Medjuck. Production Company Caravan Pictures/Northern Lights Entertainment/Roger Birnbaum Productions/ Touchstone Pictures. Time 102 mins.
On Reg 1 DVD through Walt Disney Video
On Reg 2 DVD through Touchstone BED888164

Random Hearts (1999)

Starring Harrison Ford (as Sergeant William 'Dutch' Van Den Broeck), Kristin Scott Thomas (Kay Chandler), Charles S. Dutton (Alcee), Bonnie Hunt (Wendy Judd), Dennis Haysbert (Detective George Beaufort), Sydney Pollack (Carl Broman), Richard Jenkins (Truman

Trainor), Paul Guilfoyle (Dick Montoya), Susanna Thompson (Peyton Van Den Broeck), Peter Coyote (Cullen Chandler), Dylan Baker (Richard Judd), Lynne Thigpen (Phyllis Bonaparte), Susan Floyd (Molly Roll), Bill Cobbs (Marvin), Kate Mara (Jessica Chandler), Ariana Thomas (Shyla Mumford), Nelson Landrieu (Silvio Coya), Brooke Smith (Sarah), Christina Chang (Laurie), Michelle Hurd (Susan), Reiko Aylesworth (Mary Claire Clark).

Directed by Sydney Pollack, Screenplay by Kurt Luedtke, adapted from the Warren Adler novel by Darryl Ponicsan, Original Music by Dave Grusin, Cinematography by Philippe Rousselot, Film Editing by William Steinkamp, Casting by David Rubin, Production Design by Barbara Ling, Art Direction by Chris Shriver, Set Decoration by Susan Bode, Costume Design by Bernie Pollack, Gowns (for Ms Thomas) Ann Roth, Key Makeup Artist Naomi Donne, Hair Stylist (for Ford) Michael Kriston, Makeup Artist (for Ford) Michael Laudati, stunt coordinator Mickey Giacomazzi, Produced by Sydney Pollack & Marykay Powell, Executive Producers Warren Adler & Ronald L. Schwary. Production Company Columbia Pictures Corporation/Mirage Enterprises/Rastar Pictures. Time: 133 mins.
On Reg 1 DVD through Sony Pictures
On Reg 2 DVD through Touchstone CDR28808

What Lies Beneath (2000)

Harrison Ford (Dr Norman Spencer), Michelle Pfeiffer (Claire Spencer), Diana Scarwid (Jody), Joe Morton (Dr Drayton), James Remar (Warren Feur), Miranda Otto (Mary Feur), Amber Valletta (Madison Elizabeth Frank), Katharine Towne (Caitlin Spencer), Victoria Bidewell (Beatrice), Eliott Goretsky (Teddy), Ray Baker (Dr Stan Powell), Wendy Crewson (Elena), Sloane Shelton (Mrs Templeton), Tom Dahlgren (Dean Templeton), Jayson Argento (Cafe Customer), Micole Mercurio (Mrs Frank).

Directed by Robert Zemeckis, Screenplay by Clark Gregg, from a story by Sarah Kernochan & Clark Gregg, Cinematography by Don Burgess, Film Editing by Arthur Schmidt, Original Music by Alan Silvestri, Casting by Marcia DeBonis & Ellen Lewis, Production Design by Rick Carter & Jim Teegarden, Art Direction by Stefan Dechant, Tony Fanning & Elizabeth Lapp, Set Decoration by Karen O'Hara, Costume Design by Susie DeSanto, Costume Designer (for Harrison Ford) Bernie Pollack, Key Hair Stylist Janice Alexander, Key Makeup Artist Deborah La Mia Denaver, Visual Effects Supervisor Robert Legato, Stunt Coordinator Tim A. Davison, Stunt Double (for Harrison Ford) Jon H. Epstein, Stunt Double (for Michelle Pfeiffer) Tricia Peters, Associate Producers Steven J. Boyd & Cherylanne Martin, Produced by Jack Rapke, Steve Starkey & Robert Zemeckis, Executive Producer Joan Bradshaw & Mark Johnson. Production Company 20th Century Fox/DreamWorks SKG/ImageMovers. Time 130 mins.
On Reg 1 DVD through Dreamworks Video
On Reg 2 DVD through Touchstone 20021DVD

K-19: The Widowmaker (2002)

Starring Harrison Ford (as Alexei Vostrikov), Liam Neeson (Mikhail Polenin), Joss Ackland (Marshal Zelentsov), Sam Spruell (Dmitri), Peter Stebbings (Kuryshev), Christian Camargo (Pavel), Roman Podhora (Lapinsh), Sam Redford (Vasily), Steve Nicolson (Demichev), Ravil Issyanov (Suslov), Tim Woodward (Partonov), Lex Shrapnel (Kornilov), Shaun Benson (Leonid), Kristen Holden-Reid (Anton), Dmitry Chepovetsky (Sergei), Christopher Redman (Kiklidze), Tygh Runyan (Maxim), John Shrapnel (Admiral Bratyeev).

Directed by Kathryn Bigelow, Screenplay by Christopher Kyle, from a story by Louis Nowra, Cinematography by Jeff Cronenweth & Anthony Nocera, Film Editing by Walter Murch, Original Music by Klaus Badelt, with additional music by Geoff Zanelli, Casting by Ross Clydesdale, Mali Finn & Mary Selway, Production Design by Karl Juliusson & Michael Novotny, Art Direction by Arvinder Grewal, Angela Murphy & William Ladd Skinner, Set Decoration by Ian Greig, Carol Lavallee & Dan Wladyka, Costume Design by Marit Allen, Key makeup artist Jordan Samuel, Special makeup effects artist Gordon J. Smith, Hair designer: Mr. Ford Michael Kriston, Makeup artist: Mr. Ford Michael Laudati, Special effects supervisor Tony Kenny, Visual effects supervisors John Nelson & Bruce Jones, Stunt coordinators Rick Skene, Mickey Giacomazzi & Jamie Jones, Associate producers Winship Cook, Steve Danton & Samara Koffler, Co-producers Basil Iwanyk, Steven-Charles Jaffe, Mary Montiforte,

Brent O'Connor & Mark Wolfe, Line producers Oliver Hengst & Leonid Vereschtchaguine, Produced by Kathryn Bigelow, Edward S. Feldman, Sigurjon Sighvatsson & Chris Whitaker, Executive producers Moritz Borman, Guy East, Harrison Ford, Dieter Nobbe, Volker Schauz & Nigel Sinclair. Production Company First Light Production, IMF Internationale Medien und Film GmbH & Co. 2. Produktions KG, Intermedia Films, National Geographic Society, New Regency Pictures, Palomar Pictures Corporation. Time 138 mins.
On Reg 1 DVD through Paramount Home Entertainment
On Reg 2 DVD through Paramount Home Entertainment PHE8259

Hollywood Homicide (2003)

Starring Harrison Ford (as Joe Gavilan), Josh Hartnett (K.C. Calden), Lena Olin (Ruby), Bruce Greenwood (Lt Bennie Macko), Isaiah Washington (Antoine Sartain), Lolita Davidovich (Cleo Ricard), Keith David (Leon), Master P (Julius Armas), Gladys Knight (Olivia Robidoux), Lou Diamond Phillips (Wanda), Meredith Scott Lynn (I.A. Detective Jackson), Tom Todoroff (I.A. Detective Zino), James MacDonald (Danny Broome), Kurupt (K-Ro), André Benjamin (Silk Brown), Alan Dale (Commander Preston), Clyde Kusatsu (Coroner Chung), Dwight Yoakam (Leroy Wasley), Martin Landau (Jerry Duran), Eric Idle (Celebrity), Frank Sinatra Jr. (Marty Wheeler), Robert Wagner (Himself), Johnny Grant (Himself), Smokey Robinson (Cabbie). Directed by Ron Shelton, Screenplay by Robert Souza & Ron Shelton, Cinematography by Barry Peterson, Film Editing by Paul Seydor, Original Music by Alex Wurman, Casting by Ed Johnston, Production Design by James D. Bissell, Art Direction by Christa Munro, Set Decoration by Jan Pascale, Costume Design by Bernie Pollack, Hair stylist (for Mr Ford) Michael Kriston, Makeup artist (for Mr Ford) Michael Laudati, Special effects coordinator Ken Pepiot, Visual effects supervisor Carey Villegas, Stunt coordinator Jeffrey J. Dashnaw, Stunt double (for Harrison Ford, uncredited) Gary J. Wayton, Co-producers Scott Bernstein, Allegra Clegg & Robert Souza, Produced by Lou Pitt & Ron Shelton, Executive Producers David V. Lester & Joe Roth. Producton Company Revolution

Studios, The Pitt Group. Time 116 mins.
On Reg 1 DVD through Sony Pictures
On Reg 2 DVD through Paramount Home Entertainment CDR34859

Water to Wine (2004)
Written and Directed by Willie McMillon. Starring Harrison Ford (as Jethro the Bus Driver), Malcolm Ford (Himself).

Firewall (2006)
Starring Harrison Ford (as Jack Stanfield), Virginia Madsen (Beth Stanfield), Paul Bettany (Bill Cox), Jimmy Bennett (Andrew Stanfield), Beverley Breuer (Sandra), Matthew Currie Holmes (Bobby), Eric Keenleyside (Allan Hughes), Jennifer Kitchen (Dani), Carly Schroeder (Sarah Stanfield), Ken Tremblett (Bob), Vince Vieluf (Pim), Finn Michael (Bank Executive), Rebecca Reichert (Girlfriend), with Alan Arkin, Robert Forster, Robert Patrick, Nikolaj Coster-Waldau, Zachary De Wilde, Stephen Milton, Mary Lynn Rajskub, Kett Turton.
Directed by Richard Loncraine, Screenplay by Joe Forte, Cinematography by Marco Pontecorvo, Film Editing by Jim Page, Original Music by Alexandre Desplat, Casting by Mary Gail Artz, Heike Brandstatter & Coreen Mayrs, Production Design by Brian Morris, Art Direction by Helen Jarvis, Costume Design by Shuna Harwood, Makeup artist (for Mr Ford) Michael Laudati, Visual Effects Supervised by Mark Breakspear, Produced by Armyan Bernstein, Basil Iwanyk & Jonathan Shestack, Executive Producers Bruce Berman, Graham Burke, Jeff Clifford, Dana Goldberg, Charlie Lyons & Brent O'Connor. Production Company Village Roadshow Pictures. Time 105 mins
On Reg 1 DVD through Warner Home Video
On Reg 2 DVD through Warner Home Video CDR34859

Crossing Over (2008)
Starring Harrison Ford (as Max Brogan), Sean Penn (Chris Farrell), Ray Liotta (Cole Frankel), Ashley Judd (Denise Frankel), Summer Bishil (Taslima Jahangir), Lee Horsley (Ray Cooper), Cliff Curtis (Hamid Baraheri), Jaysha Patel (Jahanara Jahangir), Alice Eve (Claire Shepard), Alice Braga (Mireya), Melody Khazae (Zahra

Baraheri), Merik Tadros (Farid Baraheri), Justin Chon (Yong Kim), Marshall Manesh (Sanjar Baraheri), Tim Chiou (Steve).
Written & Directed by Wayne Kramer, Cinematography by Jim Whitaker, Film Editing by Arthur Coburn, Production Design by Toby Corbett, Art Direction by Peter Borck, Set Decoration by Linda Lee Sutton, Costume Design by Kristin M. Burke, Produced by Wayne Kramer & Frank Marshall, Co-produced by Gregg Taylor, Executive producers Michael Beugg, Bob Weinstein & Harvey Weinstein. Production Companies The Weinstein Company, The Kennedy/Marshall Company, Movie Prose & C.O. Films. Time 113 mins.
On Region 1 DVD through The Weinstein Company
On Region 2 DVD though Eiv EDV 9640

Indiana Jones and the Kingdom of the Crystal Skull (2008)

Starring Harrison Ford (as Indiana Jones), Karen Allen (Marion Ravenwood), Cate Blanchett (Col Dr Irina Spalko), Shia LaBeouf (Mutt Williams), John Hurt (Professor Harold Oxley), Ray Winstone (George 'Mac' McHale), Jim Broadbent (Dean Charles Stanforth), Joel Stoffer (Agent Taylor), Igor Jijikine (Dovchenko), Alan Dale (General Ross), Andrew Divoff (Russian soldier), Pavel Lychnikoff (Russian soldier).
Directed by Steven Spielberg, Screenplay by David Koepp, Cinematography by Janusz Kaminski, Film Editing by Michael Kahn, Original Music by John Williams, Casting by Debra Zane, Production Design by Guy Hendrix Dyas, Art Direction by Luke Freeborn, Costume Design by Bernie Pollack & Mary Zophres, Visual Effects Supervised by Pablo Helman, Produced by Frank Marshall & Denis L. Stewart, Executive Producers Kathleen Kennedy & George Lucas, Production Company Lucasfilm and Paramount Pictures. Time 122 mins.
On Region 1 DVD through Paramount Home Entertainment: Single-Disc, Two-Disc (ASIN: B00005JPO1)
On Region 2 DVD though Paramount Home Entertainment, Single-Disc, Two-Disc

Brüno (2009)

With Harrison Ford (as himself, uncredited).

Extraordinary Measures (2009)

Starring Brendan Fraser (as John Crowley), Harrison Ford (Dr Robert Stonehill), Keri Russell (Aileen Crowley), Meredith Droeger (Megan Crowley), Diego Velazquez (Patrick Crowley), Sam M. Hall (John Crowley, Jr), Jared Harris (Dr Kent Webber), Patrick Bauchau (CEO Erich Loring), Alan Ruck (Pete Sutphen), David Clennon (Dr Renzler), Dee Wallace (Sal), Courtney B. Vance (Marcus Temple), Ayanna Berkshire (Wendy Temple), P. J. Byrne (Dr Preston), Andrea White (Dr Allegria)
Directed by Tom Vaughan, Screenplay by Robert Nelson Jacobs (based on the book by Geeta Anand), Cinematography by Andrew Dunn, Editing by Anne V. Coates, Music by Andrea Guerra, Casting by Margery Simkin & Lana Veenker, Production Design by Derek R. Hill, Art Direction by John Richardson, Set Decoration by Denise Pizzini, Costume Design by Deena Appel, Makeup Artist (for Harrison Ford) Bill Corso, Associate Producers Josh Rothstein & Jordana Glick-Franzheim, Produced by Carla Santos Shamberg, Michael Shamberg & Stacey Sher, Executive Producer Harrison Ford & Nan Morales. Production Companies CBS Films & Double Feature Films. Time 106 mins.
On Region 1 DVD through Sony Pictures
On Region 2 DVD though Sony Pictures Home Entertainment

Morning Glory (2010)

Starring Rachel McAdams (as Becky Fuller), Noah Bean (First Date), Harrison Ford (Mike Pomeroy), Jack Davidson (Dog Walking Neighbor), Diane Keaton (Colleen Peck), Vanessa Aspillaga (Anna), Patrick Wilson (Adam Bennett), Jeff Goldblum (Jerry Barnes), Jeff Hiller (Sam, Channel 9 Producer), Linda Powell (Louanne), Mike Hydeck (Ralph), Joseph J. Vargas (Channel 9 Director), Mario Frieson (Channel 9 Technical Director), Kevin Herbst (Channel 9 Associate Director), Jerome Weinstein (Fred).
Directed by Roger Michell, Screeplay by Aline Brosh McKenna, Music by David Arnold, Cinematography by Alwin H. Kuchler, Editing by Daniel Farrell, Nick Moore & Steven Weisberg, Casting by Marcia DeBonis & Ellen Lewis, Production Design by Mark Friedberg, Art Direction by Alex DiGerlando & Kim

Jennings, Set Decoration by Alyssa Winter, Costume Design by Frank L. Fleming, Costumes (for Harrison Ford) Bernie Pollack, Makeup Artist (for Harrison Ford) Bill Corso, Stunt Coordinator Peter Bucossi, Associate Producers Udi Nedivi & Lindsey Paulson, Produced by J.J. Abrams & Bryan Burk, Executive Producers Sherryl Clark & Guy Riedel. Production Company Bad Robot, in association with Goldcrest Pictures. Time 107 mins.
On Region 1 DVD through Paramount Home Entertainment
On Region 2 DVD through Paramount Home Entertainment

Cowboys & Aliens (2011)
Starring Daniel Craig (as Jake Lonergan), Harrison Ford (Woodrow Dolarhyde), Abigail Spencer (Alice), Buck Taylor (Wes Claiborne), Matthew Taylor (Luke Claiborne), Cooper Taylor (Mose Claiborne), Clancy Brown (Meacham), Paul Dano (Percy Dolarhyde), Chris Browning (Jed Parker), Adam Beach (Nat Colorado), Sam Rockwell (Doc), Ana de la Reguera (Maria), Noah Ringer Emmett (Taggart), Brian Duffy (Deputy), Olivia Wilde (Ella Swenson), Keith Carradine (Sheriff John Taggart), Brendan Wayne (Charlie Lyle), Gavin Grazer (Ed), Toby Huss (Roy Murphy), Wyatt Russell (Little Mickey), Jimmy Jatho (Saloon Patron), Kenny Call (Greavey), Walton Goggins (Hunt), Julio Cedillo (Bronc), Garret Noel (Gang Member), David O'Hara (Pat Dolan), Troy Gilbert (Red), Chad Randall (Bull McCade), Scout Schoenfeld Hendrickson (Jake's Gang Member), Raoul Trujillo (Black Knife). Directed by Jon Favreau, Screenplay by Roberto Orci, Alex Kurtzman & Damon Lindelof and Mark Fergus & Hawk Ostby (based on a screen story by Mark Fergus & Hawk Ostby, from a story by Scott Mitchell Rosenberg), Original Music by Harry Gregson-Williams, Cinematography by Matthew Libatique, Film Editing by Dan Lebental & Jim May, Casting by Sarah Finn, Production Design by Scott Chambliss, Art Direction by Christopher Burian-Mohr & Daniel T. Dorrance, Set Decoration by Karen Manthey, Costume Design by Mary Zophres, Makeup Artist (for Harrison Ford) Bill Corso, Visual Effects Supervisor for ILM Roger Guyett, Special Effects Supervisor Daniel Sudick, Stunt Coordinator Thomas Robinson Harper, Associate Producer Karen Johnson, Co-Produced by Daniel Forcey, Chris Wade & K.C. Hodenfield, Produced by Brian Grazer & Ron Howard and Alex Kurtzman, Roberto Orci & Damon Lindelof and Scott Mitchell Rosenberg, Executive Producers Jon Favreau, Bobby Cohen, Randy Greenberg, Ryan Kavanaugh, Denis L. Stewart & Steven Spielberg. Production Companies Universal Studios & Dreamworks. Time 118 mins.
On Region 1 DVD through Universal Pictures – Release date TBC
On Region 2 DVD though Paramount Home Entertainment – Release date 26 Dec 2011.

HARRISON FORD: OTHER APPEARANCES AND ACHIEVEMENTS

TV APPEARANCES

The Mike Douglas Show, 1977 – Himself
The Merv Griffith Show, 1977 – Himself
Dinah!, 1977 – Himself
The Making of Star Wars, 1977 – Himself
The Alan Hamel Show, 1977 – Himself
Star Wars Holiday Special, 1978 – Han Solo
Clapper Board, 1981 – Himself
Great Movie Stunts: Raiders of the Lost Ark, 1981 – Host
The Making of Raiders of the Lost Ark, 1981 – Himself
Return of the Ewok, 1982 – Himself/Han Solo
From Star Wars to Jedi – The Making of a Saga, 1983 – Himself
Frontline, 1983 – playing Narrator in The Lost American
Making of Indiana Jones and the Temple of Doom, 1984 – himself
Oprah, 1986 (celebrity interview w/ Harrison Ford) – Himself
Aspel & Company, 1987 – Himself
Film '89 – Himself (10 October 1989)
Premier: Inside the Summer Blockbusters, 1989 – Himself
The Making of Indiana Jones and the Temple of Doom, 1989 – Himself
Hearts of Darkness: A Filmmaker's Apocalypse, 1991 – Himself
Earth and the America Dream, 1992 – Narrator
Behind the Scenes: A Portrait of Pierre Guffroy, 1992 – Himself
Secret World of Spying, 1992 – Jack Ryan
Superstars of Action, 1993 – Himself
The Tonight Show with Jay Leno, 1993 – Himself (30 July 1993)
George Lucas: Heroes, Myths and Magic, 1993 – Himself
A Century of Cinema, 1994 – Himself
The 66th Annual Academy Awards, 1994 – Himself, presenter Best Picture
Mustang: The Hidden Kingdom, 1994 – Narrator
Jimmy Hollywood, 1994 (uncredited) – Himself
The Walt Disney Company and MacDonald's present the American Teacher Awards, 1995 – Himself
The American Film Institute Salute to Steven Spielberg, 1995 – Himself

The Charlie Rose Show, 1996 – Himself as a Guest (2 January 1996)
Film '96 – Himself (15 January 1996)
Leute heute, 1997 – Himself in "Filmfestspiele Venedig"
The Charlie Rose Show, 1997 – Himself as a Guest (25 March 1997)
The Rosie O'Donnell Show, 1997 – Himself (26 March 1997)
Late Show with David Letterman, 1997 – Himself as Guest (9 June 1997)
The Charlie Rose Show, 1997 – Himself as a Guest (22 July 1997)
Late Show with David Letterman, 1997 – Himself as Guest (28 July 1997)
Frontline: "The Lost American", 1997 – Narrator
Harrison Ford: The Reluctant Hero, 1998 – Himself
The 24th Annual People's Choice Awards, 1998 – Himself
The Rosie O'Donnell Show, 1998 – Himself (1 June 1998)
The Charlie Rose Show, 1998 – Himself as a Guest (16 June 1998)
Magic Hour, 1998 – Himself (Series 1, Episode 2)
Biography: "Steven Spielberg: An Empire of Dreams", 1998 – Himself
The Making of American Graffiti, 1998 – Himself
People Profiles: Harrison Ford, 1999 – Himself
The Stars of Star Wars: Interviews from the Cast, 1999 – Himself
The Unauthorised Star Wars Story, 1999 – Himself
E! Celebrity Profile Series, 1999 – Himself
Indiana Jones and the Last Crusade: A Look Inside, 1999 – Himself
The 71st Annual Academy Awards, 1999 – Himself (presenter, Best Picture)
The Howard Stern Radio Show (tv series), 1999 – Himself
Larry King Live, 1997/1999 – Himself
From Star Wars to Star Wars: The Story of Industrial Light & Magic, 1999 – Himself
Jane Goodall, Reason for Hope, 1999 – Himself
57th Annual Golden Globe Awards, 2000 – Himself
The Directors, 1999/2000 – Himself (various

segments on Spielberg, Pollack, Noyce, Lucas and Ivan Reitman)
AFI Salute to Harrison Ford, 2000 – Himself (honoree)
Late Night with Conan O'Brien, 2000 – Himself (25 July 2000)
Blockbuster Entertainment Awards, 2000 – Himself
HBO First Look, 2000 – Himself ("The Making of Random Hearts" and "What Lies Beneath: Constructing the Perfect Thriller")
Inside the Actors Studio, 2000 – Himself
Legends, 2000 – Himself
Derailed: Anatomy of a Train Wreck, 2001 – Himself
Lost Worlds: Life in the Balance, 2001 – Himself
AFI's 100 Years … 100 Thrills: America's Most Heart-Pounding Movies, 2001 – Host
The Concert for New York City, 2001 – Himself
R2-D2: Beneath the Dome, 2001 – Himself
Patriot Games: Up Close, 2002 – Himself
The 59th Annual Golden Globe Awards, 2002 – Himself (winner: Cecil B. DeMille Award)
Clear and Present Danger: Behind the Danger, 2002 – Himself
The Search for Life: Are We Alone? 2002 – Narrator
The Tonight Show with Jay Leno, 2002 – Himself (15 July 2002)
The Charlie Rose Show, 2002 – Himself as a Guest (19 July 2002)
Rank, 2002 – Himself (placed 19th in "The 25 Toughest Stars")
AFI's 100 Years … 100 Passions: America's Greatest Love Stories, 2002 – Himself
VH-1 Where Are They Now? 2002 – Himself
Harrison Ford: Just Another Pilot, 2002 – Himself
Revealed with Jules Asner, 2002 – Himself in "Harrison Ford Revealed"
Film 2002 – Himself
Leute heute, 2002 – Himself in Filmfestspiele Venedig
Macy's 4th of July Spectacular, 2003 – Himself
ABC World Stunt Awards, 2003 – Himself
MTV Movie Awards, 2003 – Himself
AFI's 100 Years… 100 Heroes & Villains, 2003 – Himself
60th Annual Golden Globe Awards, 2003 – Himself (presenter, Best Director)
Young Hollywood Awards, 2003 – Himself

75th Annual Academy Awards, 2003 – Himself (presenter, Best Director)
Late Night with Conan O'Brien, 2003 – Himself (13 June 2003)
The Charlie Rose Show, 2003 – Himself as a Guest (20 June 2003)
This Is Your Life, 2003 – Himself (Ford was surprising subject Vic Armstrong)
The Daily Show, 2003 – Himself (16 June 2003)
Extra, 2003 – Himself
The Stunts of Indiana Jones, 2003 – Himself
Indiana Jones: Making the Trilogy, 2003 – Himself
Brits Go to Hollywood, 2003 – Himself
Tinseltown TV, 2004 – Himself
Empire of Dreams: The Story of the Star Wars Trilogy, 2004 – Himself/Han Solo
When Star Wars Ruled the World, 2004 – Himself
The Characters of Star Wars, 2004 – Himself/Han Solo
AFI Life Achievement Award: A Tribute to George Lucas (a TV special), 2005 – Himself (speaker)
Between Two Worlds: The Making of Witness, 2005 – Himself
The 32nd Annual People's Choice Awards, 2006 – Himself
The 63rd Annual Golden Globe Awards, 2006 – Himself (presenter, Best Screenplay)
The Tonight Show with Jay Leno, 2006 – Himself (31 January 2006)
Late Show with David Letterman, 2006 – Himself as Guest (6 February 2006)
Live with Regis and Kelly, 2006 – Himself (7 February 2006)
Late Night with Conan O'Brien, 2006 – Himself (7 February 2006)
The Daily Show, 2006 – Himself (8 February 2006)
The Charlie Rose Show, 2006 – Himself as a Guest (9 February 2006)
Ellen: The Ellen DeGeneres Show, 2006 – Himself
Breakfast, 2006 – Himself (22 March 2006)
Martha, 2006 – Himself
Sunrise, 2006 – Himself
Getaway, 2006 – Himself
The Hollywood Greats, 2006 – Himself in "Harrison Ford"
Firewall: Decoded, 2006 – Himself

AFI Life Achievement Award: A Tribute to Sean Connery, 2006 – Himself
The 58th Annual Primetime Emmy Awards, 2006 – Himself
In the Mix, 2006 – Himself
SuperBowl XL, 2006 – Himself (opening the game)
Today Show, 2006 – Himself (2 June 2006)
Corazón de ... , 2005 – Himself
Star Wars: Feel the Force, 2006 – Himself
Taurus World Stunt Awards, 2007 – Himself
AFI's 100 Years... 100 Movies: 10th Anniversary Edition, 2007 – Himself
Dalai Lama Renaissance, 2007 – Himself as Narrator
Sex, Censorship and the Silver Screen, 2007 – Himself as Quote Reader
Scream Awards, 2007 – Himself
Dangerous Days: Making Blade Runner, 2007 – Himself
Fashion Forward: Wardrobe and Styling, 2007 – Himself
Deck-A-Rep: The True Nature of Rick Deckard, 2007 – Himself
Movies Rock, 2007 – Himself as Presenter
The Barbara Walters Special "Stars with Barbara Walters on Oscar Night", 2008 – Himself
Live from the Red Carpet: The 2008 Academy Awards, 2008 – Himself
Jimmy Kimmel Live!, 2008 – Himself (24 February 2008)
The 80th Annual Academy Awards, 2008 – Himself as presenter, Best Original Screenplay
Nickelodeon Kids' Choice Awards, 2008 – Himself
Indiana Jones: An Appreciation, 2008 – Himself
Indiana Jones and the Creepy Crawlies, 2008 – Himself
Le grand journal de Canal+, 2008 – Himself
The Immortal Beaver, 2008 – Himself
Nova, 2008 – Himself / Narrator in "Lord of the Ants"
The Tonight Show with Jay Leno, 2008 – Himself (9 May 2008)
Late Show with David Letterman, 2008 – Himself as Guest (20 May 2008)
Up Close with Carrie Keagan, 2008 – Himself (21 May 2008)
Late Night with Conan O'Brien, 2008 – Himself (21 May 2008)

Live with Regis and Kelly, 2008 – Himself (22 May 2008)
Late Show with David Letterman, 2008 – Himself as Guest (22 May 2008)
The View, 2008 – Himself
AFI's 10 Top 10: America's 10 Greatest Films in 10 Classic Genres, 2008 – Himself
The 60th Primetime Emmy Awards, 2008 – Himself
The Crystal Skulls, 2008 – Himself
Production Diary: Making of The Kingdom of the Crystal Skull, 2008 – Himself
Indiana Jones 4: The Return of a Legend, 2008 – Himself
Indiana Jones 4: Pre-production, 2008 – Himself
The Movie Loft, 2008 – Himself
Brüno, 2009 – Himself (uncredited)
Scream Awards, 2009 – Himself
Wings Over the Rockies, 2009 – Himself
Brace for Impact: The Chesley B. Sullenberger Story, 2010 – Himself as Narrator
Mark at the Movies, 2010 – Himself
The 67th Annual Golden Globe Awards, 2010 – Himself as Clip Presenter
The Hour, 2010 – Himself
Jimmy Kimmel Live!, 2010 – Himself (15 January 2010)
Up Close with Carrie Keagan, 2010 – Himself (21 January 2010)
Late Show with David Letterman, 2010 – Himself as Guest (21 January 2010)
Live with Regis and Kelly, 2010 – Himself (22 January 2010)
The Doctors, 2010 – Himself
Made in Hollywood, 2010 – Himself (23 January 2010)
The Charlie Rose Show, 2010 – Himself as a Guest (26 January 2010)
Breakfast, 2010 – Himself (26 February 2010)
Live from Studio Five, 2010 – Himself
Xposé, 2010 – Himself
AFI Life Achievement Award: A Tribute to Mike Nichols, 2010 – Himself
P.O.V., 2010 – Himself in "The Beaches of Agnes"
The Tonight Show with Jay Leno, 2010 – Himself (13 October 2010)
Late Show with David Letterman, 2010 – Himself as Guest (8 November 2010)
The Daily Show, 2010 – Himself (9 November 2010)
Jimmy Kimmel Live!, 2010 – Himself (11

November 2010)
Made in Hollywood, 2010 – Himself (20 November 2010)
Conan, 2010 – Himself in "A Fistful of Chowder" (2010)
Breakfast, 2011 – Himself (11 January 2011)
Daybreak, 2011 – Himself (13 January 2011)
Made in Hollywood: Teen Edition, 2011 – Himself
Best in Film: The Greatest Movies of Our Time, 2011 – Himself
Late Show with David Letterman, 2011 – Himself as Guest (21 July 2011)
Made in Hollywood, 2011 – Himself (23 July 2011)
Jimmy Kimmel Live!, 2011 – Himself (28 July 2011)
Drew: The Man Behind the Poster (post-production), 2011 – Himself

Episodic TV
The Virginian, 1962 (#5.19) – Cullen Tindall in "Modoc Kid" 02/01/67
Ironside, 1967 (#1.3) – Tom Stowe in "Past is Prologue" 12/07/67
My Friend Tony, 1969 – in "The Hazing" 02/16/69
Love, American Style, 1969 – in "Love and the Former Marriage" 11/24/69
The F.B.I., 1969 – in "The Scapegoat" 11/23/69
Dan August, 1970 – "Manufactured Man" 03/11/71
Gunsmoke, 1972 (#18.11) – Print in "Sodbusters" 11/20/72
Gunsmoke, 1973 (#18.20) – Hobey in "Whelan's Men" 02/05/73
Kung-Fu, 1974 (#2.18) – Mr. Harrison in "Cross Ties" 02/21/74
Petrocelli, 1974 (#1.4) – Tom Brannigan in "Edge of Evil" 10/02/74
Young Indiana Jones Chronicles, 1992 (#2.5) – Indiana (at 50) in "Indiana Jones and the Mystery of the Blues" 3/13/93

Producer
K-19: The Widowmaker (executive producer)
Extraordinary Measures (executive producer)

Commercials
Conservation International Public Service Announcement, 2002 – spokesperson (serves on the board of directors)
Earthshare, 2000 – Voice
Ebel Watches, 2000 – Only his hands were used
Lancia Lyora, 1999
Cell Phone, 1995
Honda, 1995
Kirin Beer (Japan), 1995 – for which he was paid over a million dollars
Oldsmobile, 1995 – narration
Sony TV, 1995

Theatre
Mainspring, 1960 – (Maine East Township High School, WI)
The Zoo Story, 196? – Jerry (Red Barn Theatre, Ripon College, WI)
Three Penny Opera, 1963 – Mack the Knife (Red Barn Theatre, Ripon College, WI)
The Fantastiks, 1963 – El Gallo/narrator (Red Barn Theatre, Ripon College, WI)
The Skin of Our Teeth, 1964 – Mr George Antrobus 4.(Red Barn Theatre, Ripon College, WI)
Take Her, She's Mine, 1964 – (Williams Bay Repertory Theater, Lake Geneva WI, US)
Sunday in New York, 1964 – (Williams Bay Repertory Theater, Lake Geneva WI, US)
Damn Yankees, 1964 – (Williams Bay Repertory Theater, Lake Geneva WI, US)
Dark Moon, 1964 – (Williams Bay Repertory Theater, Lake Geneva WI, US)
Night of the Iguana, 1964 – (Williams Bay Repertory Theater, Lake Geneva WI, US)
Little Mary Sunshine, 1964 – (Williams Bay Repertory Theater, Lake Geneva WI, US)
John Brown's Body – A Civil War Poem, 1965 – Southern Soldier (Laguna Beach Playhouse, CA US)

Theatre Backstage
Come Back Little Sheba, 1963 – (Red Barn Theatre, Ripon College, WI)
The Skin of Our Teeth, 1963 – Set Builder (Red Barn Theatre, Ripon College, WI)
Antingone, 1964 – (Red Barn Theatre, Ripon College, WI)

Theatre Director
The Zoo Story, 196? – (Red Barn Theatre, Ripon College, WI)
The American Dream, 196? – (Red Barn Theatre,

Ripon College, WI)

Other
The Search For Life – Are We Alone?, 2005
– narrator (planetarium show, pre-recorded
narration at the South Florida Museum)

Books
The Harrison Ford Story, (First edition 1984,
second edition 1985) – by Alan McKenzie
Harrison Ford: A Biography, 1986 – by Paul
Honeyford
Harrison Ford, 1987 – by Ethlie Ann Vare &
Mary Toledo
Harrison Ford: A Biography, 1987 – by Minty
Clinch
Harrison Ford, 1989 – by Jean Jacques Jélot-
Blanc
The Films of Harrison Ford, 1991 – by Edward
Gross
Harrison Ford: A Biography, 1993 – by Robert
Sellers
The Films of Harrison Ford, 1996 – by Lee
Pfeiffer, Michael Lewis
Harrison Ford, 1996 – by Alberto Ubeda
Portugues
Harrison Ford: Imperfect Hero, 1997 – by Garry
Jenkins
Harrison Ford, 1998 – by Agusti De Miguel
Harrison Ford, 1999 – by Manuel Maria Calvin
Muslares
Harrison Ford: A Biography, 2000 – by Robert
Abele
Timothy White: Portraits, 2001 – by Timothy
White & Harrison Ford
Harrison Ford, 2001 – by Patrizia Feretti
Harrison Ford: The Films, 2004 – by Brad Duke
Harrison Ford, 2007 – by Laurence Caracalla
*The Harrison Ford Handbook – Everything you
need to know about Harrison Ford*, 2010 – by
Laurie Ginn
*Off the Record Guide to the Career of Harrison
Ford*, 2011 – by Jenny Reese

Awards, Honors and Nominations

Academy Awards
Nominated 1985 Best Actor for *Mosquito Coast*
Nominated 1986 Best Actor in a Leading Role for
Witness

Academy of Science Fiction, Fantasy & Horror Films (Saturn)
Recognised 1982 Saturn Award Best Actor for
Raiders of the Lost Ark
Recognised 1985 Saturn Award Best Actor for
Indiana Jones and the Temple of Doom
Recognised 1996 Lifetime Achievement Award

AFI
Recognised 2000 – Life Achievement Award

APEX
Nominated 1988 Actor in a leading Role Action/
Mystery/Thriller – *Frantic*
Nominated 1993 Actor in a leading Role Action/
Mystery/Thriller – *The Fugitive*
Recognised 1994 Actor in a leading Role Action/
Mystery/Thriller – *Clear and Present Danger*
Nominated 1997 Actor in a leading Role Action/
Mystery/Thriller – *Air Force One*

Bambi Awards (Germany)
Recognised 1997 BambiFilm – International for
Air Force One

Blockbuster Entertainment Awards
Recognised 1994 Favorite Actor – Action on
Video for *The Fugitive*
Recognised 1995 Favorite Actor – Action,
Theatrical for *Clear and Present Danger*
Recognised 1995 Favorite Actor – Action, Video
for *Clear and Present Danger*
Nominated 1999 Favorite Actor – Action/
Adventure for *Air Force One*
Nominated 1999 Favorite Actor – Video for *Air
Force One*
Recognised 1999 Favorite Actor – Comedy/
Romance for *Six Days, Seven Nights*
Recognised 2001 Favorite Actor – Suspense for
What Lies Beneath

British Academy Awards (BAFTA)
Nominated 1986 Best Actor for *Witness*

GQ Magazine
1998 – Actor of the Year

Global Environmental Citizen Award (Harvard Medical School)
Recognised 2002 for his efforts to protect Earth's
most critical places

Golden Apple Awards
Nominated 1982 Sour Apple

Golden Globes
Nominated 1986 Best Performance by an Actor in a Motion Picture – Drama for *Witness*
Nominated 1987 Best Performance by an Actor in a Motion Picture – Drama for *The Mosquito Coast*
Nominated 1994 Best Performance by an Actor in a Motion Picture – Drama for *The Fugitive*
Nominated 1996 Best Performance by an Actor in a Motion Picture – Comedy/Musical for *Sabrina*
Recognised 2002 'Cecil B. Demille' for Outstanding Contribution to the Entertainment Field

Foster's Can Film Awards
Recognised 1997 – Best Actor

Hasty Pudding Theatricals
Recognised 1996 Man of the Year

MTV Movie Awards
Nominated 1994 Best Male Performance for *The Fugitive*
Recognised 1994 Best On-Screen Duo for *The Fugitive* (shared with Tommy Lee Jones)
Nominated 1998 Best Fight for *Air Force One* (shared with: Gary Oldman)

People's Choice Awards:
Recognised 1997 Favorite Motion Picture Actor
Recognised 1998 Favorite Motion Picture Actor
Nominated 1999 Favorite Motion Picture Actor
Nominated 1999 Favorite Motion Picture Star in a Drama
Recognised 1999 Favorite All-Time Movie Star
Recognised 2000 Favorite Motion Picture Actor
Nominated 2000 Favorite Motion Picture Star in a Drama

ShoWest Convention:
Recognised 1994 Special Award Box Office Star of the Century

Match.com Big O Awards
Recognised Best On-Screen Kiss for *What Lies Beneath* (Michelle Pfeiffer)

Mann's Chinese Theater:
Honored in 1992

Spencer Tracy Life Achievement Award (UCLA):
Recognised in 1994

Star on Hollywood Walk of Fame
Recognised June 2003 (6801 Hollywood Blvd)

World Stunt Awards:
Recognised 2003 Taurus Honorary Award

Young Hollywood Awards:
Recognised 2003 Role Model Award

Miscellany:
Ford turned down the role of Mike Stivic (Meathead) on *All in the Family* (1971) because he didn't like Archie's bigoted character … the role turned out to be Rob Reiner's big break.
Kirin Beer Commercial performance, 1995.
Playgirl Magazine's 1998 – 10 Sexiest men
One of *People* Mag's 50 Most Beautiful people in the world, 1998
Topped Harris Poll's: America's Favorite Star, 1999
People Mag's 1998 'Sexiest Man Alive'
Placed at 3 (April 2001)– in *Jane Magazine*'s Annual Entertainment Poll – Who Gets Better With Age (Top was Sean Connery)
Twenty seventh in *Film Threat Online*'s '50 Coldest People in Hollywood' (hardly an 'honor' but, it's included), 2001
Fifteenth *Empire* Mag's list of 100 sexiest stars in film history, 2001
First in *Empire* Mag's list of top 100 movie stars of all time, 2001
Arizona Republic (newspaper) reader poll – Who would you like to be president? Top Answer: Harrison Ford, 2004
Empire Magazine Poll 2004 – Greatest Living Actors #12
Conservation International – serves on the company's board of directors as a Vice Chair, 2004
Became a chairman (formerly Chuck Yeager had the honor) for the Young Eagles Program in June 2004 (has flown over 81 children to date)
Is fighting to save Meigs Field (Airfield) from turning into a park in Chicago, IL, 2004
Co-hosted the premiere of *Hotel Rwanda*, with Angelina Jolie, at the Academy of Motion Picture

Arts & Sciences in Beverly Hills, CA (12/2/04)
Placed at 88 on *Empire* (online) poll of All-Time
Sexiest Movie Stars, 2004
The Sun (UK). Number 1 Sexiest Grandparent,
2004
Bill Murray based his commercial performance
in *Lost in Translation* on Harrison Ford's Kirin
Beer commercial, 2004
Empire Magazine. 3rd biggest star in the world,
behind Tom Cruise and Robert DeNiro, 2005
In the play *Crumble* (Lay Me Down, Justin
Timberlake), Clara imagines that Harrison
Ford comes to her and tells her she's not a bad
mother, 2005
Han Solo came in 4th on Sci-Fi Channel's best
hero list, 2005 (Harry Potter was number one)
Named Honorary Chair of Indianapolis Prize
(shared), 2005
Harrison Ford had a test voice reel for the
character of Bob Parr (Mr Incredible) in *The
Incredibles*, 2005
Ford was one of the persons who made a
surprise delivery for Amazon.com's 10th
Anniversary. Literally, he delivered a customer
order personally, 2005
The house that Harrison Ford built an extra
building for, a 1940 Sherman Oaks home, just
sold for $1.9m (by Richard Dreyfuss), 2005
Knocked off the box office king throne by
Samuel L. Jackson, 2005

Harrison Ford's Worth
Salary on last 7 films (per each)
$20-25 million
K-19 was a record 25 million for 20 days of work
- 20% of the gross) ...
He's also the first actor ever to have been in
movies that made over $100 million in 4
decades.

Projects turned down:
Proof of Life
Perfect Storm
Patriot
Replaced Kevin Costner in *Air force One*

Real Life Hero
Private pilot of single engine fixed wing and
helicopter (Bell 407).
1] rescues two young women suffering from
hypothermia near his home in Wyoming,

[2] a young boy scout separated from his troupe.
(He saved the county money by volunteering his
helicopter services)
[3] helped stranded motorists fix their car.
[4] helped a woman get into her car after she
locked her keys in the car ... along with her
baby

Other distinctions
One of 50 people barred from entering Tibet
because of the film *Kundun* – his ex-wife Melissa
Mathison wrote the screenplay. On September
7th, 1995 he spoke before the Subcommittee
on Asian and Pacific Affairs, Senate Foreign
Relations regarding the plight of the Tibetans
Served food to the homeless in the "Celebrities
Help Los Angeles Mission", 1995
Master craftsman as a hobby (was known as
carpenter to the stars)
Has two false teeth. Due to an accidental fall
onto a gun on a TV appearance
The whip cracks in the song Desperation Samba
on Jimmy Buffets' Last Mango in Paris were
provided by Mr Ford
Has a species of spider named after him:
Calponia Harrisonford.
Once used a middle initial J. to differentiate
between him and a silent film star ... Ford has
no middle name. The J was dropped when it was
proven that the silent film actor was no longer
living.
Ford was also instrumental in securing a SAG
interim agreement to cover a commercial for
car-giant Fiat. Ford was slated to appear in a
Fiat commercial to be filmed and broadcast in
Europe. Filming did not commence though
until Ford was reassured an interim agreement
covered the carmaker's commercial.
Contributed $100,000 to the Strike Relief Fund
(screen actors guild)
The bullwhip used in all three Indiana Jones
movies was sold to help IONA and UNICEF
Ireland to help stop the spread of AIDS from
mother to child.
He contributed $50,000 dollars to fight the
building of a nuclear waste facility in Idaho,
1999.

School Trivia:
While in the Boy Scouts, Harrison was the camp
meteorologist delivering the weather report at

breakfast each morning
Attended M.S. Meltzer Junior High
Attended Maine East High School – graduated in 1960
1) Was the first voice heard on WMTH school radio station
2) Member of Model Railroad, Social Science and Audiovisual Clubs

Ripon College

Majored in:
English (Freshman to end of Sophomore year)
Philosophy (End of Sophomore year to end of Junior Year)
Drama (End of Junior Year)

1) To pay off debts owed in town, Harrison and a college friend started the humor magazine "The Mug". Harrison was the Art Director and created the cover illustration of a large beer mug. Note: The Mug had only one issue but they raised enough money through selling ads to pay off debts with extra money to spare.
2) Towards the end of freshman year, Harrison formed a folk band - The Brothers Gross. He played the gutbucket (an upside down washbucket rigged with a broomstick and a single bass string
3) Was a member of Sigma Nu
4) WRPN FM
5) Union Board

THE END

ACKNOWLEDGEMENTS

No book is ever a solo effort. My main collaborators in this biography were Harrison Ford (of course) through his quotes in the many interviews he has given in the decades since *Star Wars* shot him to international fame and my old *Starburst* colleague and long-time friend Tony Crawley who made available to me the notes from the many interviews he has conducted with Harrison Ford, since the late 1970s.

I would also like to thank my former *Starburst* and *2000AD* collaborator Steve Cook for whipping up the spectacular book cover in the blink of an eye.

I should make mention of the Zomba Books team who worked on the original edition of *The Harrison Ford Story* (1984), upon which the current edition is based. They are: Publisher Maxim Jakubowski who agreed on the spot to the project and Editor Emily White who had the almost thankless task of trying to make sense of my original typed (and Tippexed) manuscript. And special mention should go out to Francesca Landau who contributed to the original research and my long-time friend Phil Edwards who read through the original manuscript and made many suggestions and recommendations.

During the course of researching this project, I read or quoted from a whole host of writers: Ralph Appelbaum, Alan Arnold, David Badder, Hilary Bonner, John Brosnan, Ken Bruzenak, Vic Bulluck, James H.Burns, Mike Bygrave, Gerald Clarke, Minty Clinch, Richard Combs, Phil Edwards, Dave Farrow, Clinton Gilmore, Joan Goodman, Marianne Gray, Robert Greenburger, George Haddad-Garcia, Alex Harvey, Clive Hirchhorn, Ann Holler, David Houston, Garry Jenkins, Saul Kahan, David Lewin, Herb A. Lightman, David Litchfield, Iain F. McAsh, Milo Mitchell, Peter Noble, Kerry O'Quinn, Richard Patterson, Lee Pfeiffer & Michael Lewis, David Pirie, Dale Pollock, Tony Pratt, Alasdair Riley, Tim Satchell, Norman Spinrad, Michael Sragow, Philip Strick, Peter Sullivan, James Van Hise, Jo Weedon, Bruce Williamson, and David Wilson. Their interviews and features appeared in *American Cinematographer, The Blade Runner Souvenir Magazine, Cinefex, cinema magazine, City Limits, Daily Express, Daily Mail, Daily Mirror, Empire, Films Illustrated, The Guardian, A Journal of the Making of the Empire Strikes Back, Mail on Sunday, Monthly Film Bulletin, Movie Guide, Movie Star, Ms London, Photoplay, Playboy, Prevue, Raiders of the Lost Ark Collectors' Album, Readers Digest, Ritz, Rolling Stone, Screen International, Skywalking, Starburst, Starlog, The Sun, Sunday, Time, Time Out, The Times, US Magazine* and *Woman's Own*.

Into all this I folded in interviews conducted in collaboration with Phil Edwards with many of Ford's co-workers, including Anthony Daniels, Carrie Fisher, Richard Marquand, Syd Mead, Ivor Powell, and Ridley Scott.

If I've left anyone out, abject apologies and my thanks, too.

Alan McKenzie, October 2011

Lightning Source UK Ltd.
Milton Keynes UK
UKOW021140291211

184457UK00001B/161/P